POLITICAL AND ECONOMIC WRITINGS OF DANIEL DEFOE

General Editors: W. R. Owens and P. N. Furbank

Volume 1: CONSTITUTIONAL THEORY

Edited by
P. N. Furbank

MUNDUS
INTELLECTUALIS

LONDON
PICKERING & CHATTO
2000

Published by Pickering & Chatto (Publishers) Limited
21 Bloomsbury Way, London, WC1A 2TH

Old Post Road, Brookfield, Vermont 05036, USA

www.pickeringchatto.com

BRITISH LIBRARY CATALOGUING IN PUBLICATION DATA
Defoe, Daniel, 1660 or 1–1731
Political and economic writings of Daniel Defoe. – (The Pickering Masters)
1. Political science – Great Britain – Early works to 1800 2. Economics – Great
Britain – Early works to 1800 3. Great Britain – Politics and Government –
1714–1760 4. Great Britain – Politics and Government – 1660–1714 5. Great
Britain – Economic conditions – 17th century 6. Great Britain – Economic
conditions – 18th century I. Title II. Owens, W. R. III. Furbank, P. N. (Philip
Nicholas) 320.9′41′09032
ISBN 1851964657

LIBRARY OF CONGRESS CATALOGING-IN-PUBLICATION DATA
A catalogue record for this title is available from the Library of Congress.

Typset by Florence Production Ltd,
Stoodleigh, Devon

Printed by Bookcraft (Bath),
Midsomer Norton

THE PICKERING MASTERS

THE WORKS OF DANIEL DEFOE

General Editors:
W. R. Owens and P. N. Furbank

POLITICAL AND ECONOMIC WRITINGS
OF DANIEL DEFOE

CONTENTS

GENERAL EDITORS' PREFACE

Political and Economic Writings of Daniel Defoe is the first set of volumes in what is intended to be the most comprehensive collection of Defoe's writings ever attempted. The plan is that these eight volumes will be followed by sets grouping together *Travel, Discovery, and Historical Writings* (eight volumes); *Satire, Fantasy, and Writings on the Supernatural* (eight volumes); *Religious and Didactic Writings* (ten volumes); and *Novels* (ten volumes). The aim of the Pickering & Chatto *Works* is to give as extensive a representation as possible of Defoe's work in all the literary genres to which he contributed, with the partial exception of his voluminous periodical journalism.

There has never been a complete edition of Defoe, and such is the quantity of his writings that it seems unlikely there ever will be. The earliest important collection was *The Novels of Daniel De Foe*, an edition in twelve volumes in 1809–10 edited by Sir Walter Scott. A twenty-volume *Novels and Miscellaneous Works*, published by Thomas Tegg in 1840–1, was followed by a three-volume *Works*, edited by William Hazlitt (the Younger) in 1840–3. Between 1854 and 1865 a seven-volume edition of *Novels and Miscellaneous Works* was published in Bohn's 'British Classics' series, but a more extensive collection was the sixteen-volume *Romances and Narratives by Daniel Defoe* edited by George A. Aitken, published by Dent in 1895. An edition of *The Works*, also in sixteen volumes, edited by G. H. Maynadier, was published in New York in 1903–4, and the last multi-volume edition of Defoe to appear in the twentieth century was *The Shakespeare Head Edition of the Novels and Selected Writings*, published in fourteen volumes by Blackwell in 1927–8.

Defoe's position in English literature is in some ways a strange one. Nowadays he is mainly thought of as a novelist – the author of *Robinson Crusoe, Moll Flanders, A Journal of the Plague Year, Colonel Jack, Roxana*, etc. – but this was by no means how his contemporaries regarded him. For the most part he published anonymously, and though it became known that he wrote *Robinson Crusoe*, very few people would have known that he was also the author of *Moll Flanders* or *Roxana*. His reputation in his lifetime – and he became very famous – was as a poet, a writer on political and economic affairs, a journalist (especially in the long-running *Review*), and also as the target for a quite exceptional torrent of vituperation. (As well as being famous he made many enemies.)

But what is safe to say is that neither his contemporaries, nor his casual reader today, had or has anything like a clear picture of his work as a whole. Indeed, this is not too easy to arrive at, and for two separate reasons. The first is that, already during his lifetime, and over the two and a half centuries after his death, people have been in the habit of attributing works to him which he probably, and in some cases certainly, never wrote. This occurred on such a scale as to make it uncertain, not merely whether he is the author of certain works, but, in one or two cases, whether he wrote *any* works in a particular mode or genre. Secondly, the quantity and range of his writing, even after all deductions of dubious items from the canon, is astounding. There is nothing quite like it in English literature; for a parallel one would have to look to Voltaire.

It might be worthwhile to spell out this latter point in a certain amount of detail. Defoe's writings include the following. *Verse*: numerous lengthy satirical poems about City politics, contemporary poetry, the English national character, the crimes of the High-Church party, the glories of King William, 'reformation of manners', the follies of 'divine right' theories, and Scotland. *Political pamphlets*: a huge array of pamphlets on behalf of the Dissenters, on war and international relations, on constitutional theory, the Jacobite threat, the employment of the poor, Union with Scotland, public finance, debt and bankruptcy, the Africa and South-Sea trades, the Succession question, the fall of Robert Harley, the split in the Whig party, the Bangorian controversy, the French and English financial 'bubbles', etc., etc. *Histories*: a vast history of the Union between England and Scotland, and a lengthy history of the Church in Scotland. *Full-length treatises*: on 'projects', trade, discoveries, social reform, the history of writing, servants, street crime, magic, supernatural apparitions, the devil, sexual conduct, the tradesman, and the English gentleman. *Fantasies and pseudo-biographies*: a lunar fantasy, hoaxes about second-sight and prophesy, pretended memoirs of a French agent, and imaginary letters written by a Turkish spy. *Religious and family instruction*: voluminous dialogues concerned with the rearing of children, religious courtship, etc. *Periodicals*: as well as his famous *Review*, which ran for nine years and dealt with a wide variety of topics, six other shorter-lived journals treating of economics, politics, trade, the South Sea bubble, and morals and manners. *Novels*: eight in all.

It is important to stress, however, that this vast *oeuvre* is by no means a mere haphazard jumble. On the contrary, Defoe's outlook was in some ways remarkably coherent. He had a number of favourite theories and principles, some of them of considerable originality, and they are to be discovered equally in his writings on trade, finance, religion and politics and in his novels. The interconnections between his various writings are important to our understanding of them; only a really large-scale edition such as the present one can bring these out. In their Introductions to individual volumes, editors will do their best to indicate some of these interconnections.

Before outlining our textual policy, there is an important point to make about the works chosen for inclusion in the edition. We have already referred to the way in which anonymous works were attributed to Defoe during his lifetime, and since. The first list of his writings, which appeared in 1790, assigned him just over 100 works. During the nineteenth and twentieth centuries scholars attributed an ever-increasing number of works to Defoe, until by 1970 the total stood at a quite amazing 570 separate titles. In our book *The Canonisation of Daniel Defoe* (1988) we examined the remarkable process by which the Defoe canon had, as it seemed to us, become so grossly inflated, and in *Defoe De-Attributions* (1994) we put forward reasons for questioning the attribution of about 250 works, suggesting that until satisfactory evidence was produced for Defoe's authorship they should be dropped from the canon. In 1998 we published *A Critical Bibliography of Daniel Defoe*, in which we supplied the history of and evidence for some 270 attributions to Defoe, dividing these into two categories: works 'certainly' by Defoe, and works 'probably' by him. We did our best to make the word 'probably' mean what it says, and not merely 'possibly', or 'by tradition', etc. Since the case for each work has been put forward in the *Critical Bibliography*, we raise no questions about attribution in the present edition, and 'probable' attributions are presented side-by-side with 'certain' ones.

The textual policy adopted throughout the edition is as follows. The copy-text chosen is normally the earliest available edition, but additions and revisions in later editions published in Defoe's lifetime and over which there is reason to think he may have had control have been incorporated. Details of the copy-text and any other relevant editions will be given in a headnote preceding the Textual Notes to each work. Editors have taken a conservative approach, not attempting officiously to 'correct' or tidy up the texts by, for example, inserting possessive apostrophes, or standardising grammatical forms, or adjusting inconsistent spelling, or changing punctuation where the sense is perfectly clear as it stands. Spelling, capitalisation, use of italics, etc., have not been modernised, except that the long 's' has been replaced by the round 's', and 'VV' or 'vv' with 'W' and 'w'. The presentation of quotation marks has been regularised: quotation marks at the start of every line of a quotation have been removed and replaced by opening and closing single quotation marks, except that when a quotation runs on for more than one paragraph a quotation mark has been placed at the beginning of every paragraph.

Minor, straightforward corrections of errors in the copy-text have been carried out silently. These include glaring printer's errors such as use of wrong fonts, turned letters, or repeated words, but also impossible misspellings, or cases where the punctuation is plainly wrong and gets in the way of understanding. Similarly, where there is an Errata list, the corrections listed there are carried out silently. All other substantive emendations to the copy-text are recorded in the Textual Notes at the back of the volume. There are two classes of emendation: those incorporating changes judged to be authorial in later editions, and those made by the editor. Where there is no particular reason to think that Defoe had control over a later edition, the reading of the copy-text will be followed. The only exception would be in a case where the copy-text is clearly defective and the reading in another edition makes obviously better sense. No attempt has been made to record variant readings from later editions; only substantive emendations to the copy-text have been recorded. In cases where there is more than one edition with textual authority, the editor will assign them sigla (usually the date of publication), and will explain this in the headnote preceding the Textual Notes to that text. Emendations in works where only the copy-text carries authority will not normally involve the use of sigla, since any such emendations will be editorial. An emendation is indicated by a superscript letter.

W. R. Owens and *P. N. Furbank*

CHRONOLOGY

1660   Charles II restored to the throne. Daniel Foe born in the parish of St Giles, Cripplegate, probably in the autumn, son of James Foe, a merchant, and his wife Alice.

1662   Corporation Act requires all civic officers and magistrates to receive the sacrament according to the rites of the Church of England. Act of Uniformity, requiring conformity to a newly-published *Book of Common Prayer*, leads to the ejection of about 2000 clergy from the Church of England. The Foes follow Dr Samuel Annesley out of St Giles and worship henceforth as Dissenters. Butler, *Hudibras*, part I (II and III, 1663, 1678).

1664–72   The 'Clarendon Code', a series of acts bringing in severe penalties for religious nonconformity.

1665–6   Anglo-Dutch War begins. The Great Plague kills something like 70,000 people in London.

1666   The Great Fire of London begins on 2 September and burns for four days and nights. Bunyan, *Grace Abounding*.

1667   Milton, *Paradise Lost*, enlarged to twelve books, 1674. Treaty of Breda ends Anglo-Dutch War. Sprat, *History of the Royal Society*.

1672   Charles II issues Declaration of Indulgence suspending laws against Dissenters. Marvell, *The Rehearsal Transpros'd*.

1673   Parliament forces Charles to withdraw Declaration of Indulgence. Test Act compels all civil and military office-holders, and all members of the royal household, to repudiate transubstantiation and take the sacrament according to the rites of the *Book of Common Prayer*.

1674–9?   Defoe attends the Rev. Charles Morton's Dissenting Academy at Newington Green.

1678   Bunyan, *The Pilgrim's Progress*, part I (part II, 1684). The Popish Plot scare. Second Test Act excludes Roman Catholics from

Parliament. Dryden, *All for Love*.

1679   Whigs begin attempt to exclude James Duke of York from succession to the throne.

1680   Bunyan, *The Life and Death of Mr Badman*. Filmer, *Patriarcha*. Rochester, *Poems* (posthumous).

1681   Defoe writes religious verse meditations (unpublished). About this time decides against becoming a Presybterian minister. Dryden, *Absalom and Achitophel*. Marvell, *Miscellaneous Poems* (posthumous).

1682   About this time Defoe sets up as a wholesale hosier and general merchant. Compiles anthology entitled 'Historical Collections' (unpublished) for his fiancée. Bunyan, *The Holy War*. Dryden, *Religio Laici*. Otway, *Venice Preserv'd*.

1683   Rye House Plot. Execution of Algernon Sidney and Lord Russell.

1684   Defoe marries Mary Tuffley. Moves his business to Freeman's Yard, Cornhill.

1685   Accession of James II. Defoe bears arms in support of the Duke of Monmouth's rebellion, but escapes capture following Monmouth's defeat at Sedgemoor.

1686   James issues a General Pardon, releasing many Dissenters from prison.

1687   James issues Declaration of Indulgence granting freedom of worship to Dissenters and Roman Catholics. Halifax, *Letter to a Dissenter*. Newton, *Principia Mathematica*.

1688   James reissues Declaration of Indulgence, and orders that it be read from all parish pulpits. Seven bishops refuse, and are tried for seditious libel, but acquitted. In August or September Defoe's first extant publication appears, *A Letter to a Dissenter from his Friend at the Hague*. William, Prince of Orange, lands at Torbay. James II takes flight.

1689   William and Mary crowned. Bill of Rights enacted. Toleration Act allows freedom of worship to Protestant Dissenters, but does not grant civil rights. William forms Grand Alliance, and war with France begins. Locke, *First Letter on Toleration*. Marvell, *Poems on Affairs of State* (posthumous).

1690   (1 July) William III defeats James II at the Battle of the Boyne. Locke, *Two Treatises of Civil Government*.

1691   (Probably January) Defoe publishes *A New Discovery of an Old Intreague*, a satirical poem about City politics.

1692	(April) Defoe buys seventy civet cats from John Barksdale for £850. (June) becomes secretary-general of a company formed to finance diving-bell operations. He is bankrupted, with debts purportedly amounting to £17,000, and imprisoned for debt in the Fleet Prison. Massacre of Glencoe. L'Estrange, *Fables of Esop and other Mythologists*.
1694	About now Defoe sets up a brick and tile works at Tilbury. Triennial Act provides for Parliamentary elections every third year. Bank of England established.
1695	About this time adds a 'De' to his name. Becomes 'Accomptant' in the Glass Office, for the collection of duty on 'Glasswares, Stone and Earthen Bottles' (retains this post until about 1699). The Press Licensing Act lapses. William captures Namur from the French.
1696	Navigation Act forbids American colonists to export directly to Scotland or Ireland. A recoinage takes place. Baxter, *Reliquiae Baxterianae* (posthumous). Toland, *Christianity Not Mysterious*.
1697	(January) Defoe publishes *An Essay upon Projects*, his first full-length book. (September) Treaty of Ryswick ends war with France. Vanbrugh, *The Provok'd Wife*.
1698	Defoe publishes three pamphlets on the Standing Army controversy, and *An Enquiry into the Occasional Conformity of Dissenters*, the first of many pamphlets on this subject. (August) completion of William's first Partition Treaty. British merchant vessels begin carrying slaves to West Indies. London Stock Exchange founded. Behn, *Histories and Novels* (posthumous). Algernon Sidney, *Discourses Concerning Government* (posthumous).
1699	(May) *An Encomium upon a Parliament*, a satirical ballad. (June) William drafts second Partition Treaty.
1700	(February) *The Pacificator*, a long verse satire on literary issues. (November) two pamphlets, *The Two Great Questions Consider'd* and *The Two Great Questions Further Considered*, prompted by Louis XIV's recognition of his grandson's claim to the Spanish throne. Congreve, *Way of the World*.
1701	(January?) *The True-Born Englishman*, Defoe's famous verse satire on English chauvinism; (May) *Legion's Memorial*, a furious attack on the House of Commons in the name of the People of England; a dozen pamphlets and poems on political, religious and financial issues. (September) James II dies. Louis

XIV recognises the Pretender as king of England. (December) *The Original Power of the Collective Body of the People of England*, a considered statement of Defoe's constitutional theories. War of the Spanish Succession begins in Europe.

1702   (8 March) King William dies, being succeeded by Queen Anne. In May England declares war on France. At the general election in July the Tories win a majority. Defoe publishes three lengthy poems, a hard-hitting attack on High-flyers entitled *A New Test of the Church of England's Loyalty*, and three pamphlets inspired by the introduction in the House of Commons in November of a Bill to outlaw the practice of Occasional Conformity. The most famous, *The Shortest Way with the Dissenters*, provokes an enormous outcry from High Tories and Dissenters alike. A warrant is issued for the arrest of its author.

1703   In hiding, Defoe publishes *A Brief Explanation of a Late Pamphlet*, and *A Dialogue between a Dissenter and the Observator* expressing his exasperation at being so misunderstood by his fellow-Dissenters. On 21 May he is arrested and held in Newgate before being released on bail. On 7 July is convicted of publishing a seditious libel and committed to Newgate, fined, bound over for seven years, and made to stand in the pillory three times. On 29 July, to coincide with his first appearance in the pillory, publishes *A Hymn to the Pillory*, an impenitently satirical poem. On 8 November is released from Newgate through the good offices of Robert Harley, and enters Harley's service as confidential agent. (November) second Occasional Conformity Bill introduced, and once again it is defeated in the Lords. The great storm begins on 27 November.

1704   (January) Defoe publishes *The Dissenters Answer to the High-Church Challenge*, responding to Charles Leslie, and *An Essay on the Regulation of the Press*. On 19 February the first number of the *Review* appears (continues till 1713). Between February and August publishes nine pamphlets, and secretly launches a periodical, the *Master Mercury* (runs from August to September), satirising Admiral Sir George Rooke. Between April and May a number of High Tory ministers are replaced by moderates led by Robert Harley. (August) Defoe responds to news of the Battle of Blenheim with *A Hymn to Victory* (poem). From August to September is in East Anglia. (October) is reported as having fled from justice over his poem 'The

Address'. (November) *Giving Alms no Charity*. (November) third Occasional Conformity Bill introduced, with attempted 'tack', but this is defeated in the Commons and in the Lords. Swift, *Tale of a Tub*.

1705 In January the House of Lords invites Defoe to submit a plan regarding a registration office for seamen. (March) Defoe's *The Consolidator*, an allegorical lunar fantasy prompted by the 'tack'. In May and June a general election strengthens the Whigs. (July) *The Dyet of Poland*, Defoe's verse satire on the late Tory administration. (July–November) Defoe goes on a fact-finding tour through the English counties.

1706 (May) Battle of Ramillies. (May) Defoe publishes first of six *Essays at Removing National Prejudices against a Union with Scotland*. (July) *A True Relation of the Apparition of one Mrs Veal*, and *Jure Divino*, a poem in twelve books attacking the 'divine right' theory. (August) makes a composition with his creditors. (September, to November 1707) is in Scotland. (November) persuades a Committee of the Scottish Parliament to impose a new middle rate of excise for 'tippony ale'. (December) *Caledonia*, poem in praise of Scotland.

1707 (January) Treaty of Union is ratified by the Scottish Parliament. (January–March) Defoe publishes three pamphlets in a controversy with the Rev. James Webster, and other pamphlets on Scottish affairs. (March) Act of Union passed. (June) Defoe seeks a governmental post in Scotland (presumably because the Test Act did not apply there). (September) Swedish ambassador lays complaint against Defoe for remarks about Charles XII in the *Review*. Watts, *Hymns*.

1708 (February) Harley resigns as Secretary of State, and Defoe enters the service of Godolphin. (March) French attempt at a Jacobite invasion in Scotland. (April–November) Defoe is in Scotland. In May, a general election secures a majority for the Whigs.

1709 Early this year Defoe sets up a separate Scottish edition of the *Review*. He acts now and later as a spokesman for the Royal Africa Company. (July) Charles XII is defeated by the Russians at Pultowa and takes refuge in Turkey. In the *Review*, July–September, Defoe urges that Palatine refugees should be welcomed in England. (September) Battle of Malplaquet, with loss of 20,000 allied lives. (September–January 1710) Defoe is in Scotland. On 5 November Henry Sacheverell preaches his inflammatory High-Church sermon, *The Perils of False Brethren*. (December) Defoe signs contract with David Fearne to publish the *Scots Postman* for a year. *The Tatler* begins publication. Manley, *The New Atalantis*.

1710 (February?) *The History of the Union of Great Britain*. On 27 February trial of Sacheverell begins (he is found guilty, but escapes heavy punishment). (August) Harley becomes Chancellor of the Exchequer, following the dismissal of Godolphin, and Defoe re-enters his service. (August) *An Essay upon Publick Credit*. (September) *An Essay upon Loans*. In October the Tories win a crushing victory at the general election. (November–February 1710–11) Defoe is in Scotland, where he forms a partnership to manufacture linen tablecloths.

1711 Defoe publishes nearly twenty pamphlets on political and economic topics of the moment. In March the first number of the *Spectator* appears. (April) *The British Visions*, first of a series of hoaxing 'prophecies' of events in Europe. (May) Harley is made Lord High Treasurer and raised to the peerage. His South Sea bill passes both Houses. (September) Defoe acts as spokesman for the wine wholesalers Brooks and Hellier. Peace preliminaries signed between Britain and France. South Sea Company launched. (December) Occasional Conformity Bill passed with the help of the Whigs and discontented Tories, who defeat the government in the Lords over its peace policy. Queen dismisses Marlborough. Swift, *Conduct of the Allies*.

1712 (January) Queen creates 12 new Tory peers. Peace conference opens at Utrecht. (February) Defoe acts as spokesman for the 'keel-men' of Newcastle. Publishes about ten pamphlets, and, in May, *The Present State of the Parties in Great Britain*, a lengthy account of political and religious developments in England and Scotland. Stamp Act imposes duty on periodicals. Arbuthnot, *The History of John Bull*. Pope, *The Rape of the Lock* (in *Miscellaneous Poems and Translations*).

1713 (January) Defoe acts as spokesman for a Brass company. (April) Treaty of Utrecht ends War of Spanish Succession. Defoe is arrested on account of three ironic tracts on the Hanoverian succession. (May) Defoe launches *Mercator*, a periodical advocating trade with France (it runs to July 1714), and publishes several pamphlets on the subject. (June) Treaty of Commerce with France is rejected. Defoe publishes *A General History of Trade*. At the general election in August the Whigs are heavily defeated. The South Sea Company receives the *asiento*, giving it the right to import African slaves into Spanish colonies in the New World. Steele launches the *Guardian*, and the *Englishman*.

1714   Defoe edits the *Monitor*, April to August, a periodical defending Tory policies. (June) Schism Act passed. (July) Queen dismisses Harley. (July–September) Defoe writes for a sham rival version of the *Flying-Post*. (August) The Queen dies, being succeeded by the Elector of Hanover (George I). (September?) *The Secret History of the White Staff*, first of a three-part pamphlet ingeniously defending Harley's reputation. Mandeville, *Fable of the Bees*. Swift, *The Public Spirit of the Whigs*.

1715   (January) Defoe's *The Family Instructor*, fictional dialogues concerning religion, continued in 1718 and 1727. (February) *An Appeal to Honour and Justice*, an apologia for his own life, in which it is reported by the publisher that Defoe has suffered a fit of apoplexy and is possibly dying. First volume of Pope's *Iliad* is published. (June) Harley and Bolingbroke are impeached. (July) *An Account of the Conduct of Robert Earl of Oxford*, defending Harley. (September) death of Louis XIV. Earl of Mar raises standard of revolt at Perth. (November) Jacobites defeated at Preston and Sheriffmuir.

1716   (May) Septennial Act. (December) Townshend is replaced by Stanhope as Secretary of State. Defoe publishes three or four pamphlets on changes in the Ministry. Execution of Jacobite leaders captured at Preston the previous year.

1717   (March) Benjamin Hoadly, Bishop of Bangor, preaches a strongly Erastian sermon on 'The Nature of the Kingdom or Church of Christ'. (April) Townshend is dismissed, and Walpole resigns in sympathy. (April) Defoe publishes lengthy *Memoirs of the Church of Scotland*. (May) launches *Mercurius Politicus* (which runs to December 1720). (June) *Minutes of the Negotiations of Monsr. Mesnager*, fictitious memoirs of Louis XIV's peace-negotiator. (June–July) the Bangorian controversy rages in the press, the Bishop of Carlisle accusing Hoadly of toning down his sermon before printing it. Defoe teases Hoadly in a pseudo-Quaker *Declaration of Truth to Benjamin Hoadly*. (July) Harley acquitted of high treason.

1718   (26 April) Defoe writes to Charles Delafaye, Under-secretary of State, giving an account of his (supposed) activities on behalf of the Whig government. (August) Quadruple Alliance formed against Spain. (August) Byng defeats Spanish fleet off Cape Passaro. (August) *A Continuation of Letters Written by a Turkish Spy*, satirical reflections on divisions in Europe. (November) during the interrogation of Nathaniel Mist, witnesses attest that an inflammatory anti-government letter signed 'Sir Andrew Politick', in *Mist's Journal*, was written by Defoe.

1719   (January) Schism Act and Occasional Conformity Act repealed. (15 April) *Robinson Crusoe*. (August) *The Farther Adventures of Robinson Crusoe*. (October) the *Manufacturer* is launched (runs until March 1721). Substantial pamphlets on trade and finance.

1720   Defoe edits the *Commentator*, a miscellaneous journal (runs from January to September), followed by the *Director* (October 1720–January 1721), a periodical about the South Sea affair. (May) *Memoirs of a Cavalier*. (June) *Captain Singleton*. (August) *Serious Reflections . . . of Robinson Crusoe*. (October) the South Sea Bubble bursts. In France, John Law's 'Mississippi Company' collapses, bringing ruin to French investors.

1721   (February) Townshend is appointed Secretary of State. (April) Walpole is appointed First Lord of the Treasury. (August) an essay by Defoe's son Benjamin for the *London Journal* leads to Benjamin's arrest.

1722   (January) *Moll Flanders*. (February) *Due Preparations for the Plague*, moral and practical considerations prompted by the plague in France. (February) *Religious Courtship*, didactic treatise in dialogue form. (March) *A Journal of the Plague Year*. (August) Defoe and his daughter Hannah sign a ninety-nine year lease on a large estate in Essex, for £1000. Discovery of the Atterbury plot. (December) *Colonel Jacque*.

1724   (February) *Roxana*. (April) *The Great Law of Subordination Consider'd*. (May) *A Tour thro the Whole Island of Great Britain* (Vol. II, 1725; Vol. III, 1726). (November) execution of Jack Sheppard. (November) *A New Voyage Round the World*. Swift, *Drapier's Letters*.

1725   (June) Defoe's *Every-Body's Business is No-body's Business*, first of a series of five tracts supposedly by 'Andrew Moreton', a peevish but public-spirited old bachelor. (September) *The*

Complete English Tradesman. (October–May 1726) *A General History of Discoveries and Improvements* (in four parts).

1726   (April) *An Essay upon Literature*, about the origins of writing. (May) *The Political History of the Devil*, satirising the idea of a physical Devil and hell. (November) *A System of Magick*, a history of magic in lampooning style. Swift, *Gulliver's Travels*.

1727   (January) *Conjugal Lewdness*, on the use and abuse of the marriage-bed. (February) Spain attacks Gibraltar. (March) *An Essay on the History and Reality of Apparitions*. (June) George I dies.

1728   Defoe begins his unpublished *The Compleat English Gentleman*. (March) *Augusta Triumphans*, an 'Andrew Moreton' piece, proposing a university for London and schemes for suppressing prostitution, gambling, gin-drinking, etc. (March) *A Plan of the English Commerce*. (August) Defoe and his future son-in-law Henry Baker quarrel over his daughter Sophia's dowry. (October) newspapers report a visit by 'Andrew Moreton' to the King (George II) and Queen at Windsor, to present his scheme for preventing street-robberies (evidently a concerted publishing hoax). Gay, *The Beggar's Opera*. Pope, *The Dunciad*.

1729   Defoe's daughter Sophia marries Henry Baker. (May) Defoe publishes pamphlet on imprisonment for debt. Swift, *A Modest Proposal*. Thomson, *Britannia*.

1730   (February or March) *A Brief State of the Inland or Home Trade*, a diatribe against hawkers and pedlars. Defoe is in hiding from his creditors.

1731   (24 April) Defoe dies, in Ropemaker's Alley. (26 April) he is buried in Bunhill Fields.

Volume 1

CONSTITUTIONAL THEORY

INTRODUCTION

The Standing Army controversy

The first occasion for Defoe to write on constitutional theory was the debate that broke out in 1697, regarding the right of the monarch to maintain a standing army. In September of that year, King William's nine-years' war against France ended with the Treaty of Ryswick, and William, on his return to England, received a triumphant welcome. He was, however, by no means the popular figure he had been ten years earlier, as the saviour of England's liberties; there were rumours and scandal about his Dutch advisers, and he found himself faced with a hostile Parliament. The attack began on his right to maintain an army in peace time. In October the Whig polemicists John Trenchard and Walter Moyle published an anonymous pamphlet, *An Argument Shewing that a Standing Army is Inconsistent with a Free Government*, calling for the disbanding of all professional troops, leaving the defence of the country to a militia. Their pamphlet was answered by the Whig Lord Chancellor, Lord Somers – the debate was almost entirely a Whig affair – and a number of other writers joined in. Meanwhile a motion was passed in the House of Commons requiring all land forces raised since September 1680 to be disbanded – leaving a force of something under 10,000 men.

It was an opportunity for Defoe to come to the support of a king whom he greatly honoured, and he would contribute three pamphlets to the debate. The first, entitled *Some Reflections on a Pamphlet Lately Publish'd*, was in direct answer to Trenchard and Moyle's *Argument*. It took the line that what was at stake was not the right to maintain a 'standing army' – for that was something no right-thinking person could defend – but rather an army duly approved, for a given purpose and a stated length of time, by Parliament.

> We have a blessed happy Union between the King and the Parliament; the King offers not to invade the Peoples Liberties, nor they his Prerogative; he will desire no Army but for their safety, nor they will deny none that is.[1]

Trenchard and Moyle argued as though liberty and an army were intrinsically incompatible, as if 'the King is not to be trusted with either Men, Arms, nor Money, for the last will be the Consequence of the former'. But this, says Defoe – quite apart from being a flagrant insult to William, after all he had done to rescue and preserve the nation's liberties – was to ignore the particular excellence of the English constitution.

> We who are *English Men* have the least Reason of any People in the World, to complain of any of our Laws, or of any Publick Affairs, because nothing is or can be done, but I, and every *individual Free holder* in *England*, do it our selves, we consent to it, and tacitly do it by our *Representatives* in the Parliament. (p. 48).

From this constitutional statement of position Defoe then proceeds to offer a variety of practical arguments against Trenchard and Moyle: that in the past kings have succeeded in tyrannising without the aid of an army; that, nevertheless, the institution of kingship is hardly comprehensible without military power, and a king without an army, in present-day Europe, can hardly hope to wield any influence; that the art of war has progressed, requiring a specialised training that cannot be expected of a militia; that a militia cannot serve abroad; and that the logic used to boost the value of a militia is unsound. 'If they are strong enough to defend us from all the World, a small number of standing Troops cannot hurt us; if they are not, then we must have an Army, or be exposed to every Invader' (p. 49).

In December 1697 a second part of Trenchard and Moyle's *Argument* was published, and at much the same time *A Discourse Concerning Militia's and Standing Armies* by Andrew Fletcher. Defoe replied to both of these in *An Argument Shewing that a Standing Army, with Consent of Parliament, is not Inconsistent with a Free Government*. His argument here is based partly on foreign policy – on the theory that the safety of England depends upon alliances with foreign powers, which in turn presuppose an army ('The Defence of *England's Peace* lies in making War in *Flanders*') – and partly on history and the peculiar character of English institutions. To argue as Andrew Fletcher does, he says, and idealise the supposed 'balance' of the feudal order, in which military power was shared between

---

1 *Some Reflections on a Pamphlet*, below, p. 47.

the king and his barons, was to commit a fallacy: it amounted to no more than 'exchanging one Tyrant for Three hundred'.[2] The true 'balance' was the one between the sword and the purse-strings. It was because the People of England grew rich, through peace and trade, that they had been able to reject their hated feudal servitude and set up a Parliament. '*The Power of the Purse is an Equivalent to the Power of the Sword.*' (74)

The debate continued throughout 1698, and in November of that year Trenchard and Moyle published *A Short History of Standing Armies in England*, prompting Defoe to reply with *A Brief Reply to the History of Standing Armies in England*. Here his attack became more personal. He accused the authors of being republicans and godless Socininans, professional malcontents whose campaign of persecution against the best of kings was in the cause of mere self-advancement.

Nevertheless, the fundamental thesis underlying Defoe's Standing Army pamphlets was clear-cut and consistent, and it forms a highly important part of his general outlook. We can, in fact, find its central thesis stated, memorably, in the poem, *The True-Born Englishman*, which was to make him famous. He argues there that, as soon as James II's High-Church advisers made the slightest approach to Dutch William, they became rebels, as much as any Whig, and moreover were dishonoured for all time as oath-breakers. From other points of view, however, their action eloquently expressed a precious truth:

> *That Kings, when they descend to Tyranny,*
> *Dissolve the Bond, and leave the Subject free.*
> The Government's ungirt when Justice dies,
> And Constitutions are Non-Entities.
> The Nation's all a Mob, there's no such thing
> As Lords or Commons, Parliament or King.
> A great promiscuous Crowd the Hydra lies,
> Till Laws revive, and mutual Contract ties.

If the People then decide to choose another king, they are in conscience bound to submit to him:

> But then that King must by his Oath assent
> To *Postulata's* of the Government;
> Which if he breaks, he cuts off the Entail,
> And Power retreats to its Original.[3]

---

2 *An Argument Shewing*, below, p. 73.

3 *The True-Born Englishman* (1701), in *Poems on Affairs of State, Volume 6: 1697–1704*, ed. Frank H. Ellis (New Haven and London, 1970), ll. 804–7 and 816–19.

It is, as will be seen, a contract theory of government, with some affinities to Locke's, though also with some marked differences from his – a matter we shall come on to. One finds the theory stated or drawn upon in many of Defoe's works, and often at great length in his *Review*. It underlies all the works included in the present volume, but it finds its most complete statement in the prose tract *The Original Power of the Collective Body of the People of England* (1702), as amplified by the vast verse treatise *Jure Divino* (1706) which forms a separate volume in the Pickering & Chatto edition of *The Works of Daniel Defoe*.

The Original Power of the Collective Body of the People of England (*1702*)

During the course of 1701 King William had been locked in a furious struggle with a Tory House of Commons. In October of the previous year the King of Spain had died and, to the world's astonishment, had been found to have bequeathed his enormous dominions to the young Duke of Anjou, the grandson of Louis XIV of France. Louis had, moreover, recognised this will; and, with his encouragement, the young Prince Philip had entered Madrid, whilst the French seized most of the fortresses guarding the Spanish Netherlands. It was evidently a menacing situation, but William's new House of Commons seemed unwilling to react or to grant the King the 'supplies' necessary to build up an army, spending their energy instead on impeaching his ministers.

Events then took a surprising turn. On 29 April 1701, at the Kent Quarter-Sessions at Maidstone, the Grand Jury, justices and freeholders signed a petition humbly imploring the House to 'have regard to the voice of the people' and to vote the King 'supplies', to enable him 'powerfully to assist his allies before it is too late'. Five Kentish gentlemen were deputed to deliver this petition, and the House, highly incensed, voted it 'scandalous, insolent and seditious' and threw the petitioners into prison.

The consequences were even more dramatic, and at this point Defoe, for long an admirer and supporter of King William, became involved. A week after the arrest of the 'Kentish gentlemen', he made an appearance at Westminster, accompanied by a guard of sixteen 'gentlemen of quality', and delivered to the Speaker of the House a paper known as 'Legion's Memorial', presenting, in the most threatening tones, and as from the House's 'masters' – i.e. those who had elected them – a summary of the nation's grievances against the Commons. 'Englishmen', it said, were 'no more to be Slaves to *Parliaments*, than to a King'. There might be no recognised procedure for bringing the House to its duty, nevertheless 'the great Law of Reason says, and all Nations allow, that whatever Power is above Law, is burthensome and Tyrannical, and may be reduc'd by *Extrajudicial* Methods'. 'Our name is Legion', the memorial ended, 'and we are many'.[4] This astonishing and explosive ultimatum seems to have terrified the House. At all events no steps were apparently taken to punish its authors; the impeachments of William's ministers were dropped, and William eventually got his 'supplies'; and on the prorogation of Parliament the Kentish gentlemen were released and fêted in the City.

The principle invoked in such flaming terms in 'Legion's Memorial' is what is soberly elaborated in *The Original Power of the Collective Body of the People of England*, published at the end of the same year. Framed as a series of brief maxims, it takes as its immediate pretext a recent pamphlet by the Tory financier and MP Sir Humphrey Mackworth, entitled *A Vindication of the Rights of the Commons of England* (1701). Mackworth had asserted that all political authority in England lay with the King, Lords and Commons. Their respective powers served as checks and balances on one another, but they were 'Not to be limited by any authority beside their own', and the ordinary citizen had no right to criticise them. Defoe, by contrast, uncompromisingly asserts the 'original right' of the 'People' of England to govern themselves. They may depute this right to a monarch, a nobility and a house of representatives, but if these governors betray the 'public good', or descend into tyranny, their authority ends, and – as he had phrased it in *The True-Born Englishman* – 'power retreats to its original'. There is, and must be, 'some Power *Prior* to the Power of King, Lords and Commons, from which, as the Streams from the Fountain, the Power of King, Lords and Commons is derived'; and if the 'People' cannot retrieve this power from a bad government by peaceful means, they may reasonably resort to force or ask for help from some neighbouring nation. This is what Reason, despite all sophistries of law and precedent, infallibly suggests. 'Reason is the Test and Touch-stone of Laws, and ... all Law or Power that is Contradictory to Reason is *ipso facto* void in it self, and ought not to be obeyed.'[5]

4 *Legion's Memorial* is included in *Political and Economic Writings*, vol. 2.
5 *The Original Power*, below, p. 107.

Kings, and *a fortiori* parliaments, Defoe argues, rule by consent of the people. This was acknowledged even at the time of the crowning of Israel's first king; he was appointed by God and proclaimed by the Prophet, but he received the assent of the People. There are those who hold that kings, by succession from God's original institution of monarchy, enjoy a 'divine right' to rule, but – quite apart from the fact that no such uninterrupted succession can be proved – no nation has in practice abided by this notion.

Government is, and always has been, designed for 'the Support of the Peoples property'. Property is the foundation of power, and government loses its authority if it attempts to invade private property. But this said, Defoe makes an all-important qualification. The power or 'original right' that he speaks of is to be understood as belonging essentially to free-holders. In England, this is the basis both of the House of Lords and the House of Commons. The nobility received their title and dignities in respect of their large share in the freeholds of the nation, and the rest of the freeholders had, and have, an equal right to sit in Parliament. Their numbers being so large, however, they agreed to choose repre-sentatives to act in their name.

According to Defoe's conception, the freeholders are the proper owners of the country, the other inhabitants being merely 'sojourners' or lodgers, who must either accept the laws that the freeholders impose or leave the country. (If any single man in England were to become land-lord of the whole freehold of England, Defoe adds, with a touch of fantasy, he would be entitled to return himself to Parliament for every county, and if the king in possession were to die, he would become king himself 'by inherent Right of Property'.)

Sir Humphrey Mackworth, in his pamphlet, finds it unimaginable that the Lords and Commons could ever, ultimately, violate reason and justice – upon which Defoe comments that it may not be probable, but it is certainly not impossible. Assuming, therefore, that it actually happens, reason and justice will then declare the Constitution dissolved and power to have returned to the People. What then? Evidently the People, assem-bled in a 'Universal Mob', cannot take over government. They will have to delegate their power to a 'Convention' of people, intrusted with the task of drawing up a new constitution and appointing a new ruler; and in so far as they agree on the membership of this body, they will be committed to accepting their decisions. But what if they do not agree? Suppose the inhabitants of Cornwall were to say they wished to be ruled by a certain Cornishman. They would, at this stage of affairs, have a perfect right to do so, and no law would prevent them. It might seem a misfortune to the rest of England, but 'in the nature of the thing it could not be Unjust'.

Defoe's system, somewhat eccentric as it must seem in its extravagant claims for freehold, is remarkably clear and coherent. This particular tract was often quoted both by friends and enemies. It would be reprinted, half a century later, during John Wilkes's struggle over the rights of citizens *vis-à-vis* Government and Parliament. It was attacked by, among others, Charles Davenant, in his *Essays upon Peace at Home, and War Abroad* (1703) in which he objects to 'Appeals from the People from their Representatives', meaning approaches to the people against their representatives, to which Defoe replies that 'appeals to the People' are often made by parliaments and monarchs, so why should it not happen the other way round?[6]

Defoe's Jure Divino *(1706)*

To understand Defoe's position fully, however, one also needs to read his verse satire, *Jure Divino*, attacking the doctrine of the 'divine right of kings'. According to this theory, hereditary monarchy was the form of government prescribed by God himelf. Thus all monarchs derived their authority from that bestowed on Adam, and a monarch was, in a sense, a divine personage and was above the law. Any limitation to his prerogative was merely a concession on his part, which he could revoke at his pleasure.

This doctrine, which was to become the rallying-cry of high Tories, was, at least in its extreme form, a fairly recent invention. As Macaulay writes, 'In the middle ages the doctrine of indefeasible hereditary right would have been regarded as heretical: for it was altogether incompatible with the high pretensions of the Church of Rome'.[7] The doctrine first came to prominence in the reign of James I, subsequently being propounded by clerics such as Archbishop Ussher, Bramhall and Jeremy Taylor, and it received its classic statement in the treatise *Patriarcha* by Sir Robert Filmer: a work written somewhere about 1642, though not published until 1680.

The 'divine right' doctrine, though itself new, was linked to the older and hallowed doctrine of the church which inculcated the duty of Passive Obedience. According to this, it was never lawful for subjects to offer

---

6 *Some Remarks on the First Chapter of Dr. Davenant's Essays*, below, p. 148.
7 Macaulay, *History of England* (1858), Vol. I, p. 75.

resistance to a monarch – even were he the most depraved and merciless tyrant. *The Whole Duty of Man*, the most widely-read manual of devotion of the seventeenth century, explained the difference between Passive, as opposed to Active, Obedience thus:

> An obedience we must pay either Active or Passive: the active in the case of all lawful commands ... But when he enjoins anything contrary to what God hath commanded, we are not to give him this active obedience; we may, nay, we must refuse thus to act; ... We are in that case to obey God rather than Man. But even this is a season for the Passive Obedience; we must patiently suffer what the ruler inflicts on us for such a refusal, and not to secure ourselves, rise up against him. *For who can stretch forth his hand against the Lord's Anointed and be guiltless?*[8]

The doctrines of 'divine right' and 'passive obedience' are logically distinct but were usually held conjointly, and they were so by Filmer.

His book was published, belatedly, in the middle of the Exclusion crisis, and made a considerable impact; and it gained further adherents three years later at the time of the Rye House plot, when an attempt was made on the life of King Charles and his brother the Duke of York. On the very day that Lord Russell was executed for his part in the plot, the University of Oxford publicly adopted Filmer's doctrines, ordering the works of Buchanan, Milton and Baxter to be burnt in the court of the Schools.

All this, a product of Charles's attempt at absolutism, was of course dramatically changed by the Revolution of 1688, when the bulk of the Church of England found it possible, after all, to countenance 'stretching forth their hand against the Lord's Anointed' and to the replacing of James II by King William. This was plainly very far from 'passive obedience', or from upholding the divine right of King James by lineal succession. It might be thought no more would have been heard of 'divine right', all the more so that John Locke, in the first of his *Two Treatises of Government* (1690), delivered a devastating attack on Filmer's *Patriarcha*. At all events, if such doctrines were to survive, they would require drastic revision; and this is in fact what happened. The leaders of the moderate Anglican clergy, among them William Sherlock, Archbishops Tillotson and Tenison and Bishops Burnet and Lloyd, adopted the theory that God removed King James from the throne by a direct act of his Providence, the human actors in this event being merely his innocent instruments.[9] This could not be

8 *The Whole Duty of Man* (1659), p. 280.
9 See Gerald Straka, 'The Final Phase of Divine Right Theory in England, 1688–1702', *EHR*, 77 (1962), pp. 638–58.

said to save Filmer's doctrines, but at least it preserved the idea of the divinity of kings and kingship.

Indeed, with the coming of Queen Anne to the throne, 'divine right' doctrine enjoyed a notable revival, in particular through the writings of Charles Leslie.

Defoe and Charles Leslie

Charles Leslie (1650–1722) was, in his period, the best-known of all High-Church controversialists. Samuel Johnson said he was the only reasoner among the nonjurors, 'and a reasoner who was not to be reasoned against;'[10] though others, like Defoe's biographer Walter Wilson, have been less kind to him.[11] He was born in Ireland, the second son of the Bishop of Raphoe and of Clogher, and through the influence of the Earl of Clarendon, he was appointed to the chancellorship of Connor. His political stance was somewhat paradoxical. Then, and always, he was a staunch Anglican, with an intense and mystical attachment to episcopacy, it being his dearest wish to secure a union between the Anglican and Gallican churches. Accordingly, during his Irish period, he took a tough stance against James II's Romish innovations. On the other hand he was a convinced Filmerian, upholding wholeheartedly the duty of non-resistance to princes; and at the Revolution, not only did he refuse to take the vows, thereby wrecking his future in the Church, but he became a friend of the exiled King James, visiting him and his Queen at Saint-Germains and eventually, in 1713, joining his household.

Early in King William's reign he came to London, acting as chaplain to his friend the Earl of Clarendon, and, according to his biographer, he formed a plan to 'provide a complete armoury of defence for the Church of England against her various antagonists, within and without'. He began with systematic attacks on Deism, Quakerism, Judaism and Socinianism; then, from his *The New Association* (1702) onwards, he concentrated on the Dissenters.[12] According to this pamphlet, the Dissenters, whose academies were nurseries of rebellion, were in a conspiracy with

10 Boswell, *Life of Johnson*, ed. Birbeck Hill, IV, p. 287.

11 Wilson thought his style 'partook of the qualities of his mind, which were coarse and crabbed in the extreme'; *Memoirs of the Life and Times of Daniel De Foe* (1830), II, 30.

12 R. J. Leslie, *Life and Writings of Charles Leslie* (1885), p. 164.

self-styled 'moderate' churchmen to overthrow the Church and Government and pull down the walls of the 'new Troy', London. (By the 'walls', he meant the Corporation and Test Acts.)

Defoe, meanwhile, had in June 1702 published a tract, *A New Test of the Church of England's Loyalty*, which wrong-footed the High-Church party in cunning fashion and greatly rankled with Leslie. It said that, in all the branglings in the nation, the Church had claimed that its principle – and not only that, but its practice – had been to give 'entire and undisputed obedience'[13] to her sovereign, as the 'lively image of divine authority', and that, by contrast, it had been the very principle of the Dissenters as a body 'to disturb Government, kill Kings, and oppose Laws'.[14] It ought, therefore, said Defoe, to do much to restore harmony to the nation if he can prove that this contrast is quite illusory: that, so far as loyalty to their princes is concerned, the Church faction and the Whig faction have been about as bad as each other. The Puritans ('Dissenters, Phanaticks, or Whigs, call them as you please') broke through their loyalty and obedience to King Charles I and unjustly brought him to the block; and when the Church party found their rights and property endangered by King James, they behaved in a very similar fashion.

The implications of this are followed through, with fine irony, at the expense of the Church party. ''Tis such a Jest, such a Banter to say, We did take up Arms, but we did not kill him [King James]: *Bless us, Kill our King, we wou'd not have hurt a Hair of his Head!* Why, every Bullet shot at the Battel of the *Boyne* was a killing the King; for if you did not, 'twas because you cou'd not hit him.' It is one of Defoe's most telling pamphlets, and many of its arguments eventually reappear in the Preface to *Jure Divino*.

Defoe, by this time, had recognised Leslie as an important adversary: indeed the title of his famous satirical hoax on the High-Church party, *The Shortest Way with the Dissenters*, was probably a sly allusion to Leslie's titles *A Short and Easie Way with the Deists* and *A Short and Easie Method with Jews*. Further, in his *Brief Explanation of The Shortest Way with the Dissenters*, Defoe mentioned that Leslie's *New Association* had been one of the models for his satire. This provoked Leslie, in *The New Association Part II* (1703), to denounce *The Shortest Way with the Dissenters* as a vile piece of trickery, also to complain of Defoe's naming him – unfairly, he

13 *A New Test of the Church of England's Loyalty*, in *Political and Economic Writings*, Vol. 3, pp. 59–60.
14 Ibid.

claimed – as one of those threatening actual violence ('Gallows, Galleys, Persecution, and Destruction') against the Dissenters.[15]

As is well known, *The Shortest Way* led to Defoe's condemnation to prison and the pillory; and according to the Preface to *Jure Divino* a large part of the poem was composed while he was a prisoner in Newgate. His theme in the poem is that the motive for this tyrannical campaign was not defence of the Church – for the Church was in no danger from the Dissenters – but something much deeper. The clue was to be found in 'divine-right' doctrines: that is to say, in the real, as opposed to the pretended, meaning of those doctrines, which – in a word – was *idolatry*, the sin against the second Commandment. Tyranny and idolatry, as the history of the world shows, are so closely entwined as to be almost the same thing.

In August 1704 Leslie launched a journal, entitled *The Rehearsal*, with the direct purpose of skirmishing with Tutchin, the author of the Whiggish *Observator*, and Defoe, the author of the *Review*,[16] in defence of 'divine right doctrines'. (Parodying the *Observator*, the *Rehearsal* took the form of a dialogue between 'Countryman' and 'Observator'.[17]) As a non-juror, Leslie was in a strong moral position as compared with his more time-serving brethren. Equally, in Defoe he was faced with an untypical Dissenter, one quite as vehement against Occasional Conformity as himself. Thus their quarrel, in the pages of their journals, developed in a not altogether predictable way.

It was certainly very abusive at times. Defoe loved to annnoy Leslie with anti-High-Church rumours, and Leslie would go to exorbitant lengths to discredit them. When Defoe reported that a certain Oxford College had erected the Queen's royal arms (the motto of which was *Semper eadem*, or 'always the same') under a weathercock (!), Leslie instantly set up inquiries and managed, after much effort, to obtain written denials from the college workmen that anything of the kind had taken place. From now on he made a habit of raking this incident up, as a glaring example of Defoe's falsity.

More importantly, in the *Review* for 18 December 1705, Defoe drew a comparison between the 'dry martyrdom' of King James, at the hands of supposed exponents of 'passive obedience', and the 'wet martyrdom'

---

15 This was perhaps justified in a literal sense, but Leslie's language about the Dissenters at the end of *The New Association* is in fact almost as furious as Sacheverell's.

16 The *Review* began publication in February 1704.

17 Later, after 'Observator' has been dismissed with ignominy, between 'Countryman' and 'Rehearsal'.

of King Charles I, at the hands of the Puritans. The difference, he said, appeared to him remarkably small. Leslie responded to this ruthless witticism with the greatest indignation,[18] and from now on it became another pretext for the exchange of insults.

At a certain point, however, it occurred to both writers that there might be some profit in politer behaviour. Defoe was at work on *Jure Divino*, and it was in a way an advantage to him to have, in Leslie, such an articulate spokesman for 'divine right' doctrines. It helped to clear his own mind as regards Filmer's theory that all kingship derived its authority from Adam, and again over the thorny issue of the Israelites' choice of Saul as king. It enabled him to press the question, to which Leslie could not really find a convincing answer, whether basing the Queen's right to the throne purely on *inheritance*, as Leslie and his followers did, was not actually treasonable, considering how much stronger a claim to the throne was possessed by her brother the Pretender. Moreover, Leslie sometimes made intelligent criticisms. He had, for instance, quite cogent things to say against Defoe's theories (very idiosyncratic as they were) about property and the political rights of free-holders. (See *ante* p. 22). Defoe, Leslie announced with triumph, had deserted the people in favour of the free-holders: a comment not altogether off the mark.[19] He was, on the other hand, ready to do justice to Defoe's argument that Queen Anne had a 'divine right' to the throne, but the right was not 'inherent in her person'.

The two had, in short, begun to listen to each other's arguments. Defoe argued in the *Review* (13 July 1706) that an English monarch's right to the throne is not consecrated till the moment in the coronation ceremony when the People are asked whether they will have him or her as ruler. To this Leslie replies, not unreasonably, that the ritual was simply not meant to be taken literally. If anyone were actually to answer 'No' at this stage, they would most certainly be hurled into jail.

Leslie was also struck, as one is oneself, by a curious ambiguity in what Defoe says about Locke and Algernon Sidney. Defoe is explaining

18 'Can this be *Endur'd!*' he wrote, in the *Rehearsal* for 5 January 1706. 'Is not the *Wet Martyrdom* (as he in *Ridicule* calls it) and the Horrible *Sin* of it, as lying upon the whole *Nation*, once every Year, in a most *Solemn* Manner *Deprecated*, and that by Law, and to be forever *Observ'd*, because of its *Heinousness*, and the *UN-EXAMPL'D Wickedness* of it ... And shall we now be told by a vile Varlet come *Reeking* from the *Calves-Head-Club*, or *Kit-Kat*, That this whole *Scene of Observing* the 30th of *January* (which they call the *Madding-Day*), is all *Farce and Grimace*, and a *Mocking of God*; for that We are *Guilty* of a *Dry-Martyrdom* as *Criminal* as the *Other* that was Wet!'

19 See *Rehearsal*, 3 August 1706.

that his own theories about the origin of government are, perhaps, somewhat novel; and he continues:

> I know, what Mr. Lock, Sidney and others have said on this Head, and I must confess, I never thought their Systems fully answer'd – But I am arguing by my own Light, not other Mens; and therefore my Notions may be new, yet I beg the Favour to be heard, and if confuted, no Man shall be sooner silenc'd than I.[20]

As Leslie points out, it is not clear from this whether Defoe is saying that no-one had ever been able to answer Locke and Sidney (something that Leslie would strongly deny, having devoted many issues of the *Rehearsal* to answering Locke),[21] or rather that their systems had not 'answered', i.e. had not proved convincing.[22] He assumed, for polemical purposes, that Defoe must have meant the latter. For, in their recent debates, had not Defoe allowed that the first monarchies were 'patriarchal' and 'primogenial'?

Defoe's point had actually been that, though these original monarchies had most probably been patriarchal in character, it was not because God had issued any directive in the matter. Reason had arrived at this solution unaided. Leslie, however, seizes on this as a major concession and declares, triumphantly, that he has '*Converted* the Now *Celebrated DE FOE* himself, who has, under his Hand, fairly given up to me *Lock*, *Sidney*, Milton &c. and all their *Schemes*. And it cannot be Deny'd to be an *Instance* of his *Sincerity*, when he found he was not able to *Defend* them any longer.'[23]

This, one may suppose, was not how Defoe would have seen matters. But by now he has been despatched to Scotland, and for the moment his debate with Leslie ends.

Defoe's Succession Pamphlets

The great issue between Defoe and Leslie, over the nature of Queen Anne's right to the throne – was it hereditary or merely Parliamentary and consensual? – revived with great force in 1713. A Tory ministry led

---

20 *Review*, 10 September 1706, in *Defoe's Review*, [facsimile] ed. Arthur W. Secord, 22 vols (New York, 1938).
21 See *Rehearsal* between April and September 1705.
22 See *Rehearsal*, 18 September 1706.
23 *Rehearsal*, 13 November 1706.

by Robert Harley had by this time been in power for some three years, and rumours were rife that, though it still paid lip-service to the Act of Settlement and the Hanoverian succession, it was intending a sell-out to France, with whom in secret it had for some time been in friendly relations, and to the Pretender. The danger seemed all the more real in that it was known that Queen Anne, no friend to the Hanoverians, would in her heart have preferred her Stuart brother to succeed. Thus it was becoming an urgent question whether, if the Queen were to die, the Act of Settlement would in fact be upheld.

This was the cue for Defoe to put Leslie and Filmer's 'divine right' doctrines to ironic use. Between February and April 1713 he published three provocatively-titled pamphlets, with the dual purpose of raising the spectre of a Jacobite takeover, as a real and frightening threat, and of defusing Whig propaganda on the subject by comic exaggeration.

In the first, *Reasons against the Succession of the House of Hanover*, Defoe draws an ingenious parallel between the choice that might face the country upon Queen Anne's death and the situation which followed the death of Edward VI. A few weeks before his death, the devoutly Protestant Edward had settled the succession to the throne on the young Lady Jane Grey, a great-grand-daughter of Henry VII and a convinced Protestant. She was thus the legal incumbent, and Mary Tudor, though with a far stronger hereditary claim, was the Pretender. Nevertheless, the ill-fated Lady Jane was only allowed to reign for nine days and subsequently came to the block. The nation, out of its devotion to 'divine' hereditary right, had showed its preference for the 'Bloody Papist Persecuting Queen *Mary*'.

> Such was their Zeal for the Hereditary Right of their Royal Family, that they chose to fall into the Hands of *Spanish* Tyranny, and of *Spanish* Popery, and let the Protestant Religion and the hopes of its Establishment go to the D—l, rather than not have the Right Line of their Princes kept up.[24]

Similarly, the followers of the Pretender today must be saying to themselves:

> You call such a Man the Pretender but is he not the Son of our King? And if so, what is the Protestant Religion to us? Had we not much better be Papists than Traytors? Had we not much better deny our God, our Baptism, our Religion and our Lives, than deny our lawful Prince, our next Male in a Right Line? (p. 172).

24 *Reasons against the Succession*, below, p. 171.

Being good Protestants, moreover, those who helped bring in Mary Tudor were ready to pay the price – on the bonfires at Smithfield. No doubt then, Defoe's pamphlet argues maliciously, the same is true of those present-day Protestants who wanted to bring in the Pretender. Their intention was to be burnt at the stake – 'or they would not do it to be sure' (p. 172).

But while such as these have a voice in affairs, the pamphlet asks, can right-thinking folk wish the Hanoverian succession to take place? 'What! Would you bring over the Family of *Hannover* to have them Murther'd?' (p. 171).

The ensuing pamphlet, *And What if the Pretender should Come?* (published a month or so later) exploits a similar vein of irony. It expounds the manifest advantages to the nation if the Pretender were allowed to succeed to the throne. If, as people say, the power and invincibility of the French king are so much to be dreaded, what better remedy than to make him England's fast friend? The Scots could then hope to see the dissolution of the Union, about which they complain so loudly, and return to their old situation – of being perfectly free and depending on no-one but France. The Pretender would wisely cancel all public debts and would receive all taxes himself, thus relieving the country of the need for troublesome parliaments, also giving himself the opportunity to set up a noble standing army. Such would be the happy fruits of 'divine right' doctrines.

It is one of his most inventive essays in irony. As always with Defoe's best satire, it spreads its fire. Attacking the Jacobites offers him, simultaneously, the chance to pick off various targets nearer home. With all the crimes and oppressions of which the despotic Louis XIV is accused (he makes his imaginary Jacobite ask) does he not encourage manufacture and cultivate learning on a scale unknown in England? Has not France made unparalleled increases in prosperity under his rule? It is what Defoe himself has often insisted on naggingly in the past, though in a different cause. The device of quoting the views of that 'Scandalous Scribler' Mr *Review* works with great effectiveness. Let us consider his comment, earlier made in the *Review* (16 September 1712), that the question of the legitimacy of the Pretender is not significant – a remark improved by his imaginary Jacobite into his 'openly grant his Legitimacy'. It is a telling illustration of how words will be twisted by polemicists, and an excellent introduction to Defoe's constitutional theories, as well as a rebuke to the crudeness of current Whig arguments. But also, of course, in the way that he expands it, it is an unobtrusive but most ferocious insult to King James's widow. 'If the person we contend about be the Lawful true son of King *James's* Queen, the Dispute whether he be the Real Son of the King will be quite out of the Question'.[25]

Then, how sparkling are certain sly jokes in this pamphlet, like the argument that, under the Pretender's rule, country gentlemen will no longer continually be being harrassed to come up to Westminster, 'whether they can spare the Money or no for the Journey, or whether they must come *Carriage Paid*' (p. 202).

The last of the pamphlets, *An Answer to a Question that No Body thinks of*, makes a less obvious use of irony. It argues – with conspicuous coolness towards the Harley ministry, by which Defoe was still employed – that the ministry cannot be suspected of working for the Pretender, since, for the moment anyway, it is not in its interest do so; that Louis XIV is, for the moment, under too many obligations to Queen Anne to promote the interests of the Pretender; that the Toleration, the Scottish kirk and the Protestant faith, the public credit, and the liberties, privileges and property-rights of Britons, are all, for the moment, secure. But (this becomes the pamphlet's bodeful refrain) *what if the Queen should die?* The Revolution settlement, the pamphlet is arguing, is in serious danger unless immediate steps are taken to buttress and reinforce it.

It must seem reckless on Defoe's part, considering the dire price he had paid for *The Shortest Way with the Dissenters*, to have indulged in irony again, to this extent, on a burning public issue. But then, Defoe was a reckless man, and he nearly paid the same, or a worse, price again. The Whig pamphleteers William Benson and Thomas Burnet, together with Defoe's enemy Ridpath of the *Flying-Post*, laid a complaint against these 'Jacobite' pamphlets to Lord Chief Justice Parker, and Defoe was arrested at his home and spent a weekend in Newgate. He then made matters worse by criticising Parker's conduct over the affair in the pages of the *Review*, while the case was still *sub judice*, and on 22 April 1713 he was once again arrested and committed to the Queen's Bench prison. The outcome could have been very serious for him, though by good fortune and with help from Harley, he eventually managed to obtain a 'general pardon' from the Queen.[26]

---

25 *And What if the Pretender should Come?*, below, p. 190. See also note 1 to *And What if the Pretender*, p. 275.
26 See James Sutherland, *Defoe* (1937), pp. 195–9.

Defoe and Locke

Defoe is sometimes spoken of as a disciple of Locke. This seems rather to over-emphasise the influence. It is not, of course, in doubt that Defoe knew Locke's *Two Treatises on Government*,[27] and by his tantalising remark – that he never thought the systems of Locke and Sidney 'fully answer'd' – he could well be meaning that no-one had successfully refuted them. (He writes that Sidney's *Discourses* 'remain unanswerable to this day'.[28]) Nevertheless, he insists that he is 'arguing by my own Light, not other Mens', and this is certainly the impression that he makes. He of course maintains, in broadly Lockean fashion, that political authority ultimately lies with the People, and that by the 'People' is really meant property-owners. But beyond this, the systems of Locke and Defoe, though they do not positively contradict each other, are framed in noticeably different terms. For one thing, a leading concept in Locke is the 'State of Nature'. As he represents it, the 'State of Nature', being governed by 'the law of Nature', is, in theory at least, a perfectly viable condition for human existence. The individuals in it are free and equal, and each has the 'right' or 'power' to punish someone who offends against the law of nature, as well as to seek reparation for any damage he may have caused. The State of Nature has, however, its inconveniences, for it can easily degenerate into a 'State of War', in which one human being attempts to enslave others. (Liberty, we are to understand, means not being subjected to another human being's will.) This is why humans give up the State of Nature and, by mutual agreement, institute civil government. But – and this is the polemical force of Locke's scenario – we are not to suppose that the State of Nature is thereby relegated to prehistory. For princes of modern nations are still, visibly, in a State of Nature as regards one another. Equally, a despotic ruler is in a State of War with his subjects.

Now Defoe, by contrast, makes no use of the concept of a State of Nature, and for the good reason that, in his eyes, government is 'natural'. As he writes in *Jure Divino*,

> The *Laws of Government* were stamp'd on high,
> *Came down from Heav'n* for Men to manage by,
> And bear the Image of Divine Authority.

27 In *Jure Divino* (1706) he quotes (Book VII, p. 27) from the same speech made by James I to Parliament that Locke cites in Chapter 18 of the *Second Treatise* and was very probably alerted to it by reading Locke (though he gives a page reference, which is more than Locke does).

28 *Jure Divino* (1706), Book IV, p. 28.

> The Characters are *Capital and plain,*
> *Printed by Nature* on the Mind of Man.[29]

Government, that is to say, is a natural necessity.

> Society to Regulation tends,
> As naturally as Means pursue their Ends;
> The Wit of Man could never yet invent,
> A Way of Life without a Government.[30]

It follows from this that, though Defoe sometimes speaks of the 'rights' or 'native rights' of the people or of property-owners, the notion of rights is by no means as important for him as it is for Locke. Locke's arguments repeatedly turn on what a man 'can' or 'cannot' do (in the sense of having or not having the right to). A man, he says, 'cannot' enslave himself to another, since he does not possess such an 'arbitrary power over his own life', and therefore there 'cannot' be any such compact of enslavement between him and a tyrant or arbitrary ruler.[31] It is a metaphysical mode of reasoning alien to Defoe, whose own arguments tend more towards *Realpolitik* and the lessons of history. It is significant that, in *The Original Power of the Collective Body of the People of England* (1702), there is a second title in which the word 'Power' is replaced by the word 'Right', as if the two terms were indistinguishable.

It is noticeable, too, that, whereas Locke speaks of 'the law of nature', giving the word a juridical sense,[32] Defoe normally refers to the 'laws of nature' in the plural and includes physical laws among them. Indeed, in general, he uses the word 'laws' just as often in the sense of 'regular concatenations of cause and effect' as of 'commandments'. Since God created Nature, we are to suppose him the original author of these 'laws of nature', but he does not interfere with their working.

As for the question of property, nowhere in his poem does Defoe allude to Locke's memorable theory that 'Whatsoever then he [any man] removes out of the state that nature hath provided and left it in, he hath mixed his labour with, and joined to it something that is his own, and thereby makes it his property'.[33] On the other hand, as we have

---

29 Ibid, III, 19.
30 Ibid, II, 10.
31 See for instance Chapters 11 and 15 of the *Second Treatise, passim.*
32 'It is certain there is such a law, and that, too, as intelligible and plain to a rational creature and a studier of that law as the positive laws of commonwealths, nay, possibly plainer' (*Second Treatise*, Chapter 2).
33 *Second Treatise*, Chapter 5.

seen (p. 22), he puts forward a highly individual theory about the political rights of freeholders, and there is no close analogue to this in Locke.

Yet, after all, there is a notable resemblance between the two writers – not so much in what they did, as in what they did not do. J. G. A. Pocock, in his *The Ancient Constitution and the Feudal Law* (1957), has pointed out the central originality of Locke's *Two Treatises*: it is that nowhere in them is there any mention of English history.

Whiggish political theory, throughout the century, had been essentially historical in character. It held that English Common Law had subsisted, fundamentally unchanged, from an immemorial past and that it enshrined an 'ancient constitution' of a parliamentary, or quasi-parliamentary, kind. These Common Law liberties, so the theory ran, even antedated the Norman Conquest (for did not William I, in his coronation oath, pledge himself to perpetuate the laws of Edward the Confessor?); and, in resisting royal absolutism (for instance at the time of the Exclusion crisis in the 1670s) Whigs were fighting to defend these ancestral liberties. As a theory it had done great service for the opponents of James I, and again for the Levellers; but as historical scholarship developed – the nature of feudalism coming to be better understood and the authenticity of what passed as the 'laws of Edward the Confessor' growing more more and dubious – the theory was losing ground, indeed becoming something of a liability. Hence the value, and extreme effectiveness, of Locke's approach, which, breaking with previous tradition, based its arguments entirely upon reason and 'natural rights'.

Pocock speculates that Locke may have been simply, and abnormally, uninterested in history and in 'Edward the Confessor and Magna Carta and the rest of it'. If so, he was greatly unlike Defoe, who was evidently deeply interested in history. He claimed to have 'read all the Histories of Europe that are Extant in our Language, and some in other Languages',[34] and Books VIII–X of *Jure Divino* are framed as a sort of historical pageant, portraying monarchies from Nimrod and Ninus to his own day. But in this poem, as in his polemics in the *Review*, his interest in history does not run along conventional Whig lines. Its pervasive themes are the ludicrousness of the doctrine of 'passive obedience' to tyrants, and the absurdity of any claim that monarchical authority has been passed on uninterrupted through the ages. Accordingly, for his purposes, what is significant about England's Saxon ancestors is not so

---

34 *The Two Great Questions Further Consider'd*, in *Political and Economic Writings*, Vol. 5, p. 46.

much their bequeathing of liberties and parliamentary institutions as their ruthlessness and treachery as conquerors and the bloodstained history of usurpation of their royal line.

Defoe on Cabinet Government

In May 1704 Robert Harley was appointed Secretary of State and offered Defoe employment in a secret-service capacity; and in response, some time between July and August, Defoe drew up a remarkable memorandum, in which (perhaps picturing himself as Richelieu to Harley's Louis XIII) he offered his employer political advice at the highest level. High among his priorities was 'intelligence', and in the ensuing years he would go to great lengths to build up a nationwide intelligence network for Harley. This, however, was merely a practical aspect of a quasi-constitutional reform or revolution that he was urging on Harley: i.e. that he should introduce Cabinet government, and that, by corollary, he should make himself Prime Minister.

In the reign of Charles II, and more particularly during William III's absences from England, a 'Cabinet council' came to be a recognised element in administration, but by this was meant merely a working committee of the Privy Council. It was, that is to say, still strictly part of the royal administration. What Defoe proposed was, by contrast, a secret, or semi-secret, committee of the Secretary of State's office, able to put important measures into a complete form before they were presented for the monarch's approval in Council, and thus significantly diminishing the influence of the Crown. It was, indeed, the system that came to be established later in the century – though with the large difference that the 'Cabinet' was made ultimately responsible to Parliament.

As for the post of 'Prime Minister': it was not, nor is it still, a recognised part of the British constitution, though it became such an important one in practice; and it did not develop quite in the way that Defoe envisaged. The tradition inaugurated by Robert Walpole, who is usually spoken of as the first 'Prime Minister', was for this function to be attached, not to the Secretaryship of State, but to the post of First Lord of the Treasury. Nevertheless, Defoe's foresight in these matters is very striking, and it is hard not to think that it had its influence on Harley, and through him on the course of history.

SOME

REFLECTIONS

On a Pamphlet lately Publish'd,
Entituled, AN

ARGUMENT

Shewing that

A Standing Army

Is inconsistent with

A Free Government,

AND

Absolutely Destructive to the
Constitution of the *English*
MONARCHY.

––––––––––––––––

Hard words, Jealousies and Fears,
Sets Folks together by the Ears.[1]
Hudibras Lib.1.

––––––––––––––––

LONDON:
Printed for *E. Whitlock* near *Stationers-Hall.* 1697.

The Preface.

Mr. ABCDEFG,[2]

    SIR,

Since I am to Address to you Incognito, *I must be excus'd if I mistake your Quality; and if I treat you with more or less Civility than is your due, with respect to the Names or Titles, by which you may be Dignified or Distinguish'd; but as you are in Print, you give your self a just Title to the scandalous Name of a Pamphleteer, a Scribler, a seditious broacher of Notions and Opinions, and what not, for as is the Book such is the Author.*

I confess you are something difficult to be known, for your Note is so often chang'd, and your Trumpet gives such an uncertain sound, that no man can prepare himself to the Battle; sometimes you talk like a Common Wealths Man,[3] sometimes you applaud our present Constitution, sometimes you give high Encomiums *of the King; and then under the Covert of what Kings may be, you sufficiently Banter him; sometimes the Army are* Ragamuffins, *sometimes Men of Conduct and Bravery; sometimes our Militia are brave Fellows, and able enough to Guard us, and sometimes so inconsiderable, that a small Army may Ruine us, so that no Man alive knows where to have you.*

Possibly I may not have made a particular Reply to a long Rapsody of Exclamatory Heads; for indeed, Sir, *Railing is not my Talent: Had I more time to consult History, possibly I might have illustrated my Discourse with more lively instances; but I assure you I have not look'd in a Book during the Composure, for which reason I desire to be excus'd if I have committed any Errors, as to the Dates of any of my Quotations.*

If I were a Member of the Army, I wou'd thank you mightily for the fine sweet words you give them at the end of your Book: you have a pretty way with you of talking of Kings, and then you don't mean this King; and then of Armies, but you don't mean this Army; no, by no means, and yet 'tis this King that must not be trusted with Men nor Arms, and 'tis this Army that must be Disbanded; and his Majesty is exceedingly obliged to you, Sir, *for your usage of him as a Soldier; for 'tis plain you are Disbanding him as well as the Army.*

But of all things I magnifie you, Dear Sir, *for that fine turn of Argument, that not to Disband the Army is the way to bring in King* James; *but to Disband them is the most effectual way to hinder them. You have read, no doubt, of the Fable, how the Sheep were perswaded to dismiss the Dogs who they had hired to defend them against the Wolves; the Application,* Sir, *is too plain; and this is the Clause makes me suspect you for a* Jacobite.

Well you have driven furiously, and like Jehu[4] *called all the World to see your Zeal for the Lord; but like him too you have not Demolished the high Places; you have Demolish'd the Army, but you have not provided against* Jacobitism; *you take care to leave the King naked to the Villany of Assassines, for you are not for leaving him so much as his Guards; and you take care to leave the Nation naked to the insults of an Enemy, and the King and the People must defend themselves as well as they can. This is the way indeed to teach us Obedience with a Rod of Iron, and to make us pass under the Axes and Harrows of a barbarous Enemy.*

All your Plea is Liberty, an alluring word; and I must tell you, Liberty or Religion has been the Mask for almost all the Publick Commotions of the World: but if Freedom be the English *Man's Right, you ought to have given the King and his Parliament the Freedom of Debating this matter by themselves, without putting your self upon them to raise a Controversie, where for ought you know there may be no occasion.*

What, is there no way but an entire Disbanding the whole Army? Can no Expedient be found out to secure us from Enemies abroad, and from Oppression at home, &c. no way but this, Sir, *How do you know what a Parliament may do?*

Parliaments are Magnipotent, tho' they are not Omnipotent, and I must tell you, Sir, the Commons of England *are not a Body that can be Enslaved with* 20000 *Men; and all that have ever attempted it, formed their own Ruine in it, and I hope ever will do so; but* the Wicked fear where no fear is, and fly when none pursues.

I wish he wou'd let us know his Character, that we might judge of the Manners by the Man, for I am sure we cannot judge well of the Man by the Manners.

Your most Humble Servant,
D. F.[a]

REFLECTIONS ON A LATE
SCANDALOUS PAMPHLET, ENTITULED,
AN ARGUMENT AGAINST A
STANDING ARMY.

SOME Men are so fond of their own Notions, and so impatient in the Pride of their own Opinions, that they cannot leave Business of Consequence to them to whom it specially and peculiarly belongs, but must, with as much Brass as Impertinence, meddle with a Cause before it comes before them, tho' it be only to show they have more Wit than Manners.

I observe this by the way, before I enter the List of Argument which a Nameless Author of a most Scandalous Pamphlet, call'd, *An Argument against a standing Army.*

If the Author of that Pamphlet be, as he wou'd be thought, a true honest spirited English-man, who out of his meer Zeal for the Safety, Liberty, and Honour of his Country, has made this false Step, he is the more to be consider'd: But if so, why shou'd he fear his Name? The days are over, *God be thank'd*, when speaking Truth was speaking Treason: Every Man may now be heard. What has any Man suffer'd in this Reign for speaking boldly, when Right and Truth has been on his side? Nay, how often has more Liberty been taken that way than consisted with good Manners, and yet the King himself never restrain'd it, or reprov'd it; witness Mr. *Stephen's* unmannerly Books,[5] written to the King himself.

But since the Author Conceals himself from all the World, how can we guess him any thing but a Malecontent, a Grumbletonian, *to use a foolish term*, a Person dissatisfied with his not being Rewarded according to his wonderful Merit, a *Ferg—*, a *Man—*,[6] or the like. Or a down-right *Jacobite*, who finding a French War won't do, wou'd fain bring in Fears and Jealousies to try if a Civil War will. I confess I cannot affirm which of these; but I am of the Opinion he is the latter of the two, because his Insinuations are so like the Common Places of that Party, and his Sawcy Reflections on the King's Person, bear so exact a Resemblance to their usual Treatment of him, that it seems to be the very stile of a Malignant.

I may be readily answer'd to this (I confess) *Let me be what I will, what's that to you, Answer my Argument; If the Doctrine be true, let the Devil be the Parson; Speak to the Point.*

In good time I shall: And to begin with him, I agree with him in all he says, or most part at least of his Preamble, saving some trifling Matters of Stile and of Notion, and we won't stand with him for small things. And thus I bring him to his Fourth Page without any trouble; for indeed he might have spar'd all the Three Pages for any great signification they have, or relation to what comes after.

The Fifth Paragraph in his Fourth Page, and indeed the Substance of the whole Book brings the Dispute to this short Point; *That an Army in* England *is inconsistent with the Safety of the Kingdom; That Liberty and an Army are incompatible; That the King is not to be trusted with either Men, Arms, nor Money, for the last will be the Consequence of the former; lest he that has ventur'd his Life in the Extremest Dangers for us, shou'd turn our Devourer and destroy us.* A great deal of very handsome Language he bestows upon the King on this account, calling him, with a tacit sort of necessary Consequence, *Wolf, Beast, Tyrant,* and the like.

He tells us, *Page* 3. *All the Nations round us have lost their Liberty by their permitting standing Armies; and that they permitted them from Necessity or Indiscretion.* If from Necessity, 'twas their Misfortune not their Fault. If from Indiscretion, that was their Fault indeed.

But he is not pleas'd to give us one Instance of any People who were brought under that Necessity, and lost their Liberty by it; and yet if he had, 'twas no Argument, but that if we were reduc'd to the same Necessity, we must run the risque of it: Of which more by and by.

In the same Page he lays down the Draught of our Constitution, *Depending on a due Ballance between King, Lords and Commons;* and affirms from thence, *That this Constitution must break the Army, or the Army destroy this Constitution:* and affirms absolutely, with a Confidence Peculiar to himself, *That no Nation can preserve its freedom, which maintains any other Army than such as is composed of a Militia of its own Gentry and Freeholders.* And being gotten into a Positive vein, he says, *What happen'd yesterday, will come to pass again; and the same Causes will produce like Effects in all Ages.* And indeed all is alike true, since nothing is more frequent, than for the same Causes to produce different Effects; and what happened yesterday may never happen again while the World stands, of which King *James* is a visible Instance. But to descend to Particulars.

I shall give you only this remarkable Instance; King *Henry* VIII made as vigorous and irregular Efforts to destroy the Religion of the Kingdom (as then 'twas establish'd) as ever King *James* did, and perhaps his Methods were more than ordinarily parallel; he Govern'd this Nation with as absolute a despotical Power, though the Constitution was then the same as it is now, as ever King *Charles* II. or King *James* II. attempted to have done, and yet the Effects were not Abdication, or calling in a Foreign Aid. I could go back to other Kings of this Nation, whose Stories might illustrate this; but the Gentleman is Historian good enough, I perceive, to know it; and by the way, 'tis to be observed also, that he did this without the help of a Standing Army: From whence I only observe, as all the present use I shall make of this Instance, that there are ways for a King to tyrannize without a standing Army, if he be so resolv'd: *è contra*,[7] there may be ways to prevent it with an Army, and also that I think this proves, that *the same Causes does not always produce the same Effects*; and a little further, *if the same Causes will produce the like Effects in all Ages*, why then, Sir, pray lay by your Fears, for if ever King *William* (which we are sure he won't) or any King else, goes about to destroy our Constitution, and overturn our Liberties, as King *James* did, the People will call in a Foreign Aid, and cause him to run away, as they did then; *for what happened Yesterday will come to pass again, and the same Causes will produce the like Effects in all Ages*.

Page the Sixth he begins very honestly, with a Recognition of our Security under the present King, and softens his Reader into a Belief of his Honesty, by his Encomiums on his Majesty's Person, which would be well compar'd with his Seventeenth Page, to shew how he can frame his Stile to his Occasion; but in short, concludes, that when he is dead, we know not who will come next; nay, the Army may come and make who they please King, and turn the Parliament out of Doors and therefore in short, we ought not to trust any thing to him, that we wou'd not trust to the greatest Tyrant that may succeed him. So that our Condition is very hard, that the Person of a King is no part of the Consideration, but *a King, be he Angel or Devil, 'tis all one, is a Bugbear, and not to be trusted*. A fine Story indeed, and our great Deliverer (as he calls the King) must not regret this, but be contented: that *now he has cleared the World of all our Enemies, but himself*, he should be esteem'd the great *Charibdis*[8] which the Nation was to be split upon, and we must entirely disarm him, *as a Wolf who ought not to be trusted with Teeth*; for these are his own Words.

Then he tells us, *No Legislators*[9] *ever establisht a Free Government, but avoided this, as the Israelites, Athenians, Corinthians, Accaians, Lacedemonians, Thebanes, Sammites, Romans.* Now 'tis notoriously known, that all these were first establish'd Commonwealths, not Monarchies: and if this Gentleman wou'd have us return to that Estate, then I have done with him; but I appeal to himself, if all these Governments, when they became Regal, did not maintain a Millitary Power more or less: Nay, God himself, when the *Israelites* would have a King, told them this would be a Consequence: as if it might be inferr'd as of absolute necessity, that a Military Power must be made use of with a Regal Power; and as it may follow *no King, no Army,* so it may as well follow, *no Army no King.* Not that I think an Army necessary to maintain the King in his Throne, with regard to his Subjects, for I believe no Man in the World was ever *the Peoples King* more than his present Majesty. But I shall endeavour a little to examine by and by, what the King and Nation, so as Matters now stand in the World, wou'd be without an Army.

But our Adversary rests not here, but Page 7. he proceeds; truly he *wou'd not have the King trusted with an Army; no, nor so much as with Arms, all the Magazines too must be taken from him.* And referring to the Estates, mentioned before, he says, *They knew that the Sword and the Sovereignty marcht Hand in Hand, and therefore a general exercise of the People in Arms, was the Bulwark of their Liberties, and their Arms,* that is, Magazines of Amunition, &c. for the Term is now changed, *were never lodg'd in the Hands of any but the People:* for so the following Words directly imply. *The best and bravest of their Generals came from the Plough, and contentedly return'd to it again when the War was over.* We shou'd have made a fine War against *France* indeed, if it had been so here. And then he goes on with Instances of Nations who lost their Liberties when ever they deviated from these Rules. At the end of these Examples, our Author tells all the world in short what he would be at: For there he has, like God Almighty, divided the World, and he has set the *Sheep on his right hand, and the Goats on his left;* for he has reckon'd up all the Monarchal Governments in the World, with a *Go ye cursed into the most abandon'd Slavery,* as he calls it; and all the Commonwealths in the World, on the other side, with a *Come ye blessed into freedom from Kings standing Armies,* &c.

Nay he has brought *Algiers* and *Tunis* in for People who enjoy their Liberty, and are free. I suppose he has never been there: and truly, I believe the Freedom he mentions here, wou'd be very like that, or like the *Days when there was no King in* Israel, *but every Man, did what was right in his own Eyes.*

Thus far I have follow'd him only with Remarks in general to Page 13. he proceeds then to tell us the Danger of an Army, and the Misfortune of all Countries to be forc'd sometimes to take up Arms against their Governours. A Man ought to be an universal Historian to affirm that, and I have not time to examine it. Now from hence he draws this Assertion, *That 'tis therefore necessary to put us into a Capacity always to be able to Correct our Kings, that we may have no occasion for it; for when we are enabled to do it, we shall never be put upon it.* The English is this, Keep your King so weak that he may always be afraid of you, and he will never provoke you to hurt him. *For,* says he, *the Nation shall be sure to live in Peace which is most capable of making War: But if the King has* 20000 *Men before-hand with us,* observe it [*with us*] in totidem verbis[10] I leave his meaning to be construed, *the People can make no Efforts without the Assistance of a Foreign Power.*

Another Consequence of an Army is, *They may come and force the People to choose what Members they please, to sit in Parliament, or they may besiege the Parliament-House, and the like.* Now it happened that both these things have been done in *England,* and yet the People preserved their Liberties, which is a Demonstration beyond the Power of Words, from his old Maxim, *What happen'd Yesterday, will come to pass again,* and *like Causes will have like Effects:* The choice of Members of Parliament were obstructed, and the House of Parliament was besieged and insulted by the Soldiers, and yet the People were not depriv'd of their Liberties; therefore it may be so again, *for what happen'd Yesterday will come to pass again.*

Page 14. He descends to a particular, which reverst, I think, is a lively Instance what a vigorous Opposition may do against a far greater Force than 20000 Men: *If King* Charles *the First,* says he, *had had but* 5000 *Men, the People cou'd never have struck a Stroak for their Liberties.*

Turn this Story, and let us but recollect what Force the Parliament had, and what the King had, and yet how many Stroaks he struck for his Crown.

The Parliament had the Navy, all the Forts, Magazines and Men in their Hands: The King, when he erected his Standard at *Nottingham,* had neither Ships, Men, Arms, Ammunition or Money, but seem'd to be turn'd loose into the Field, to fight with the Commons of *England,* and all the Militia was in the Hands of the Parliament by the Commission of Array, and yet the King was ready in *Keynton Field,* and at the Head of an Army, sooner than the Parliament were ready to fight him, nor do the Writers of that Side pretend to call that a Victory.

Then he comes to King *James*, and says he, *If he had not attempted Religion, but been contented with Arbitrary Power, we shou'd ha' let him bound us Hand and Foot; and tho' King* James *had all the Nation, and his own Army against him, yet we account the Revolution next to a Miracle.* To this I reply, No, Sir; no Miracle at all on that Score; for the Nobility, Gentry, and People of *England* did not question but they shou'd reduce him to reason, else they had never call'd in the present King, for they did not expect him to work Miracles, but to procure a Free Parliament, &*c.* as is at large express'd in his Majesties Declaration. But here lay the Miracle of the Revolution:

The Providential Removal of the *French* Kings Forces to the Siege of *Philipsburgh*, against all manner of Policy, when if he had made but a feint on the Frontiers of the *Dutch*, they could neither have spar'd their Troops nor their Stadtholder.

The wonderful Disposition of the Wind and Weather which lockt up King *James*'s Fleet, so as to make the Descent easie and safe.

And at last the Flight of King *James*, and the Re-settlement of the whole Kingdom without a Civil War, which was contrary to the Expectations of all the World; this was that which was next to Miraculous.

Now we must come to examine his Quotations, by which I must be excus'd to guess at the rest of his Instances, which indeed, generally speaking, are chosen very remote; he tells us, a very small Army is capable to make a Revolution; *Oliver Cromwel* left behind him but 17000, *Oportet Mendacem esse Memorem*;[11] *Oliver Cromwel* did not work the Revolution which he brought to pass on the Parliament with less than 35000 Men, and if he left but 17000 behind him, which nevertheless I do not grant, there must be reckoned the Army left in *Scotland*, with General *Monk*, which was at least 12000, and the Settlement in *Ireland*, which at least also took off from the old Army above 10000 Men more, besides those which had chang'd Parties and laid down their Arms: As to the *Pretorian* Soldiers,[12] I don't read that they by themselves made any Revolution in the *Roman* Empire. *Julius Cæsar* had a much greater Force when he March'd out of *Gaul*; and they were great Armies who Declared *Galba, Otho* and *Vespasian* Emperors. Then as to the *Ottoman* Empire, of which this Author, I suppose, knows very little; the *Janisaries* have not been less in that Empire till this War, than 70000 Men; what he calls the *Court Janisaries* I know not, but when *Selimus* Depos'd and Murther'd his Father *Amurath*,[13] you will find above 50000 *Janisaries* and *Spahis* in the Action; but if an Army of 17000 Men can enslave this Nation, as he foolishly supposes, our Militia are good for much at the same time.

As to his Paragraph, *p.* 15. wherein he says, we are told, this Army is to be but for a time, and not to be part of our Constitution. I must say to him, I never have been told so, but I am of the Opinion, and shall acquiesce in it, that such an Army and no other, as the King and Parliament shall think needful for our Preservation shall be kept on Foot, so and so long as the said King and Parliament shall think fit; and from them I dare say no Danger can befal our Liberty. We have a blessed happy Union between the King and the Parliament; the King offers not to invade the Peoples Liberties, nor they his Prerogative; he will desire no Army but for their safety, nor they will deny none that is: But here is an Author, who in the beginning of his Pamphlet says, the Safety of the Kingdoms depends upon a due Ballance; and at the same time tells us, our Armies, no nor our Magazins, are not to be trusted with the King; is that a due Ballance?

Then he tells you, that saying the Purse is in the Hands of the People, is no Argument at all, and that an Army will raise Money, as well as Money raise an Army; he suggests indeed that 'tis *too desperate a Course,* as well he may; for I wou'd only ask him, if he thinks an Army of 20000 Men could suppress this whole Kingdom, and live upon Free Quarter on the Inhabitants by Force. I wou'd put him in mind of the Alarum *Ship Money*[14] made in *England,* and yet King *Charles* had then an Army and no Parliament Sitting. Then he supposes a shutting up the *Exchequer,* for indeed he is upon the Point of *Supposing* every thing that has but a *Possibility* in it, and what if the *Exchequer* should be shut up? why this Gentleman wants to be told that the Money is not in *Specie* in the *Exchequer,* and it must be raised and brought thither by the Help of the Army; so that all that amounts to the same thing as the other, raising Money by Troops of Horse, which has been try'd in *England,* to the Destruction of the Contrivers; *and what has been,* he says, *will always be again.*

From this he proceeds to an insolent saucy Banter on his Majesty's Person, *whose Vertue,* he says, *we ought not to hazard by leading it into Temptation: Our Heroes,* he says, *are of a course Allay,*[15] and he has observed most Men to do all the Mischief they can, and therefore he is for dealing with them as with Children and Mad Men, that is, take away all Weapons from them, by which they may do either themselves or others any Mischief; *as the Sheep who addrest to* Apollo, *that for the future the Wolves might have no Teeth.*

His placing this in the Plural, the Courtiers, is too thin a Screen to blind any Man's Eyes; but 'tis as plain as if it had been said in so many

Words, that all this is meant directly of the King; for who is it we have been speaking of? *'tis the King, who is not to be trusted with an Army, or with the Arms of the Kingdom;* *'tis the King* who must be the Tyrant, and must raise Money, and shut up the Exchequer, and the like; and he speaks here of nothing but what the King only can be supposed to do.

In Confutation of his 18th Page, I could very plainly demonstrate, that even a Slavery under a Protestant Army would differ very much from a Slavery under a Popish and French Army. *England* has felt the First, and seen others feel the last: there is a Difference in Slavery, *Algiers* is better than *Sally*;[16] and there are Degrees of Misery; and this is no putting an Epethite[17] upon Tyranny, ask the Protestants of *Languedoc* if the *French Dragoons* were not worse than the *Spanish Inquisition*: But this is Foreign to the Point, it does not appear to any considerate Person, that here is any of these Slaveries in view, and therefore, I thank God, we are not put to the Choice.

I shall leave him now, and discourse a little in Particular of the thing it self, and what other Pretensions he makes will meet their Answer in the process of the Story as they come in my way.

As I said at the Beginning, *what's all this to us?* we who are *English Men* have the least Reason of any People in the World, to complain of any of our Laws, or of any Publick Affairs, because nothing is or can be done, but I, and every *individual Free holder* in *England*, do it our selves, we consent to it, and tacitly do it by our *Representatives* in the Parliament; and since then our Liberties, aye and our Lives are committed to them, who are you, Sir? that you shou'd run before you are sent, and dictate to the *Collective Body of the Nation*, what they ought or ought not to do? If *the House of Commons* think fit to continue 50000 Men, there is no doubt but they will find ways so to keep them at their dispose, that even that Army shall be the Preserver of our Liberties, not the Destroyer of them, and to them let us leave it.

But 'tis the King is the Bugbear, *a Royal Army shall destroy us, but a Parliament Army shall protect us*. Page 11. *Commonwealths*, he says, *may have Armies, but Kings may not*. Now if putting Arms into the Hands of Servants is so fatal, why it's as dangerous to make a general Muster of the Militia, as 'twas to the *French* in the *West-Indies*, to give their Arms to their Servants, a standing Militia regulated and disciplin'd, such as the *Vaudois or Miquelets*, why that's *a Standing Army, and shall be as insolent as they, if you give them an Opportunity, and a Standing Army,* as they may be regulated, *shall be as safe and as far from Tyrannizing as they*.

And with this Gentleman's leave, I believe I could form a Proposal how an Army of 20000 Men might be kept in *England*, which should be so far from being destructive of, that, they should on all Occasions be the Preservers and Protectors of the Peoples Liberties, in case of a *Court Invasion*, for that is the Out cry; I confess, I do rather beg the Question here, than produce my Schemes of that Nature, because I do not think it becomes me to dictate to my Superiors, who without Question, know better what to do in that great Concern of the Government, than I could direct.

The Question here may be more properly, What sort of an Army we talk of? If 'twere an Army Independant of the People, to be paid by the King, and so entirely at his absolute dispose. If 'twere to be an Army of 50000 Men, why then something may be said; but our Gentleman has not talk'd of above 20000, and I presume he speaks of that without any Authority too, and at the same time talks of the Valour and Performances of the Militia, and wou'd have Sixty thousand of them settled and regulated. This Argument of the Militia is strangely turn'd about by him; sometimes they are such Hero's that they are able to defend us, and why should they not, and the like, *page* 20, 21. and sometimes so weak that 20000 Men *will ruine us all*; nay, any thing of an Army. If they are strong enough to defend us from all the World, a small number of standing Troops cannot hurt us; if they are not, then we must have an Army, or be exposed to every Invader.

I wonder therefore this Gentleman does not descend to show us a time when the Militia of any Country did any Service *singly*, without the help of the Regulated Troops; I can give him a great many Instances when they did not. The best time that ever the Militia of *England* can boast of doing any Service, was in our Civil War; and yet I can name a Gentleman, who is now alive, who was an Officer of Horse in the Parliament Army, he was posted by the General at *a Defile*, to dispute the Passage of some of the King's Horse, who advanc'd from *Warrington Bridge* in *Cheshire*, finding himself prest, he sent away to the General for some Foot to support him: He sent him a Company of Foot of the Militia, and a Detachment of Dragoons; the Foot were plac'd behind the Hedges to line the Pass where they might have fir'd almost under Covert, as behind a Breast-work; but as soon as ever the King's Horse appear'd, without firing one shot, they run all away. These were Regulated Militia. But our Author gives us three Instances of Countries, whose Militia defend them; and three more of the bravery of a Country Militia, which Instances I must a little examine.

Poland, Switzerland, and the *Grisons* are an Instance of Nations who defend themselves against powerful Neighbours without a standing Army. As to *Poland*, I shall shew afterwards at what a rate they have defended themselves. The *Swiss* and *Grisons* subsist between formidable Enemies, just as the Duke of *Savoy* defends himself between the *French* and the *Spaniards*, or as *Hamburgh* between the *Danes* and the Dukes of *Zel*, or as *Geneva* between the *French* and the *Savoyard*; not but that either side is able to devour them, but because when ever one side Ataques them, the others defend them; for 'tis neither sides Interest to see the others have them.

But now we come to the Militia, the *London* Apprentices in the late War, and the *Vaudois* and *Miquelets* in this. As to the *London* Auxiliaries, which they call Apprentices, they behav'd themselves very well, but it was in Conjunction with the Regulated Troops, when I must also say, the King's Army at that time were but raw, and not much better than themselves.

The *Vaudois* are *Les Enfans perdue*,[18] a People grown desperate by all the Extremities which make Cowards fight; a small handful of Ruin'd Men, exasperated by the Murder of their Families, and loss of their Estates, and are to be lookt upon as Men metamorphised into Dragons and Furies; and yet even the *Vaudois* have never fought but on Parties, Skirmishes, Surprizes, Beating up Quarters, and the like, back'd with Retreats into inaccessible Rocks, and skulking behind the Cliffs, from whence, like Lightning, they break out on the Enemy, and are gone before they could well find where they were.

The *Miquelets* in *Catalonia* are another Instance, and these are but People, who by the Advantages of the Mountains, lye in wait to intercept Convoys, and surprize Parties, and have done the *French* exceeding Damage, on account of the Distance of the *French* Armies in that Country from their Magazines; for 'tis necessary to state Matters very exactly, to debate with so cunning a Disputant. But for the Service of either the *Vaudois* or *Miquelets* in the open Field, it has not been extraordinary. As to the Militia in *Ireland*, all their Fame is owing to despicable wretched Conduct of the *Irish*; for what Army but that of a Rabble of *Irish*, could *Iniskilling* and *London-Derry*[19] have stood out against, at the rate they did. So that these Wonders of the Militia are all Phantosms, and not applicable to the present Case at all.

I shall a little urge here by way of Reply, That there seems to be a Necessity upon the People of *England* at this time, to stand in a Posture of Defence more than usually; if I cannot prove this, then I say nothing.

First, This Necessity arises from the Posture of our Neighbours: *In former times*, says our Authour, *there was no difference between the Citizen, the Souldier, and the Husband-man*; but 'tis otherwise now, *Sir*, War is become a Science, and Arms an Employment, and all our Neighbours keep standing Forces, Troops of *Veteran* Experienced Soldiers; and we must be strangely expos'd if we do not.

In former times the way of Fighting was Common to all, and if Men ran from the Field to the Camp, so did their Neighbours, and 'twas as good for one as another. But how did the *Romans* preserve their *Frontiers*, and plant their Colonies? That was not done by Citizens of *Rome*, but by Legionary Troops; and shall we Disarm, while our Neighbours keep standing Armies of Disciplin'd Souldiers on foot? Who shall secure us against a sudden Rupture? Whoever will give himself the trouble to look into the Treaties of *Westphalia* and *Nimeguen*,[20] and to Examine the Conduct of the *French* King, they will find, He did not then account Leagues such Sacred things as to bind him against a visible Advantage; and why should *we lead him into Temptation*? Let any one but reflect on the several Treaties between him and the Duke of *Lorrain*, the Duke of *Savoy*, and the *Spaniards*; after which ensued, the Prize of all *Lorrain*, the taking of all *Savoy*, and the taking of the City and Country of *Luxemburgh*; let them look on his surprising the Principality of *Orange*, directly contrary to the Peace of *Nimeguen*, and the like, and is this a Neighbour to live by Naked and without an Army? Who shall be Guarrantee that the *French* shall not insult us, if he finds us utterly Disarmed.

To answer this Necessity says this wise Gentleman, *We will have an Equivalent*; why, *we will not have a Land Army, but we will have a Sea Army*, that is, *a good Fleet*. A fine Tale truly, and is not this some of Mr. *Johnson*'s false Heraldry,[21] as well as 'tother? Is it not all one to be Slaves to an Army of Musqueteers, as a Rabble of Tarrs? Our very Scituation, which the Author is in his Altitudes about, and blesses his *God Neptune for* at such a rate; that very Scituation exposes us to more Tyranny *from a Navy, than from an Army*: Nay I would undertake, if I were Admiral of a good Fleet, to Tyrannize more over this Nation, than I should if I were General of 40000 men. I remember 'twas a great cry among the *Jacobite Party*, about four Year ago; what a vast Charge are we at about a War for the Confederates, *Damn the Confederates*, let us keep a good Fleet, and we are able to defend our selves against all the World; let who will go down, and who will go up, no Body will dare to meddle with us: But God be thanked, the King knew better than these, what was the true Interest of *England*; a War in *Flanders* is a War in

England, let who will be the Invaders; for a good Barrier between a Kingdom and a powerful Enemy, is a thing of such Consequence, that the *Dutch* always thought it well worth the Charges of a War to assist the *Spaniard*; for thereby they kept the War from their own Borders and so do we.

In defending this silly Equivalent of a Fleet, he has the Vanity to say, *If our Fleet be well mann'd, 'tis a ridiculous thing to think of any Princes Invading us*; and yet we found it otherwise. This very War we found King *James* invaded *Ireland*, and the *French* sent him an Aid of 8000 Men, who stood their Ground so well at the Battle of the *Boyn*, that if King *James* had done his part as well, it might have been a dearer Victory than it was; after this he fetch'd those 8000 off again; and after that sent Monsieur St. *Ruth*; and after that a Relief to *Limerick*, tho' it came too late; and all this notwithstanding we had the greatest Fleet at Sea, that ever *England* had before that time, since it was a Nation.

Thus Experience Bafles this foolish Equivalent, for Armies are not Transported with so much Difficulty; and the Six hundred Sail the P. of *Orange* brought with him, had not been absolutely necessary for 14000 Men; but there were vast Stores, Artillery, Arms, and heavy Baggage with them, which are not always necessary; for we know Monsieur *Pointy*[22] carried 4500 Men with him, on his Expedition to *Cartagena* in but 16 Ships; and the 8000 Men before-mentioned, sent to *Ireland*, were carried in not above 35 or 38 Sail.

Another wretched Equivalent, which this Author would have us trust to, is the *Militia*; and these he magnifies, as sufficient to defend us against all the Enemies in the World; and yet at the same time so Debases them, as to make them nothing in Comparison of a small Army: Nay, he owns, that *notwithstanding these we are undone, and our Liberties destroyed, if the King be trusted but with a few Guards*. This is such a piece of Logick as no Man can understand.

If a Militia be regulated and *Disciplin'd*, I say they may enslave us as well as an Army; and if not, they cannot be able to defend us; if they are unable to Defend us, they are insignificant; and if able, dangerous; *But*, says the Author, *there is no danger from the Militia, for they are our selves, and their Officers are Country Gentlemen of Estates*: And is not our Army full of *English* Gentlemen, of Estates and Fortunes; and have we not found them as inflexible to the Charms of Tyranny, when closetted in the late Reign; and as true to the Protestant Interest and Liberties of *England*, as any Country Gentlemen, or Freeholders, or Citizens in *England*. Did they not lay down their Commissions, did they not venture to disobey his illegal Commands? when the Cowardly Citizens address'd him with their nauseous Flattering, fulsome Harrangues; thank'd him for their Bondage, and gave up their Charters and Priviledges, even before he ask'd for them; *These are the Persons that must guard our Liberties*; and they would be finely Guarded, *God help us*. I remember a Speech which I have to show in *Manuscript* of Sir *Walter Rawleigh*, on the Subject of the *Spanish* Invasion, which comes directly to this Case. The Author of this Pamphlet, to instance in the prodigious Navy that is necessary to bring over a small Army, tells us, the *Spanish Armado* Embark'd but 18000 Men, but he forgot that they were to take the Prince of *Parma* on Board from *Flanders* with 28000 old Low Country Soldiers more; with which Army, as Sir *Walter Rawleigh* observ'd to that Gentleman, it was no improbable thing to think of Conquering this Kingdom; and Queen *Elizabeth* was so sensible of it, that she often told Sir *Walter*, that if they had not been beaten at Sea, they had been all undone, for her Armies were all Tumultuary Troops, Militia, and the like.

To proceed, I'll grant all the Improbabilities which he suggests of the *French King's* reviving a War, which has been so fatal to him: And as to King *James* Coming, truly I'll allow the Militia are fittest at all times to deal with him; but to use his own Method of *Supposing the worst*, I'll *suppose* the *French King* waving the Ceremony of a *League*, and a *Declaration of War*, when he has recovered Breath a little, shou'd as much on a sudden as can be, break with us single, and pour in an Army of 50000 Men upon us; I'll suppose our Fleet may be by accident so lockt in, as King *James's* was, *for what has been may be*, and they take that Opportunity, and get on Shore, and to oppose their Army, truly we raise the Militia, a Fine Shew they wou'd make, but what wou'd they do against 60 Batalians of *French* and *Swiss* Infantry? wou'd this Gentleman *venture to be hang'd if they run all away and did not fire a Gun at them*? I am sure I wou'd not.

But on the other Hand, if the Militia are a sufficient Guard against a *Foreign Power*, so they are against a *Home Power*, especially since this *Home Power* may be kept down to a due Ballance, so as may but suffice to keep us from being insulted by a *Foreign Enemy*; for Instance, suppose the King were to entertain in constant Pay, 20000 Men, including his Guards and Garrisons, the Militia of *England* Regulated and Disciplin'd, join'd to these, might do somewhat, but by themselves nothing. I can give him innumerable Instances of the Services of the Militia, but I never heard or read of any real Bravery from them, but when join'd with Regular Troops.

To Instance once for all, 'tis notorious that when the Prince of *Conde* attackt the Citizens of *Paris* at *Charenton*,[23] that Populous City being all in an Uproar, sent a Detachment of 20000 Men to dislodge the Prince, who with 1500 Horse and Dragoons, drove them all away, and they never lookt behind them, till they got within the City Wall.

Another Necessity for keeping up a certain Number of Troops, is the vast Expence and Difficulty of making a New-rais'd Army fit for Service; I am bold to say, as the Nature of Fighting is now chang'd, and the Art of War improv'd, were the King now to raise a New Army, and to be Commanded by New Officers, Gentlemen who had seen no Service, it should cost him Three Years Time, and 30000 Mens Lives to bring them into a Capacity to face an Enemy. *Fighting is not like what it has been*; I find our Author is but a *Book Soldier*, for he says, *Men may learn to be Engineers out of a Book*; but I never heard that a *Book Gunner* could *Bombard a Town*; the Philosophy of it may be Demonstrated in Scales and *Diagrams*, but 'tis the Practice that produces the Experiments; 'tis not handling a Musket, and knowing the Words of Command, will raise a Man's Spirit, and teach him to Storm a Counterscarp; Men must make the Terrors of the War familiar to them by Custom, before they can be brought to those Degrees of Gallantry. Not that there is an intrinsick Value in a *Red Coat*; and yet the Argument is not at all enforced by the Foul Language he gives the Souldiers, while they are fighting in *Flanders*, and laying down their Lives in the Face of the Enemy to purchase our Liberty; 'tis hard and unkind to be treated by a rascally Pamphleteer with the Scandalous Term of *Ragamuffins*, and *Hen-roost Robbers*. I am no Soldier, nor never was, but I am sensible we enjoy the present Liberty, the King his Crown, and the Nation their Peace, bought with the Price of the Blood of these *Ragamuffins*, as he calls them, and I am for being civil to them at least.

I might descend a little to examine what a strange Country *England* would be, when quite dismantled of all her Heroes (as he calls them); truly were I but a Pirate with a Thousand Men, I wou'd engage to keep the Coast in a Constant Alarm. We must never pretend to bear any Reputation in the World: No Nation would value our Friendship, or fear to affront us. Not our Trade Abroad would be secure, nor our Trade at Home. *Our Peace*, which we see now establish'd on a good Foundation, what has procur'd it? a War, and the Valour of our Arms, speaking of Second Causes. And what will preserve it? truly nothing but the Reputation of the same Force; and if that be sunk, how long will it continue? Take away the Cause, and our Peace, which is the Effect, will certainly follow.

Let me now a little examine the History of Nations who have run the same risque this Gentleman would have us do, and not to go back to remote Stories of the *Carthaginians*, who the *Romans* could never vanquish till they got them to dismiss their *Auxiliary Troops*, the Citizens of *Constantinople*, who always deny'd their Emperor the Assistance of an Army, were presently ruin'd by the *Turks*. We will come nearer home: The Emperor *Ferdinand* II.[24] over-run the whole Protestant Part of *Germany*, and was at the point of Dissolving the very Constitution of their Government, and all for want of their having a *Competent Force* on foot to defend themselves; and if they had not been deliver'd by the Great *Gustavus Adolphus*,[25] *God Almighty must have wrought a Miracle to have sav'd them*. Next look into *Poland*, which our Author reckons to be one of the *Free Countries who defend themselves without a standing Army*. First he must understand, for I perceive he knows little of the Matter, that *Poland* has not defended it self; or if it has, it has been at a very sorry rate, God knows, much such a one as we should do without an Army, or at much such a rate as we did of old, when the *Picts* and *Scots* were our Hostile Neighbours. Pray let us see how *Poland*, which enjoys its freedom without a standing Army, has defended it self: First, It has been ravag'd on the side of *Lithuania* by the Effeminate *Muscovites*, and tho' the *Poles* always beat them in the Field, yet they had devoured their Country first before the *Polanders* Militia could get together. On the other hand, the *Tartars*, in several volant Excursions, have over-run all *Upper Poland*, *Ukrania* and *Volhinia*, even to the Gates of *Crakow*; and in about Fifty years 'tis allow'd they have carried away a Million of this *wretchedly free People* into Slavery, so that all *Asia* was full of *Polish* Slaves.

On the East side *Carolus Gustavus*,[26] King of *Sweden*, over-run the whole Kingdom, took *Warsaw*, *Crackow*, and beat King *Casimir* out of the Country into *Silesia*, and all in one Campaign, and only indeed for want of a *Force ready* to meet him upon the Frontiers; for as soon as *Casimir* had time to recover himself, and Collect an Army, he lookt him in the Face, and with an Invinsible Resolution fought him wherever he met him: But the ruin of the Country was irreparable in an Age.

To come nearer home, and nearer to the Matter in hand, our Neighbours the *Dutch*, in the Minority of the present King, and under the manage of *Barnavelt*'s Principles[27] reviv'd in the Persons of the *De Witts*, to preserve their Liberties, as they pretended they would suppress the Power of the House of *Orange*, and Disband their old Army which had establish't their Freedom by the Terror of their Arms; and to secure themselves, they came to a regulated Militia, the very thing this

Gentleman talks of: Nay, this Militia had the Face of an Army, and were entertain'd in Pay; but the Commissions were given to the Sons of the principal Burghers, and the Towns had Governors from among themselves. This is just what our Gentleman wou'd have; and what came of this? These brave Troops were plac'd in Garrisons in the Frontier Towns: And in the Year 1672. the *French* King, this *very individual French King now regnant*, during the continuance of the *Sacred Peace of Westphalia*, enters the Country at the Head of *two dreadful Armies*, and these Soldiers, that were the Bulwark of the Peoples Liberties, surrendred the most impregnable Towns, garrison'd some with 2000, some 3000 Men, nay some with 6000, without striking a stroke, nay faster than the *French* cou'd well take Possession of them; so that in about Forty days he had taken 42 strong Towns, which would cost him Seven years to take now, tho' no Army were in the Field to disturb him; and then the People saw their Error, and gave themselves the Satisfaction of Tearing to Pieces the Authors of that pernicious Advice.

And truly, I think these Instances are so lively, that I wonder our Author, who I perceive is not so ignorant, as not to know these things, shou'd not have provided some Answer to it, for he could not but expect it in any Reply to him.

These things may a little tell us what is the *Effects of a Nations being disarm'd* while their Neighbours are in Arms, and all this must be answer'd with *a Fleet*; and that may be answer'd with this, *We may be invaded notwithstanding a Fleet*, unless you can keep up such a Fleet as can Command the Seas in all parts at the same time, or can, as Queen *Elizabeth* did, forbid your Neighbours to build Ships. But the *French* King is none of those, and his Power at Sea is not be slighted: Nor is it so small, but it may with *too much ease* protect an Invasion, *and it is not safe to put it to that hazard*.

Another Necessity of an Army seems to me to lye among our selves: There are Accidents which require the help of an Army, tho' the King and People were all of a Mind, *and all of a side*. King *James* and his Parliament had a full understanding, and they were as Vigorous for him, as ever Parliament was for a King, and yet what had become of both if he had not had *Regular Troops* to have resisted the Duke of *Monmouth*?[28] If they had been to be raised *then*, he must have gone to *France* then, as he did now, or have stay'd at home and have far'd worse; for they wou'd hardly have us'd him so tenderly as the present King did to my knowledge.

I am loth to mention *the Jacobite Party* as an Argument worth while, to maintain any thing of force, but just enough to prevent *Assassinations and private Murthers on the King's Person;* for as they never dar'd *look him in the face* when powerfully assisted by the *French;* so I dare say they will never have the Courage to disturb our Peace *with Sword in hand;* what they do, will be by Caballing to foment Distrusts and Discontents to embroil, if possible, the King with his People or by private villainous Assassinates to destroy him, and by that means to involve the whole Nation in *Blood and Disorder.*

I allow the Speech of Queen *Elizabeth* to the Duke *D'Alançon* was very great and brave in her; but pray had Queen *Elizabeth* no *standing Army?* On the contrary, she was never without them; she never had less in the *Low Countreys,* in aid of the *Dutch,* in *France* in aid of the King of *Navar,* and in her Wars in *Ireland,* than 30000 Men; and all the difference was, that she kept them abroad, employ'd for the Assistance of her Neighbours, and had them absolutely at Command; and so sensible she was of the want of them on the approach of the *Spanish Armado,* that she never left her self so bare of them afterwards: and therefore to compare her Enemies and ours, and her Force with ours, without an Army, as he does *p.19.* is a *Deceptio visus*[29] upon our Understanding, and a presumption that no body has read any History but himself.

Then we come to K. *Charles* the Second's time in *p.26.* and *then,* he says, *we thought a much less Army than is now contended for a grievance.* To which I answer, *Quatenus*[30] *an Army,* they were not thought a Grievance, but attended with the Circumstances of Popish Confederacies and Leagues, and *a Popish Successor*[31] *in view,* and then *visibly managing them* they might be thought so; and yet the *Grand Jury* presenting them, made them no more a Grievance than if they had presented the Parliament which granted an establisht number of Troops to King *Charles.*

Another bold Assertion he makes *p.27. That a standing Army is the only way to bring in K.* James. This is a strange preposterous Supposition, and has no Argument brought to prove it, but the uncertain capricious Humour of the Souldiery, who in all Ages have produc'd violent Revolutions, may bring it to pass; that is in short, *the Thing is possible,* and that is all he can say; and 'tis every jot as possible, that K. *William* himself should change his Mind, *Abdicate the Throne,* and *Call in K. James again,* therefore *pray let us have no King at all,* for really when all is done *these Kings are strange things, and have occasion'd more violent Revolutions in the World than ever have been known in unarm'd Governments.* Besides, if we had no King, then a *standing Army* might be safe enough; for he tells you, *in Commonwealths they may be allow'd,* p.11. *but in Monarchies they are the Devil and all:* Nay he gives two Instances when we had Armies turn'd out their Masters, *Oliver Cromwel* and *General Monk* and yet both these were in the time of *a Commonwealth*. Now I would know if ever an Army turn'd out their King; as for K. *James* his instance is false, he really run away from his Army, his Army did not turn him out; 'tis true, part of it deserted: but I am bold to say, had K. *James*, with the Remainder, made good his Retreat, *Soldier like*, either to *London*, or, [illegible] *Canon of Portsmouth*, or to both, which he might ha' done, for no Body pursued him, till the *French King* had reliev'd him, *it might have been a Civil War to this Hour*.

And thus I have followed him to his last Page, I think I have not omitted any of his material Arguments or Examples; whether he is answered or not, in point of Argument, I leave to the Reader: what I have discovered in his Sophistical straining of Arguments, and misapplying his Quotations to gild by his Wit the want of his Proofs is what I thought needful; his malicious Spirit every where discovers it self, and to me he seems to be a discontented unsatisfied sort of a Person, that is for any thing but what shou'd be, and borrows the Pretence of Liberty, to vent his Malice at the Government: Nor is it a new Invention, when ever any Person had a mind to disturb the *Roman Government*, Liberty was always the Word, and so it is now.

Conclusion.

I Shall say no more as to Argument, but desire the Favour of a Word in General, as to the present Controversy.

To me it seems one of the most impudent Actions that ever was suffered in this Age, that a Private Person shou'd thus attack the King, after all that he has done for the Preservation of our Liberties and the Establishing our Peace, after all the Hazards of his Person and Family, and the Fatiegues of a bloody War, to be represented at his Return, as a *Person now as much to be feared as King* James *was; to be trusted no more than a Mad Man*, and the like, before he so much as knows whether there shall ever be any Dispute about the Matter, or no.

Has the King demanded a Standing Army? Has he propos'd it? Does he insist upon it? How if no such thought be in him? 'Tis a Sign what a Government we live under, and 'tis a Sign what Spirit governs some Men, who will abuse the most indulgent Goodness. It had been but time to have wrote such an Invective upon the King and the Army, when we had found the Parliament of *England* strugling to disband them, and the

King resolute to maintain them: But *This*! when the King and the House are all Union and Harmony! 'tis intollerable, and the King ought to have some Satisfaction made him, and I doubt not but he will.

I am not, nor, I think, I have no where shown as if I were for the Government by an Army; but I cannot but suppose, with Submission to the House of Commons, that they will find it necessary to keep us in a Posture of Defence Sufficient to maintain that Peace which has cost so much Blood and Treasure to procure, and I leave the Method to them, and so I think this Author ought to have done. I do not question but in that great Assembly all things will be done for the Maintenance of our Liberty with a due respect to the Honour and Safety of his Majesty; that is possible: They have shown themselves the most steady and Zealous for his Interest and the Publick, of any Body that ever filled that House; and I could never see, and yet I have not been a slight observer of Affairs neither, I say, I could never see the least symptom of an Inclination in the King's Actions, to dislike or contradict what they offered: has he not left them to be the entire judges of their own Grievances, and freely left them to be as entire judges of the Remedies? Has he ever skreened a Malefactor from their Justice, or a Favourite from their Displeasure? Has he ever infring'd their Priviledges? and as to who shall come after, we have his Royal Declaration[32] at his coming to these Kingdoms; *That his Design was to establish our Liberties on such Foundations, as that it might not be in the power of any Prince for the future to invade them*, and he has never yet attempted to break it: And how is this to be done? not at the direction of a Pamphlet, but by the King, Lords and Commons, who have not taken a false Step yet in the Matter; To them let it be left, and if they agree, be it *with an Army*, or *without an Army*; be it *by a Militia regulated*, or *by an Army regulated*, what is that to him?

I have indeed heard much of *a Militia regulated into an Army*, and truly I doubt not, but *an Army might be regulated into a Militia*, with Safety and Honour to the King, and the Peoples Liberties. But as I have said, *I leave that to the Government to determine*, and conclude with only this Observation; If ever the Gentleman who is the Author of this Pamphlet be trac'd, I verily believe he will appear to be one, who thinking he has deserv'd more Respect from the Government than he has found, has taken this Way to let them know, they ought to have us'd them better or us'd him worse.

AN

ARGUMENT

Shewing, That a

𝔖𝔱𝔞𝔫𝔡𝔦𝔫𝔤 𝔄𝔯𝔪𝔶,

With Consent of

PARLIAMENT,

Is not Inconsistent with a

Free Government, &c.

---

2 Chron. 9. 25.

And King Solomon *had four thousand Stalls for Horses and Chariots, and twelve thousand Horsemen; whom he bestowed in the Chariot-Cities, and with the King at* Jerusalem.[a]

LONDON:
Printed for *E. Whitlock* near *Stationers.* 1698.

THE PREFACE.

THE Present Pen and Ink War rais'd against a Standing Army, has more ill Consequences in it, than are at first Sight to be Discern'd. The Pretence is specious, and the cry of Liberty is very pleasing; but the Principle is Mortally Contagious and Destructive of the Essential Safety of the Kingdom; Liberty and Property, are the Glorious Attributes of the English *Nation; and the dearer they are to us, the less Danger we are in of Loosing them; but I cou'd never yet see it prov'd, that the danger of loosing them by a small Army was such as we shou'd expose our selves to all the World for it. Some People talk so big of our own Strength, that they think* England *able to Defend it self against all the World. I presume such talk without Book; I think the prudentest Course is to prevent the Trial, and that is only to hold the Ballance of* Europe *as the King now does; and if there be a War to keep it abroad. How these Gentlemen will do that with a* Militia, *I shou'd be glad to see Proposed; 'tis not the King of* England *alone, but the Sword of* England *in the Hand of the King, that gives Laws of Peace and War now to* Europe; *And those who would thus wrest* [a] *the Sword out of his Hand in time of Peace, bid the fairest of any Men in the World to renew the War.*

The Arguments against an Army have been strongly urg'd; and the Authors with an unusual Assurance, Boast already of their Conquest, tho' their Armour is not yet put off. I think their Triumph goes before their Victory; *and if Books and Writing will not, God be thanked the Parliament will Confute them, by taking care to maintain such Forces, and no more, as they think needful for our safety abroad, without danger at home, and leaving it to time to make it appear, that such an Army, with Consent of Parliament, is not inconsistent with a Free Government,* &c.

AN ARGUMENT, SHEWING, THAT A STANDING ARMY, WITH CONSENT OF PARLIAMENT, IS NOT INCONSISTENT WITH A FREE GOVERNMENT, &c.

IN the Great Debates about a Standing Army; and in all the Arguments us'd on one side and 'tother, it seems[a] to me, that both Parties are Guilty of running into the Extreams of the Controversie.

Some have taken up such terrible Notions of an Army, that take it how you will, call it what you will; be it Rais'd, Paid or Commanded by whom you will, and let the Circumstances be alter'd never so much, the Term is synonimous, an Army is an Army; and if they don't Enslave us, the Thanks is not to our good Conduct; for so many Soldiers, so many Masters: They may do it if they will; and if they do not do it now, they may do it in another Reign, when a King shall arise who knows not *Joseph*,[1] and therefore the Risque is not to be run by any means: From hence they draw the Consequence, *That a Standing Army is Inconsistent with a Free Government*, &c. which is the Title to the Argument.

This we find back'd by a Discourse of *Militia*'s,[2] and by a Second part of the Argument,[3] *&c.* and all these Three, which seem to me to be wrote by the same Hand, agree in this Point in General, That the War being at an end, *no Forces at all* are to be kept in Pay, *no Men* to be Maintained whose Profession is bearing Arms, whose Commission is to Kill and Slay, as he has it in *the Second Part*; but they must be Dismist, as Men for whom there is no more Occasion against an Enemy, and are dangerous to be kept up, least they find Occasion against our selves.

The Advocates for the Necessity of a *Standing Army*, seem to make light of all these Fears and Jealousies; and Plead the Circumstances of the Kingdom, with Relation to our Leagues and Confederacys abroad, the Strength of our Neighbours, a Pretender to the Crown in Being, the Uncertainties of Leagues, and the like, as Arguments to prove an Army necessary. I must own these are no Arguments any longer than those Circumstances continue, and therefore can amount to no more than to argue the necessity of an Army for a time, which time none of them has ventured to Assign, nor to say how, being once Establish'd, we shall be sure to be rid of them, in case a new King shou'd succeed before the time be expir'd, who may not value our Liberty at the rate his present Majesty has done.

I desire calmly to consider both these Extreams, and if it be possible, to find out the safe *Medium*[4] which may please us all.

If there be any Person who has an ill Design in pushing thus against the Soldery, I am not to expect, that less than a Disbanding the whole Army will satisfie him; but such who have no other End than preserving our Liberties entire, *and leaving them so to Posterity*, will be satisfied with what they know is sufficient to that End; *for he who is not content with what will fully answer the End he proposes, has some other End than that which he proposes*. I make no Reflections upon any Party, but I propose to direct this Discourse to the Honest well meaning English-Freeholder, who has a share in the *Terra firma*, and therefore is concern'd to preserve Freedom to the Inhabitant that loves his Liberty better than his Life, and won't sell it for Money; and this is the Man who has the most reason to fear a Standing Army, for he has something to loose; as he is most concern'd for the Safety of a Ship, who has a Cargo on her Bottom.

This Man is the hardest to be made believe that he cannot be safe without an Army, because he finds he is not easie with one. To this Man all the sad Instances of the Slavery of Nations, by Standing Armies, stand as so many Buoys to warn him of the Rocks which other Free Nations have split upon; and therefore 'tis to this Man we are to speak.

And in order to state the Case right, we are to distinguish first between *England* formerly, and *England* now; between a Standing Army able to enslave the Nation, and a certain Body of Forces enough to make us safe.

England now is in sundry Circumstances, different from *England* formerly, with respect to the Manner of Fighting, the Circumstances of our Neighbours, and of our Selves; and there are some Reasons why a Militia are not, and perhaps I might make it out cannot be made fit for the Uses of the present Wars. In the Ancient Times of *England*'s Power, we were for many years the Invaders of our Neighbours, and quite out of fear of Invasions at home; but before we arriv'd to that Magnitude in the World, 'tis to be observed we were hardly ever invaded, but we were conquer'd, *William* the Conqueror was the last; and if the Spaniard did not do the same, 'twas because God set the Elements in Battel array against them, and they were prevented bringing over the Prince of *Parma*'s Army;[5] which if they had done, 'twould have gone very hard with us; but we owe it wholly to Providence.

I believe it may be said, that from that Time to this Day, the Kingdom has never been without some Standing Troops of Souldiers entertain'd in pay, and always either kept at Home or employ'd Abroad; and yet no evil Consequence follow'd, nor do I meet with any Votes of the Parliament against them as Grievances, or Motions made to Disband them, till the Days of King *Charles* the First. Queen *Elizabeth*, tho' she had no *Guard du Corps*,[6] yet she had her *Guards du Terres*.[7] She had even to her last hour several Armies, *I may call them*, in Pay among Forreign States and Princes, which upon any visible Occasion were ready to be call'd Home. King *James* the First had the same in *Holland*, in the Service of *Gustavus Adolphus* King of *Sweden*, and in the Unfortunate Service of the King of *Bohemia*;[8] and that Scotch Regiment, known by the name of *Douglas*'s Regiment, have been, (*they say*) a Regiment Two hundred and fifty Years. King *Charles* the First had the same in the several Expeditions for the Relief of *Rochel*,[9] and that fatal Descent upon the Isle of *Rhe*, and in his Expeditions into *Scotland*; and they would do well to reconcile their Discourse to it self, who say in one place, *If King* Charles *had had Five thousand Men, the Nation had never struck one stroak for their Liberties*; and at the same time say, in another place,[a] *That the Parliament were like to have been petitioned out of doors by an Army a hundred and fifty Miles off, tho' there was a Scotch Army at the Heels of them*: for to me it appears that King *Charles* the First had an Army then, and would have kept it, but that he had not the Purse to pay them, of which more may be said hereafter.

But *England* now stands in another Posture, our Peace at Home seems secure, and I believe it is so: but to maintain our Peace abroad, 'tis necessary to enter into Leagues and Confederacies: Here is one Neighbour[10] grown too great for all the rest; *as they are single States or Kingdoms*, and therefore to mate him, several must joyn for mutual Assistance, according to the Scotch Law of Duelling, *that if one can't beat you ten shall*. These Alliances are under certain Stipulations and Agreements, with what Strength and in what Places, to aid and assist one another; and to perform these Stipulations, something of Force must be at hand if occasion require. That these Confederacies are of absolute and indispensible necessity, to preserve the Peace of a weaker against a stronger Prince, past Experience has taught us too plainly to need an Argument.

There is another constant Maxim of the present State of the War; and that is,* *carry the War into your Enemies Country, and always keep it out of your own.* This is an Article has been very much opposed 'tis true; and some, who knew no better, would talk much of the fruitless Expence of a War abroad; as if it was not worth while to defend your Confederates Country, to make it a Barrier to your own. This is too weak an Argument also to need any trouble about; but this again makes it absolutely necessary to have always some Troops ready to send to the assistance of those Confederates if they are invaded. Thus at the Peace of *Nimeguen*,[11] six Regiments were left in *Holland*, to continue there in time of Peace, to be ready in case of a Rupture. To say, that instead of this we will raise them for their assistance when wanted, would be something, if this potent Neighbour were not the *French* King, whose Velocity of Motion the *Dutch* well remember in 1672.[12] But then, *say they*, we may send our Militia. First, *The King can't command them to go*; and Secondly, if he could, *no body wou'd accept them*; and if they would go, and would be accepted of, *they would be good for nothing*:[13] If we have no Forces to assist a Confederate, who will value our Friendship, or assist us if we wanted it? To say we are Self-dependent, and shall never need the Assistance of our Neighbour, is to say what we are not sure of, and this is certain it is as needful to maintain the Reputation of *England* in the Esteem of our Neighbours, as 'tis to defend our Coasts in case of an Invasion; for keep up the Reputation of our Power, and we shall never be Invaded.

If our Defence from Insurrections or Invasions, were the only necessary part of a future War, I shou'd be the readier to grant the Point, and to think our Militia might be made useful; but our business is *Principiis Obsta*,[14] to beat the Enemy before he comes to our own door. Our Business in case of a Rupture, is to aid our Confederate Princes, that they may be able to stand between us and Danger: Our Business is to preserve *Flanders*, to Garrison the Frontier Towns, and be in the Field in Conjunction with the Confederate Armies: This is the way to prevent Invasions, and Descents: And when they can tell us that our Militia is proper for this work, then we will say something to it.

I'll suppose for once what I hope may never fall out, That a Rupture of this Peace shou'd happen, and the *French*, according to Custom, break

---

* *This is a Maxim which the* French *have always observed, who have ever taken Care to make their Army live at their Enemy's Charge.*[a]

suddenly into *Flanders*, and over-run it, and after that *Holland*, what Condition wou'd such a Neighbourhood of such a Prince, reduce us to? If it be answer'd again, Soldiers may be rais'd to assist them, I answer, as before, let those who say so, read the History of the *French* King's Irruption into *Holland* in the year 1672. where he conquer'd Sixty strong fortified Towns in six Weeks time: And tell me what it will be to the purpose to raise Men, to fight an Enemy after the Conquest is made?

'Twill not be amiss to observe here that the Reputation and Influence the *English* Nation has had abroad among the Princes of *Christendom*, has been always more or less according as the Power of the Prince, to aid and assist, or to injure and offend, was Esteem'd. Thus Queen *Elizabeth* carried her Reputation abroad by the Courage of her *English* Souldiers and Seamen; and on the contrary, what a ridiculous Figure did King *James*, with his *Beati Pacifici*, make in all the Courts of *Christendom*? How did the Spaniard and the Emperor *banter* and *buffoon* him? How was his Ambassador asham'd to treat for him, while Count *Colocedo* told Count *Mansfield*,[15] *That his New Master* (meaning King *James*) *knew neither how to make Peace or War*? King *Charles* the First far'd much in the same manner: And how was it altered in the Case of *Oliver*?

> *Tho' his Government did a Tyrant resemble,*
> *He made* England *Great, and her Enemies tremble.*
>   Dialogue of the Horses.[16]

And what is it places the present King at the Helm of the Confederacies? Why do they commit their Armies to his Charge, and appoint the Congress of their Plenipotentiaries at his Court? Why do Distressed Princes seek his Mediation, as the Dukes of *Holstien*, *Savoy*, and the like? Why did the Emperor and the King of *Spain* leave the whole Management of the Peace[17] to him? 'Tis all from the[a] Reputation of his Conduct and the *English* Valour under him; and 'tis absolutely necessary to support this Character which *England* now bears in the World, for the great Advantages which may and will be made from it; and this Character can never Live, nor these Allyances be supported with no Force at Hand to perform the Conditions.

These are some Reasons why a Force is necessary, but the Question is, What Force? For I Grant, it does not follow from hence, that a great Army must be kept on Foot in time of Peace, as the Author of the Second Part of the Argument says is pleaded for.

Since then no Army, and a great Army, are Extreams equally dangerous, the one to our Liberty at Home, and the other to our Reputation Abroad, and the Safety of our Confederates; it remains to Inquire what *Medium* is to be found out; or in plain *English*, what Army may, with Safety to our Liberties, be Maintained in *England*, or what Means may be found out to make such an Army serviceable for the Defence of us and our Allies, and yet not dangerous to our Constitution.

That any Army at all can be Safe, *the Argument denies*, but that cannot be made out; a Thousand Men is an Army as much as 100000; as the *Spanish* Armado is call'd, *An Armado*, tho' they seldom fit out above Four Men of War; and on this Account I must crave leave to say, I do Confute the Assertion in the Title of the Argument, that a Standing Army is Inconsistent with a Free Government, and I shall further do it by the Authority of Parliament.

In the Claim of Right, presented to the present King, and which he Swore to observe, as the *Pacta Conventa*[18] of the Kingdom, it is declar'd, *in hac verba,*[19] *That the Raising or Keeping a Standing Army within the Kingdom in time of Peace, unless it be by Consent of Parliament, is against Law.*

This plainly lays the whole stress of the Argument,[a] not against the thing it self, *A Standing Army*, nor against the Season, *in time of Peace*, but against the Circumstance, *Consent of Parliament*; and I think nothing is more Rational than to Conclude from thence, that a Standing Army in time of Peace, with Consent of Parliament, is not against Law, and I may go on, nor is not Inconsistent with a Free Government, nor Destructive of the *English* Monarchy.

There are Two Distinctions necessary therefore in the present Debate, to bring the Question to a narrow Compass.

First, *I distinguish between a Great Army and a small Army. And*
Secondly, *I distinguish between an Army kept on Foot without Consent of Parliament, and an Army with Consent of Parliament.*

And whereas we are told, an Army of Soldiers is an Army of Masters, and the Consent of Parliament don't alter it, but they may turn them out of doors who Rais'd them, as they did the Long Parliament: The First distinction answers that; for if a great Army may do it, a small Army can't; and then the Second Distinction regulates the First. For it cannot be supposed, but the Parliament when they give that Consent which can only make an Army Lawful, will not Consent to a larger Army then they can so Master, as that the Liberties or Peoples of *England*, shall never be in danger from them.

No Man will say this cannot be, because the Number may be supposed as small as you please; but to avoid the Sophistry of an Argument, I'll suppose the very Troops which we see the Parliament have not Voted to be Disbanded; that is, those which were on Foot before the Year 1680.[20] No Man will deny them to be a Standing Army, and yet sure no Man will imagine any danger to our Liberties from them.

We are ask'd, if you establish an Army, and a Revenue to pay them, *How shall we be sure they will not continue themselves?* But will any Man ask that Question of such an Army as this? Can Six Thousand Men tell the Nation they won't Disband, but will continue themselves, and then Raise Money to do it? Can they Exact it by Military Execution? If they can, *our Militia must be very despicable.* The keeping such a Remnant of an Army does not hinder but the Militia may be made as useful as you please; and the more useful you make it, the less danger from this Army: And however it may have been the Business of our Kings to make the Militia as useless as they could, the present King never shew'd any Tokens of such a Design. Nor is it more than will be needful, for 6000 Men by themselves won't do, if the Invasion we speak of should ever be attempted. What has been said of the Appearance of the People on the *Purbeck fancied Invasion,*[21] was very true; but I must say, had it been a true One of Forty Thousand Regular Troops, all that Appearance cou'd have done nothing, but have drove the Country in order to starve them, and then have run away: I am apt enough to grant what has been said of the Impracticableness of any Invasion upon us, while we are Masters at Sea; but I am sure the Defence of *England*'s Peace, lies in making War in *Flanders.* Queen *Elizabeth* found it so; her way to beat the *Spaniards*, was by helping the *Dutch* to do it. And she as much Defended *England* in aiding Prince *Maurice*, to win the Great Battel of *Newport*,[22] as she did in Defeating their *Invincible Armado.* Oliver *Cromwel* took the same Course; for he no sooner declared War against *Spain*, but he Embark'd his Army for *Flanders*: The late King *Charles* did the same against the *French*, when after the Peace of *Nimeguen*, Six Regiments of *English* and *Scots* were always left in the Service of the *Dutch*, and the present War is a further Testimony: For where has it been Fought, not in *England*, God be thanked, but in *Flanders*? And what are the Terms of the Peace, but more Frontier Towns in *Flanders*? And what is the Great Barrier of this Peace, but *Flanders*; the Consequence of this may be guess'd by the Answer King *William* gave when Prince of *Orange*, in the late Treaty of *Nimeguen*; when, to make the Terms the easier, 'twas offered, *That a Satisfaction shou'd be made to him by the* French, *for his Lands in* Luxemburgh; to which the Prince generously [a] reply'd, *He would part with all his Lands in* Luxemburgh *to get the* Spaniards *one good Frontier Town in* Flanders. The reason is plain; for every one of those Towns, tho' they were immediately the *Spaniards*, were really Bulwarks to keep the *French* the further off from his own Country; and thus it is now: And how our Militia can have any share in this part of the War, I cannot imagine. It seems strange to me to reconcile the Arguments made use of to magnifie the Serviceableness of the Militia, and the Arguments to enforce the Dread of a Standing Army; for they stand like two Batteries one against another, where the Shot from one dismounts the Cannon of the other: *If a small Army may enslave us, our Militia are good for nothing; if good for nothing, they cannot defend us*, and then the[a] Army is necessary: *If they are good, and are able to defend us, then a small Army can never hurt us*, for what may defend us Abroad, may defend us at Home; and I wonder this is not consider'd. And what is plainer in the World than that the Parliament of *England* have all along agreed to this Point, That a Standing Army in time of Peace, *with Consent of Parliament*, is not against Law. The Establishment of the Forces in the time of K. *Charles* II. was not as I remember ever objected against in Parliament, at least we may say the Parliament permitted them if they did not establish them: And the Present Parliament seems enclin'd to continue the Army on the same foot, so far as may be suppos'd from their Vote to disband all the Forces raised since 1680. To affirm then, *That a Standing Army*, (without any of the former Distinctions) *is Inconsistent*, &c. is to argue against the General Sense of the Nation, the Permission of the Parliament for 50 years past, and the Present apparent Resolutions of the best Composed House that perhaps ever entred within those Walls.

To this House the whole Nation has left the Case, to act as they see cause; to them we have committed the Charge of our Liberties, nay the King himself has only told them His Opinion, with the Reasons for it, *without leading them at all*; and the Article of the *Claim of Right* is left in full force: For this Consent of Parliament is now left the whole and sole Judge, Whether *an Army* or *no Army*; and if it Votes an Army, 'tis left still the sole Judge of the Quantity, *how many*, or *how few*.

Here it remains to enquire the direct Meaning of those words, *Unless it be by Consent of Parliament*, and I humbly suppose they may, among other things, include these Particulars.

1. *That they be rais'd and continued not by a Tacit, but Explicite Consent of Parliament; or, to speak directly, by an Act of Parliament.*
2. *That they be continued no longer than such Explicite Consent shall limit and appoint.*

If these two Heads are granted in the word *Consent*, I am bold to affirm, Such an *Army is not Inconsistent with a Free Government*, &c.

I am as positively assur'd of the Safety of our Liberties under the Conduct of King and Parliament, while they concur, *as I am of the Salvation of Believers by the Passion of our Saviour*; and I hardly think 'tis fit for a private Man to impose his positive Rules on them for Method, any more than 'tis to limit the Holy Spirit, whose free Agency is beyond his Power: For the King, Lords and Commons, can never err while they agree; nor is an Army of 20 or 40000 Men *either* a Scarcrow enough to enslave us, while under that Union.

If this be allow'd, then the Question before us is, What may conduce to make the Harmony between the King, Lords and Commons eternal? And so the Debate about an Army ceases.

But to leave that Question, since Frailty attends the best of Persons, and Kings have their *faux Pas*, as well as other Men, we cannot expect the Harmony to be immortal; and therefore to provide for the worst, our Parliaments have made their own Consent the only Clause that can make an Army Legitimate: But to say that an Army directly as an Army, without these Distinctions, is destructive of the *English* Monarchy, and Inconsistent with a Free Government, *&c.* is to say then that the Parliament can destroy the *English* Monarchy, and can Establish that which is Inconsistent with a Free Government; which is ridiculous. But then we are told, that *the Power of the Sword was first placed in the Lords or Barons, and how they serv'd the King in his Wars with themselves and their Vassals, and that the King had no Power to Invade the Priviledges of the Barons, having no other Forces than the Vassals of his own Demeasnes to follow him*: And this Form is applauded as an extraordinary Constitution, *because there is no other Limitation of a Monarchy of any Signification than such as places the Sword in the hand of the Subject: And all such Governments where the Prince has the Power of the Sword, tho' the People have the Power of the Purse, are no more Monarchies but Tyrannies: For not only that Government is tyrannical which is tyrannically exercis'd, but all Governments are tyrannical which have not in their Constitution sufficient Security against the Arbitrary Power of their Prince*; that is, which have not the Power of the Sword to Imploy against him if need be.[23]

Thus we come to the Argument: Which is not how many Troops may be allow'd, or how long; but in short, *No Mercenary-Troops at all can be maintain'd without Destroying our Constitution, and Metamorphizing our Government into a Tyranny.*

I admire how the Maintainer of this Basis came to omit giving us an Account of another Part of History very needful to examine, in handing down the True Notion of Government in this Nation, *viz.* of Parliaments. To supply which, and to make way for what follows, I must take leave to tell the Reader, that about the time, when this Service by Villenage and Vassalage began to be resented by the People, and by Peace and Trade they grew rich, and the Power of the Barons being too great, frequent Commotions, Civil Wars, and Battels, were the Consequence, nay sometimes without concerning the King in the Quarrel: One Nobleman would Invade another, in which the weakest suffered most, *and the poor Man's Blood was the Price of all*; the People obtain'd Priviledges of their own, and oblig'd the King and the Barons to accept of an *Equilibrium*; this we call a Parliament: And from this the Due Ballance, we have so much heard of is deduced. I need not lead my Reader to the Times and Circumstances of this, but this Due Ballance is the Foundation on which we now stand, and which the Author of the Argument so highly applauds as the best in the World; and I appeal to all Men to judge if this Ballance be not a much nobler Constitution in all its Points, than the old *Gothick* Model of Government.

In that the Tyranny of the Barons was intollerable, the Misery and Slavery of the Common People insupportable, their Blood and Labour was at the absolute Will of the Lord, *and often sacrificed to their private Quarrels*: They were as much at his beck as his Pack of Hounds were at the Sound of his Horne; whether it was to march against a Forreign Enemy, or *against their own Natural Prince*: So that this was but exchanging one Tyrant for Three hundred, for so many the Barons of *England* were accounted at least. And this was the Effect of the Security vested in the People, against the Arbitrary Power of the King; which was to say the Barons took care to maintain their own Tyranny, and to prevent the Kings Tyrannizing over them.

But 'tis said, *the Barons growing poor by the Luxury of the Times, and the Common People growing rich, they exchang'd their Vassalage for Leases, Rents, Fines, and the like.*[24] They did so, and thereby became entitled to the Service of themselves; and so overthrew the Settlement, and from hence came a *House of Commons*: And I hope *England* has reason to value the Alteration. Let them that think not reflect on the Freedoms the Commons enjoy in *Poland*, where the *Gothick* Institution remains, and they will be satisfied.

In this Establishment of a Parliament, the Sword is indeed trusted in the Hands of the King, and *the Purse in the Hands of the People*; the

People cannot make Peace or War without the King, nor the King cannot raise or maintain an Army without the People; and this is the True Ballance.

But we are told, *The Power of the Purse is not a sufficient Security without the Power of the Sword*: What! not against Ten thousand Men? To answer this, 'tis necessary to examine how far the Power of the Sword is in the Hands of the People already, and next whether the Matter of Fact be true.

I say the Sword is in part in the Hands of the People already, by the Militia, who, as the Argument says *are the People themselves*. And how are they Ballanc'd? 'Tis true, they are Commissioned by the King, but they may refuse to meet twice, till the first Pay is reimburst to the Countrey: And where shall the King Raise it without a Parliament: that very Militia would prevent him. So that our Law therein Authorizing the Militia to refuse the Command of the King, tacitly puts the Sword into the Hands of the People.

I come now to Examine the Matter of Fact, *That the Purse is not an Equivalent to the Sword*, which I deny to be true; and here 'twill be necessary to Examine, How often our Kings of *England* have Raised Armies on their own Heads, but have been forced to Disband them for want of Moneys, nay, have been forced to call a Parliament to Raise Money to Disband them.

King *Charles* the First is an Instance of both these: for his First Army against the *Scots* he was forced to Dismiss for want of Pay; and then was forced to call a Parliament to Pay and Dismiss the *Scots*; and tho' he had an Army in the Field at the Pacification, and a Church Army too, yet he durst not attempt to Raise Money by them.

I am therefore to affirm, *that the Power of the Purse is an Equivalent to the Power of the Sword*; and I believe I can make it appear, if I may be allowed to instance in those numerous Armies which *Gaspar Coligny*, Admiral of *France*, and *Henry* the Fourth King of *Navar*, and *William* the First Prince[a] of Orange brought out of *Germany* into *France*, and into the Low Countries, which all vanished, and could attempt nothing for want of a Purse to maintain them: But to come nearer, what made the Efforts of King *Charles* all Abortive, but *Want of the Purse*? Time was, he had the Sword in his Hand, when the Duke of *Buckingham* went on those Fruitless Voyages to *Rochell*, and himself afterwards to *Scotland*, he had Forces on Foot, a great many more than Five Thousand, which the Argument mentions, but he had not the Purse, at last he attempted to take it without a Parliament, *and that Ruin'd him*. King *Charles* the

Second found the Power of the Purse so much out-ballanced the Power of the Sword, that he sat still, and let the Parliament Disband his Army for him, *almost whether he would or no.*

Besides the Power of the Purse in *England* differs from what the same thing is in other Countries, because 'tis so Sacred a thing, that *no King ever touch'd at it but he found his Ruine in it.* Nay, 'tis so odious to the Nation, that whoever attempts it, must at the same time be able to make an Entire Conquest or nothing.

If then neither the *Consent of Parliament*, nor the *smallness of an Army proposed*, nor the Power of *the Sword in the Hands of the Militia*, which are the People themselves, nor *the Power of the Purse*, are not a sufficient Ballance against the Arbitrary Power of the King, what shall we say? Are Ten Thousand Men in Arms, without Money, without Parliament Authority, hem'd in with the whole Militia of *England*, and *Dam'd by the Laws*? Are they of such Force as to break our Constitution? I cannot see any reason for such a Thought. The Parliament of *England* is a Body, of whom we may say, *That no Weapon Formed against them cou'd ever Prosper*;[25] and they know their own Strength, and they know what Force is needful, and what hurtful, and they will certainly maintain the *First* and Disband the *Last.*

It may be said here, *'Tis not the fear of Ten Thousand Men, 'tis not the matter of an Army, but 'tis the* Thing *it self; grant a Revenue for Life, and the next King will call it,* My Revenue, *and so grant an Army for this King, and the next will say,* Give Me my Army.

To which I Answer, That these things have been no oftner ask'd in Parliament than deny'd; and we have so many Instances in our late Times of *the Power of the Purse*, that it seems strange to me, that it should not be allowed to be a sufficient Ballance.

King *Charles* the Second, as I hinted before, was very loath to part with his Army Rais'd in 1676. but he was forced to it for want of Money to pay them; he durst not try whether when *Money had Raised an Army, an Army cou'd not Raise Money.* 'Tis true, his Revenues were large, but Frugality was not his Talent, and that ruin'd the Design. King *James* the Second was a good Husband, and that very Husbandry had almost Ruin'd the Nation; for his Revenues being well managed, he maintain'd an Army out of it. For 'tis well known, the Parliament never gave him a Penny towards it; but he never attempted to make his Army Raise any Money; if he had, 'tis probable his Work had been sooner done than it was.

But pray let us Examine abroad, if *the Purse has not Governed all the Wars of* Europe. The *Spaniards* were once the most powerful People in

Europe; their Infantry were in the Days of the Prince of *Parma*, the most Invincible Troops in the World. The *Dutch*, who were then his Subjects, and on whom he had Levied immense Sums of Money, had the 10th Penny[26] demanded of them, and the Demand back'd by a great Army of these very *Spaniards*, which, among many other Reasons caused them to Revolt. The Duke *D'Alva* afterwards attempted for his Master to raise this Tax by his Army, by which he lost the whole *Netherlands*, who are now the Richest People in the World; and the *Spaniard* is now become the meanest and most despicable People in *Europe*, and that only because they are the Poorest.

The present War is another Instance, which having lasted Eight Years, is at last brought to this Conclusion, *That he who had the longest Sword has yielded to them who had the longest Purse.*

The late King *Charles* the First, is another most lively Instance of this Matter, to what lamentable Shifts did he drive himself? and how many despicable Steps did he take, rather than call a Parliament, which he hated to think of. And yet, tho' he had an Army on Foot, he was forced to do it, *or starve all his Men*; had it been to be done, he wou'd have done it. 'Tis true, 'twas said the Earl of Strafford propos'd a Scheme, *to bring over an Army out of* Ireland, *to force* England *to his Terms*; but the Experiment was thought too desperate to be attempted, and the very Project Ruin'd the Projector; such an ill Fate attends every Contrivance against the Parliament of *England*.

But I think I need go no further on that Head: The Power of Raising Money is wholly in the Parliament, as a Ballance to the Power of Raising Men, which is in the King; and all the Reply I can meet with is, *That this Ballance signifies nothing, for an Army can Raise Money, as well as Money Raise an Army; to which I Answer*, besides what has been said already; *I do not think it practicable in* England: The greatest Armies, in the Hands of the greatest Tyrants we ever had in *England*, never durst attempt it. We find several Kings in *England* have attempted to Raise Money without a Parliament, and have tryed all the means they could to bring it to pass; and they need not go back to *Richard* the Second, to *Edward* the Second, to *Edward* the Fourth, to *Henry* the Eighth, or to *Charles* the First, to remind the Reader of what all Men who know any thing of History are acquainted with: But not a King ever yet attempted to Raise Money, by Military Execution, or Billetting Soldiers upon the Country. King *James* the Second had the greatest Army and the best, as to Discipline, that any King ever had; *and his desperate Attempts on our Liberties show'd his good Will*, yet he never came to that Point. I won't deny, but that our

Kings have been willing to have Armies at Hand, to back them in their Arbitrary Proceedings, and the Subjects may have been aw'd by them from a more early Resentment; but I must observe that all the Invasion of our Rights, and all the Arbitrary Methods of our Governors, has been under pretences of Law. King *Charles* the First Levy'd Ship-Money as his due, and the Proclamations for that purpose cite the pretended Law, that in Case of Danger from a Foreign Enemy, Ships shou'd be fitted out to Defend us, and all Men were bound to contribute to the Charge; *Coat* and *Conduct Money*[27] had the like Pretences; Charters were subverted by *Quo Warrantoes*,[28] and Proceedings at Law; Patriots were Murther'd under Formal Prosecutions, and all was pretended to be done legally.

I know but one Instance in all our *English* Story, where the Souldery were employ'd as Souldiers, in open Defyance of Law, to destroy the Peoples Liberties by a Military Absolute Power, and that stands as an Everlasting Brand of Infamy upon our Militia; and is an Instance to prove, beyond the Power of a Reply, *That even our Militia, under a bad Government, let them be our selves, and the People, and all those fine things never so much*, are under ill Officers and ill Management *as dangerous as any Souldery whatever*, will be as Insolent, and do the Drudgery of a Tyrant as effectually.

In the Year [1682] when Mr. *Dubois* and Mr. *Papillon*, a Member of the Present Parliament, were chosen Sheriffs of *London*, and Sir *John Moor*, under pretence of the Authority of the Chair, pretended to nominate one Sheriff himself, and leave the City to choose but one, and confirm the Choice of the Mayor, the Citizens struggled for their Right* and stood firm to their Choice, and several Adjournments were made to bring over the Majority of the Livery, but in vain: At length the Day came when the Sheriffs were to be sworn, and when the Livery-men assembled at *Guild-hall* to swear their Sheriffs, they found the Hall Garrison'd with a Company of Trained-Bands under Lieutenant Coll. *Quiney*, a Citizen himself, and most of the Soldiers, Citizens and Inhabitants; and by this Force the Ancient Livery-men were shut out, and several of them thrown down, and insolently used, and the Sheriffs thrust away from the Hustings, and who the Lord Mayor pleased was Sworn in an open Defiance of the Laws of the Kingdom, and Priviledges of the City.†[29] *This was done by the Militia to their Everlasting Glory*, and I do not remember the like done by a Standing Army of Mercenaries,

---

* *This old Custom is reviv'd again, and tamely submitted to by the City in Spight of the Law, and in Contempt of the Resolution of those Days.*[a]

† *An Emblem of Legal Tyranny.*[b]

in this Age at least. Nor is a Military Tyranny practicable in *England*, if we consider the power the Laws have given to the Civil Magistrate, unless you at the same time imagine that Army large enough to subdue the whole *English* Nation at once, which if it can be effected by such an Army as the Parliament now seem enclined to permit, we are in a very mean Condition.

I know it may be objected here, that the Forces which were on Foot before 1680 are not the Army in Debate, and that the Design of the Court was to have a much greater Force.

I do not know that, but this I know, that *those Forces were an Army*, and the Design of all these Opponents of an Army is in so many words, against *any Army at all*, small as well as great; a Tenet absolutely destructive of the present Interest of *England*, and of the Treaties and Alliances made by His Majesty with the Princes and States of *Europe*, who depend so much on his Aid in Guard of the present Peace.

The Power of making Peace or War is vested in the King: 'Tis part of his Prerogative, but 'tis implicitly in the People, because their Negative as to Payment, does really Influence all those Actions. Now if when the King makes War, the Subject shou'd refuse to assist him, the whole Nation would be ruin'd: Suppose in the Leagues and Confederacies His Present Majesty is engag'd in for the Maintenance of the present Peace, all the Confederates are bound in case of a Breach to assist one another with so many Men, say Ten thousand for the *English* Quota, more or less, where shall they be found? *Must they stay till they are Rais'd?* To what purpose would it be then for any Confederate to depend upon *England* for Assistance?

It may be said indeed, if you are so engag'd by Leagues or Treaties, you may hire Foreign Troops to assist till you can raise them. This Answer leads to several things which would take up too much room here.

Foreign Troops require Two things to procure them; Time to Negotiate for them, which may not be to be spar'd, for they may be almost as soon rais'd; Time for their March from *Germany*, for there are none nearer to be hir'd, and Money to Hire them, which must be had by Parliament, or the King must have it ready: If by Parliament, that is a longer way still; if without, that opens a worse Gate to Slavery than t'other: For if a King have Money, he can raise Men or hire Men when he will; and you are in as much danger then, and more than you can be in now from a Standing Army: So that since giving Money is the same thing as giving Men, as it appear'd in the late K. *James*'s Reign, both must be prevented, or both may be allow'd.

But the Parliament we see needs no Instructions in this Matter, and therefore are providing to reduce the Forces to the same *Quota* they were in before 1680, by which means all the fear of Invading our Liberties will be at an end, the Army being so very small that 'tis impossible, and yet the King will have always a Force at hand to assist his Neighbours, or defend himself till more can be Raised. The Forces before 1680 were an Army, and if they were an Army by Consent of Parliament, they were a Legal Army; and if they were Legal, then they were not inconsistent with *a Free Government, &c.* for nothing can be Inconsistent with *a Free Government*, which is done according to the Laws of that Government: And if a *Standing Army* has been in *England* Legally, then I have proved, *That a Standing Army is not Inconsistent with a Free Government*, &c.

A

BRIEF

REPLY

TO THE

HISTORY

OF

Standing Armies

In *ENGLAND*.

With some Account of the Authors.

LONDON:
Printed in the Year 1698.

THE PREFACE.

IN *all Ages of the World, and under the Best of Governments, there were always some Persons to be found, who either for Envy at the Prosperity of some; Ambition, Popular Vanity, or Private Ends, took Occasion to appear as Male-contents, and set themselves to Expose and Censure the Actions of Their Governors: History is so full of Instances of this Nature, that 'twould be an affront to the Gentlemen I am dealing with, to suppose them ignorant of 'em.*

In Our Age, where Nick Names are so much in fashion, we have call'd them Murmurers, Grumbletonians *and the like, of whom one of our Poets has said not improperly.*

And should King *Jesus* Reign, they'd Murmur too.[1]

'Twould not ha' been foreign to the Purpose, as an Answer to the History of Standing Armies, *to have Entertain'd the World with a* History of these Dissenters to Government, the Murmurers of the World; who always look with sowre Faces upon the Magistrates, and cry out of so much as the little Fingers of their Superiors. *But we have not room for it here; nor to descend too far into the General Character of them; but 'tis necessary to observe, that these sort of People have one inseparable* Adjunct, *as an Essential and Chief Prop both of their Nature and Design; They always Cry* Wo, Wo, *and fright themselves and the World with sad Tidings. Religion, or Liberty, or both, are infallibly the* Ensigns of their Order. *And I wonder we have not Ribbands in their Hats, with* No Popery, No Slavery, *or* No Standing Armies, No Lords of the Treasury, *&c.*

If the Bottom of this Case was to be Examined, and the Authors dealt with in their own way, Preferment always lists them on the t'other side: And tho' I do not say these Gentlemen who write so strenuously for Liberty, would do so; yet they have told us plainly who did, Viz. The Lord Strafford,[2] *and* Noy,[3] *and I could name them some more. King Charles the First, say they, began* the Custom of making an Opposition to himself in the House of Commons, the Road to Preferment; *and how came it about?* Truly, because

83

he found they were Mercenary, and made a Noise that their Mouths might be stopp'd; this has been too much a Method since, no doubt.

'For Parliament-Men to rail at the Court,
And get a Preferment immediately for't.'[4]

But how comes it to pass, because private Ends lie so generally at the bottom of such Clamour, that we never found them proof against the Offer?

And here I could give innumerable Instances of great Ones, on the other hand, who as soon as ever the Court-Favour has fail'd them, and they found themselves not Rewarded according to their Merit, turn'd Popular, Champions for the Peoples Liberties, and Railers at the Court. I do not say, I mean by this, the Lords S—— D—— Mr. H—— Mr. H——[5] or any body else in particular; but whoever the Coat fits, let them wear it.

This Evil Spirit of Discontent is now at Work under the best Reign, and the mildest Government that ever England *knew; particularly so, in suffering the Affairs of the Government to be thus disputed in Print, by, not an Author or Single Person, but a whole Club of Mistaken Politicians,[6] who in any Reign but this would have been us'd as they deserv'd.*

Had such a Cabal of the best Men in the Nation attempted the like in Queen Elizabeth's *Reign, who we must all acknowledge was a true* English *Queen, and Govern'd the Nation with a Matchless Prudence, they would have been very severely handled; but full Liberty is given them now to say almost any thing; and truly they take the Extent of it, even to Indecency and Ill Manners. For they Treat the King himself with Jeers and Banter, and make Ridiculous Encomiums on him, to expose His Majesty to very Scurrilous Reflections.*

This is so mean a Way of Writing, that I shall not descend to Returns in kind, but shall use them like Gentlemen, whether they behave themselves so or no, and leave that to themselves.

A BRIEF REPLY TO
THE HISTORY OF
STANDING ARMIES.

THE Outcry against an Army in *England* is carried on with so high a hand, that nothing can be said to it with any hope of Effect on the Complainants. They go on with their own Arguments, never thinking any thing that is or can be said to them, worth while to take notice of: For it seems to be more their Design to render the Government suspected, than to argue fairly whether it be really true or not, That an Army must be our ruine.

I have considered their former Books according to their Desire, and to which they refer in this, and the several Answers to them; some of which seem to me to carry a great Weight with them; but to them are of so small a Consequence, that they do not think them worth a notice.

They have now given the World what they call a *History of Standing Armies*, in which they have been guilty of some Mistakes, some Omissions, and some Contradictions; and tho' the Historical part might very well have been omitted, as being nothing at all to the purpose; yet 'tis very proper to tell them,

First, 'Tis a Mistake that the *Spaniards* did any thing to purpose in the Seventeen Provinces with 9000 Men, which they call a *Standing Army*; and if they please to review *Strada* and *Bentivoglio*[7] their own Author, they will find that the Duke *D'Alva* and *Don Lewis de Requescens* had very great Armies at the Battle near *Groningen*, against Count *Lodowick* of *Nassau*, and at the Sieges of *Harlem* and *Mons*; the Duke *D'Alva*[8] brought Fourteen thousand Men with him at first; raised Twenty-four thousand more at another time against the Siege of *Mons*; and when the Count *D'Egmont* presented the Petition[9] against the Foreign Forces, they alledg'd the *Spaniards* had Thirty thousand Men in Pay, besides the Troops of the Country.

As to other Armies, I wonder the Authors did not instance the small Forces with which the *Spaniards* conquer'd the Mighty Empires of *Mexico* and *Peru*; in all which Work, I never yet read that they had above 800 Horse and 5750 Foot.

Armies, as well as every thing else, are great or small in proportion; and 4000 Archers in *Cheshire* rais'd by *Richard* the Second, though they only made way to their Master's Ruin, were really a more formidable Force than Twenty thousand men in Arms can be now.

The Authors (for I am inform'd their Name is *Legion*) have carri'd on their History to Queen *Mary*, and there break off, and tell us, the Standing Forces were then 1200 men, in Queen *Elizabeth*'s Reign 3500; where, by the way, 'tis to be noted, they grant, that it has all along been allowed to have a Standing Force in *England* for above 140 Years past; for we are not now arguing the Quantity, but the Thing, *A Standing Army*: And they have often in former Papers asserted, That any Standing Forces are destructive of our Constitution, and inconsistent with the *English* Liberty; and yet our Constitution consisted very well in Queen *Elizabeth*'s time. – Nor have these Gentlemen given their Quotations faithfully; for they have been told, and are not ignorant, That, First, whereas Queen *Mary* had but 1200 men, she shamefully lost *Calais* to the *French*, for want of Strength to relieve it. Indeed if she had rais'd the Militia, they might ha' kept the *French* from coming on to take *Dover*, but if she had had 10000 men in Pay, *Calais*, which had been ours for some Ages before, had been ours still; and if it had, the Loss of *Dunkirk*[10] had not been so much to our disadvantage. Then, as to Queen *Elizabeth*, they omit that she always had a very good Army in the *Low-Countries*, which to her was a Nursery of Soldiers: And in the time of her apprehension of an Invasion, I would ask how many she transported hither for her own Defence; for the Armies she prepar'd, at *Tilbury* Camp 44000, and 20000 at *Plimouth*, were not all Militia, but Soldiers disciplin'd and train'd in the Wars in *Ireland* and *Holland*.

What the Authors say Queen *Elizabeth* did, and with what Glory she reign'd, and how she left us when she died, is all true, and much more; and what her Revenue was, and what Taxes she had, for ought we know may be so: But I hope these Gentlemen will excuse me for saying they very much misrepresent the Case, when they would tell us what Revenues she had; as if those Revenues perform'd all the Great Things she did: They ought to have told us also what Taxes she had, and how she took from the *Spaniard* above 60 Millions of Pieces of Eight at several times, at the *West-Indies*, at *Cadiz*, and at Sea; which together with what Subsidies, Customs of Towns, and Interests the *Dutch* paid her, were Infinite: And with this she did all those great things, and with this she always kept an Army on foot, and left them so after the Peace; by the same token that King *James* let 3000 of them starve and desert for want of Subsistence, on the *Dutch* refusing to pay the Garisons of the *Brill*, *Ramekins* and *Flushing*.

I shall not enter into the History of King *James* the First, King *Charles* the First, or his Sons; the Historical part does not argue either way in this Case, as I understand the Point: The Question before us is not so much what has been, or has not been, but what is now needful to be done; and I wish these Gentlemen would admit a calm Argument; in which Case I offer to prove, First, That 'tis absolutely necessary to have some Standing Force; and then, That with Consent of Parliament 'tis not Illegal.

I remember one Reply[11] to the former Argument entred into the Historical part of the matter, and undertook to prove, That every Government in *England* had for many Years maintain'd some Standing Force; and 'tis too true to be denied.

Then they descend to examine the Reign of King *James* the First, and of K. *Charles* the First; and tho' they grant they had no Armies, yet they reckon up all the Tyrannies and Oppressions they were guilty of; how they Enslav'd the Nation, Buffoon'd the Parliament, Oppress'd the Subjects, Levied Taxes; but all without a Standing Army: Nay, when King *Charles* the First affronted the *House of Commons*, he was fain, as these Authors themselves say, to Rifle the Taverns, Gaming-houses, and Brothel-houses, to pick out 3 or 400 Men; which if true, tho' I do not see it deserves any credit; yet 'tis plain he could have no Army, no, not so much as any Guards. Now if all this can be done by a King without an Army, why then the having an Army can do no more; the Mischief does not lie in an Army, but in the Tyrant.

The Authors conclude of King *Charles* the First *having No Army to support him, his Tyranny was precarious, and at last his ruin*. And may we not say so of his Son, who had a great Army, and as Mercenary as any *English* Army ever was? And yet tho' he had an Army to support him, *his Tyranny was precarious, and at last his ruin*: So that *Tyranny* is a Weed that never throve in *England*; it always poison'd the Planter; and an Army, or no Army, it is all one.

This is only toucht at, to let the World know, that these Gentlemen have not been faithful Historians; for that they have not fairly stated the Case, but left out such things as are really true, because against their purpose; which is not a fair way of Arguing.

But if the Case must be debated, I think 'tis very proper to reduce it to Two Heads:

First, Whether a Standing Army, in time of Peace, may not be
  Lawful?
Secondly, Whether it be not Expedient?

As to the first Question, it has really been prov'd in a small Discourse formerly published, entituled, *An Argument*, shewing that a Standing Army is not inconsistent, *&c.* which these Gentlemen never thought fit to Answer, and now do tacitly acknowledge to be true, but say 'tis nevertheless dangerous: However, if it may be Legal then, it cannot be true that 'tis destructive of our Liberty and Constitution; for that can never be destructive of our Constitution which can be Legal; That were to make a thing Lawful and Unlawful at the same time.

A Standing Army, with Consent of Parliament, is a Legal Army; and if the Legislative Power erect an Army, 'tis as much a Qualification to the Army, as a Charter is to a Corporation; for what else do these Gentlemen call an Establishment? that cannot be Illegal which is done by Parliament. The Titles of a *Bankrupt House of Lords*, a *Pensioner House of Commons*, a *flattering Clergy*, and a *prostituted Ministry*, are virulent Phrases, and savour both of Passion and Ill Manners. We have them not now, nor am I convinc'd we ever had, nor hope we ever shall.

And yet if they were so, they are the Parliament of *England*; and what they do, is the Act of the whole Kingdom, and cannot be Illegal.

I shall not spend time to prove what the Authors own, and cannot deny. I therefore lay down the first Head as proved before, and granted by our Adversaries;

That a Standing Army in time of Peace with Consent of Parliament, is not inconsistent with a Free Government, and is a Legal Army.

The Second main Argument is, Whether it be necessary? for all things that are lawful, are not expedient. Whether there be so much need of an Army, as that we should run the hazards that we are told we shall be expos'd to, from them.

That we have very great Reason to be always in a Posture fit to maintain the Peace purchased now[12] with so much Blood and Treasure, I believe no Body will dispute. Whether with or without an Army, I don't yet debate. That an Army was the procuring Cause of this Peace, I hope it will be allow'd me; and that had we not appear'd in a very powerful Figure, the Terms had not been so good, and *Lewis* the 14*th* would not have parted with so many Vast Countries, Impregnable

Fortifications, and Sovereign Titles; our Army in Conjunction with our Allies have under God's Providence obtain'd this. Now, whether it be proper to let go this Lyon upon Parole, and tying the *French* King by his Honour only, which he has not formerly valued at much in such Cases; Disband our Forces, and rely upon the League? This is the direct Question.

If the King of *France* were so much to be depended upon, the *Spaniard* and the *Emperor* need not have strain'd so hard for the strong Towns of *Brisac, Friburg, Philipsburgh, Mons, Aeth, Luxemburgh*, and *Charleroy*, which are very chargeable to keep, and no real Profit to them; and the King of *France* would readily have given up *Franche-Compte, Burgundy*, and vast Territories of Land instead of them, with large Revenues and Advantages; but these are given as Pledges of the Peace, and are maintain'd by the Confederates at a vast Charge, that they might have a sufficient Strength to oblige the *French* King to perform the Stipulation of the League.

Now I do not know what vast Securities these Gentlemen may flatter themselves with; but to me it seems one of the most ridiculous things in the World to be wholly Disarm'd at such a time, when all the Nations in the World have Forces in Pay.

I am willing to give the Gentlemen of the Club all the Latitude in Argument they can desire, and therefore I'll grant that the *French* King has surrendred all the Towns and Countries he was to surrender, though he really has not. That King *James* is neither in Power nor Person at all formidable, nor indeed worth mentioning in the Case. That the King of *Spain* is not Dead, nor like to be so. That these are not, nor ever were Arguments for a Standing Force, at least not singly considered.

But notwithstanding all this, I cannot but say that some competent Standing Force is absolutely necessary to preserve that Peace which has cost the Nation so dear; and it would seem a most unaccountable Weakness to run the hazard of it, and expose us to the uncertainty of it: We say, *Temptation makes a Thief*. There is nothing in the World will be so likely to make the Peace precarious and allure the *French* to break it, as to find us Naked and Defenceless.

If it be true, that an Army may be dangerous at Home, 'tis as true, that having no Army must be fatal Abroad: The danger of an Army is uncertain, and may be none; the damage of the contrary is infallible. 'Tis not saying we have formerly Conquer'd *France*, and therefore ought not to be so frighted with Apprehensions of it now all the *French* Fools they say are Dead. *France* now, without Reflection upon *England*, is much too strong a Match for any single Nation in *Europe*, and the only means to

89

keep her within bounds, is by Confederacies, and *Leagues Offensive*; how these can be maintain'd without *Quota's* of Forces ready to unite, is a Mystery too dark for my Understanding. Indeed the King may say to his Confederates, 'Truly my Subjects won't trust me with any Soldiers, and therefore I must pay my proportion in Money.' But other Countries may refuse to keep up Forces as well as we, and so a League would be to small purpose indeed. These things have been offer'd before now, and in better Terms, and the Gentlemen with whom we argue have thought fit to forget to speak to them.

But now we are Banter'd about a Fleet and a Militia, and these are the Equivalents with which all the pretences of a Standing Army are to be Answer'd. Indeed a Fleet well ordered is a good thing; and a Militia well regulated, *That Black Swan, that unheard-of thing*, if ever it could be had would be a good thing too. But pray, Gentlemen, give some people leave to understand things in the World as well as you: Suppose this Fleet and this Militia to be all that you can pretend, what would this be to a War in *Flanders*? 'Tis the carrying the War into *Flanders*, that is our great Interest; the Barrier of Strong Towns there is our best Security against *France* in the World: Now suppose the *French* King should with 80000 men fall into those Countries like a Tempest, as he did in 1672, without declaring War, would our Militia go over with the King to help our Confederates? Or could our Fleet relieve *Charleroy*? Would raising an Army, though it could be done in forty days, as you say King *Charles* did, be quick enough? 'Tis strange these things are not worth while to consider: Why does the *French* King keep up an Army? 'Tis not for fear, but to increase his Glory; and for that very reason it would be preposterous for us to be naked.

England has always gone hand in hand with the Times; and Arm'd or not Arm'd, as her Neighbours did, and must always do so: in the Days when we kept no Forces at home, our Neighbours kept none abroad, and then there was no need of it, we were as well provided as they; but now they are all strong in Men, and shall we be naked! that is certainly to be exposed?

'Tis Argued, 'an Army may soon be raised; King *Charles* the Second raised an Army in Forty Days, and the present King very speedily.' I would but desire these Gentlemen to Examine, how it fared with both those Armies? I saw them both and they were composed of as jolly, brave, young Fellows as ever were seen; but being raw, and not us'd to hardship, the first Army lay, and rotted in *Flanders*, with Agues and Fluxes, the very first Campaign; and the last did the like at *Dundalk*;[13] and so 'twill always fare with any Army of *English* Men, 'till they have been abroad, and inur'd to the Service. I appeal to any Man, who knows the Nature of our Men; they are the worst raw Men in the World, and the best when once got over it.

But to return to the Point: If 'tis necessary to preserve our Peace, and maintain the Leagues and Confederacies, which are the Bands and Barrs of it; if 'tis necessary to be always ready to prevent an Affront of an Enemy? if 'tis necessary to support the Reputation of our *English* Power? 'tis necessary then to be, not only in a posture to Defend our selves at home, but to Defend our Confederates abroad, and to assist them in any sudden Insult from the Enemy; and this can be done neither by a Fleet, nor a Militia.

But to come further: We have been Invaded in *England*, notwithstanding our Fleet; and that many times. *Henry* the Seventh Landed with an Army in spight of *Richard* the Third and his Fleet. The Duke of *Monmouth* Landed in the *West*, tho' King *James* had a very good Fleet: And had not King *James*'s standing Army, tho' that was but Two Thousand Men, there routed them; I appeal to all Men to judge, what could the Militia have done to him? Now I'le suppose the Duke of *Monmouth* had been a *French* Man, or any thing, he had time to Land and Invade us, and unlade his Arms, and might have sent his Ships away again, and never have been hindred by our Fleet; and had he been but 5000 Regular Men, he had beat King *James* out of his Kingdom. Again, his Men were raw, a meer Militia, and you see what came of it, they were Defeated by a quarter of their Number, tho' I must say, they were better than any of our Militia too, by much.

Again, the *Prince of Orange* Landed his whole Army quickly, notwithstanding a Fleet, and had leisure enough to have sent away all his Ships again: So that 'tis a mistake, to say we cannot be Invaded if we have a Fleet, for we have been Invaded tho' we have had a good Fleet; and Demonstration is beyond Argument. And I would undertake, without Vanity, to Invade *England*, from any part beyond Sea, without any fear of the Fleet, unless you will have a Fleet able to block up your Neighbours Ports; and when you hear of any Ships fitting out any where, send and forbid them, as Queen *Elizabeth* did to *Henry* the 4th of *France*.

Now if I could come safe on Shore, notwithstanding the Fleet, then, if you have no Army to oppose me with, but your Country Militia, I would but ask any understanding Soldier, how many Men he would require to Conquer the whole Nation? Truly, not a great many; for,

I dare say, 40000 of the best Militia we have, back'd with no disciplin'd Troops, would not Fight 8000 old Soldiers: The Instance of the *Iniskilling Men*[14] in *Ireland* will not bear here; for, on the one hand, they were Men made desperate by the ruin of their Families and Estates, and exasperated to the highest degree, and had no recourse for their Lives but to their Arms; and on the other hand, the *Irish* were the most despicable scandalous Fellows the World ever saw; Fellows that shut their Eyes when they shot off their Musquets, and *tied Strings about their right Hands to know them from their left*: These are wretched Instances, and only prove what we knew before, that the Militia are always brave Soldiers when they have to do with Children or Fools; but what could our Militia have done to the P. of O.'s[15] old *Veteran* Troops, had they been willing to have opposed him; truly just as much as King *James* did, *run away*.

The Story of making them useful has been much talk'd of, and a Book was printed[16] to that purpose; it were a good Project, if practicable, but I think the Attempt will never be made by any wise Man, because no such will go upon Impossibilities.

War is no longer an Accident, but a Trade, and they that will be any thing in it, must serve a long Apprenticeship to it: Human Wit and Industry has rais'd it to such a Perfection; and it is grown such a piece of Mannage, that it requires People to make it their whole Employment; the War is now like the Gospel, Men must be set apart for it; the Gentlemen of the Club may say what they please, and talk fine things at home of the natural Courage of the *English*, but I must tell them, Courage is now grown less a Qualification of a Soldier than formerly; not but that 'tis necessary too, but Mannagement is the principle Art of War. An Instance of this may be had no farther off than *Ireland*; what a pitiful piece of Work the *Irish* made of a War all Men know: now 'tis plain the *Irish* do not want Courage, for the very same Men, when sent abroad, well Train'd, and put under exact Discipline, how have they behav'd themselves in *Piemont* and *Hungary*, they are allow'd to be as good Troops as any in the Armies.

And if the state of Things alter, we must alter our Posture too, and what then comes of the *History of Standing Armies*? Tho' there had never been any in the World, they may be necessary now, and so absolutely necessary, as that we cannot be safe without them.

We must now examine a little the Danger of a Standing Army at home; in which it will appear, whether the Gentlemen of the Club are in the right, when they turn all the Stream of the Government into one Channel, as if they all drove but one Wheel, and as if the whole Design of the King and his Ministers were to obtain the despotick Power, and to Govern by an Army.

They do indeed Caress the King sometimes with large Encomiums; but on the other hand, they speak it as directly as English can express, They intimate to us, that 'he design'd the Government by an Army, even before he came over; and therefore in his Declaration omited to promise the Disbanding it.' I wish these Gentlemen would leave out their Raillery, as a thing that never helps an Argument, – as Mr. *Dryden* says.

> – *For Disputants, when Reasons fail,*
> *Have one sure Refuge left, and that's to rail.*[17]

However, we shall not treat them in the same manner. I cannot think all those Artifices of the Court, (for a Standing Army) are true, and some of them are plain Forgeries. '*To tell us the Parliament thought*, they might have mannaged their part of the War by Sea. That the word *Authority of Parliament* was urg'd to that Article of the Declaration of Right, about Standing Armies, by such as design'd so early to play the Game of a Standing Army: That the Kingdom of *Ireland* was neglected, and *London-Derry* not Reliev'd, that a pretence for a greater Army might be fram'd.'[18] These are horrid suggestions, and savour only of ill Nature; and it may be very easy, had I leisure to examine, to prove to those Gentlemen, that the Parliament had as great a Sense of the necessity of Force to reduce *Ireland*, as the King had, and were as forward to grant Supplies for it. When the King told the House, that 'twas not advisable to attempt it without 20000 Men, If these Gentlemen had ask'd who advised his Majesty to say so, I could ha' told them, Duke *Schomberge*[19] himself did it; a Man who was much a Soldier, and as honest as ever Commanded an Army; a General of the greatest Experience of any of his Age, who no Man could despise without our Reproach to his Judgment; a Man us'd to Conquering of Kingdoms and Armies; and yet he thought it very unsafe to Fight with that Army at *Dundalk*. And we were beholding to his Conduct for the saving the whole Nation by that Caution, tho' Thousands lost their Lives by it, and some foolishly reflected on him for want of Courage; which 'twas thought, cost him his Life at the *Boyne*. King *James* had 50000 Men in *Ireland*, furnished with every thing necessary but a General; and can any body say, that to attempt reducing them with less than 20000, was a pretence to get an Army.

This is straining a Text, a Trade (without reflection) which our Adversaries are very ready at; but which is more useful for them, in their *Socinian* Principles, than in their Politicks.

By this, I must beg leave to tell the Gentlemen, it most plainly appears, that they drive at Villifying the present Establishment, rather than at the Liberty they talk so much of.

The next absurdity I find, is *Page* 23. Where, tho' they do not affirm, because like cunning Disputants, they won't hamper themselves in Argument, yet they plainly intimate, that all the omissions of our Fleet were design'd to produce this Argument from it, that a Fleet is no Security to us. As if his Majesty, or his Ministers, should Order our Fleet to do nothing Considerable, and spend Six or Seven years, and as many Millions of Mony, only to be able to say to the Parliament, *that a Fleet is no Security to us.* This is such a thing, that I cannot pass over, without desiring these Gentlemen to Examine a little, whether his Majesty has not, on the contrary, more improv'd our Fleet and Shipping, than any King before him ever did? Whether he has not built more Ships, and by his own Fancy, peculiar in that way, better Ships than any of his Predecessors? Whether the Docks, the Yards, the Stores, the Saylors, and the Ships, are not in the best Condition that ever *England* knew? Whether the King has not in all his Speeches to the Parliament, and in all the state of the Navy laid before them, put forward, to his utmost, the greatness of the Navy? Whether the Decoration of the Navy and Stores, are not regulated by him, to a degree never before put in practice; and whether, now the war is over, he has not taken care to have the greatest Fleet in the World, and in the best posture for Action? And is all this to let us know that a Fleet is no Security to us? I blush for these Gentlemen, when I think they should thus fly in the Faces of their own Arguments; and abuse the Care his Majesty has taken for that Security, which they ought to look on, with as much satisfaction, as our Enemies do with Concern.

Besides, I do not remember that ever the King, or any of his Ministers, offered to lessen the value of a good Fleet in any of their Speeches, or Discourses; if so, to what end have they been so careful of it, and why have we a Registring Act to secure Men for it, and a Royal Foundation at *Greenwich* Hospital to incourage them? why so many Bounties given to the Sea-men, and such vast Stores laid in to increase and continue them?

But must we not distinguish things? Our Defence is of two sorts, and so must be our Strength. Our Fleet is an undeniable defence and security for us; and we will grant, to oblige them, whether so or no, that both the Fleet and our Militia, which they are so fond of, are as great a Security at home as they can desire; but 'tis plain, and they cannot pretend to deny it, they are neither of them any thing to *Flanders*; which all the World will own must be the Scene of a War when ever it begins, unless they would have it brought home to us[a]. To say we may assist with Mony, is to say nothing; for Men may be wanting as much as Mony; and are so too, and have been so this War at an unusual rate.

These Arguments might be inlarg'd, even to a Twelve-penny Book, like the Author's, if the Printer desir'd it; but short as they are, they cannot be rationally confuted.

'The Gentlemen who argue thus against Force, have taken upon them to lay down a Method, how to assist *Spain*, in case of a War, by bringing Soldiers from *Final*;'[20] not letting us know, if we did not enquire, that those Forces must Sail by *Thoulon*, and that we must have a great Fleet in the *Straights* for that Service, or they will be prevented; nor not enquiring which way those Troops shall come at *Final*, while the Duke of *Savoy* possesses *Montferrat*, and all the higher part of *Italy* for the *French*: If they could argue no better than they can guide a War, if their Logic was not better than their Geography, they would make poor work of their Argument.

But because they seem to understand such things, I would fain ask these Gentlemen, if a War should break out now in the Empire, between the Papists and the Protestants, which a Man, without the Spirit of Prophesie, may say is very likely; pray which way would these Gentlemen have the King aid the Protestants in the *Palatinate*, what Service could our Fleet and Militia do in this Case. Why, say our Gentlemen, *we may aid them with Mony*. So did King *James* the First, after a most wretched manner, tho' his own Daughter was to lose her Patrimony by it; and the Protestant Interest in *Germany*, which now is in more hazard than ever it was since *Gustavus Adolphus* his time, must be supported by the Leagues and Confederacies, which our King must make, and our Forces uphold, or 'tis a great question whether it will be supported at all.

England is to be considered in several Capacities, though these Gentlemen seem to confine themselves to *England*; within it self *England* is, at this time, the Head of two Leagues, both which are essentially necessary to the preservation of our Welfare: One a League of Property, and the other of Religion. One a League against *French* Slavery, and the other a League against *German* Popery; and we can maintain neither of these without some Strength. I could tell these Gentlemen, That while they would disarm us to protect our Liberties, they strike a fatal Stroke at our Religion, which, I confess, I ought not to expect they should value, because I know their Principles to be both Irreligious and Blasphemous.

After all that has been said, 'twere not amiss to examine what this Army is we speak of, and how to be maintain'd; for these Gentlemen argue all along upon a great Army, enough to subject a Kingdom; and to raise it up to a magnitude, they have gone into *Ireland* and *Scotland*, and rak'd into the Settlement of those Kingdoms to muster up a great Army; though after all, their Calculations are wrong, almost a third part. In short, they have reckon'd up small and great to make up the number. To which it is convenient to reply.

First, What Forces are maintain'd in *Scotland* and *Ireland*, is nothing to the purpose; for both the Parliaments of those Kingdoms have concurr'd; and found it necessary, though these Gentlemen think otherwise.

Secondly, If the King does see it proper to have some Forces ready on such Occasions as we have discours'd, but, to ease us of our Jealousies and Fears, keeps them in other Kingdoms, and with consent of those Kingdoms; is not the *English* Nation so much the more oblig'd to him for his tenderness of their Safety and Satisfaction?

Thirdly, Why do not the Gentlemen as well argue against his having the Stad-holdership of *Holland*, by virtue of which he can, when ever he pleases, command over Ten or Twenty Thousand Men from thence, to enslave us when there is no War abroad. For it seems the Distance of the Army is no safety to us.

To go on, we have the War at an end, the King has dismiss'd the foreign Troops, disbanded Ten Regiments at home, besides Horse and Dragoons; most of the Scots abroad, sent Twelve Regiments to *Ireland*, and broke them there, and reduced the Army to so small a degree, as that much cannot be fear'd from them, nor fewer can hardly consist with our Safety; and yet these are the Grievances we are to be so terrify'd at, that nothing but Slavery must be the consequence.

Neither has any attempt been made to make this Army perpetual, nor has any number been prescrib'd. But such an Army, so proportioned, so qualified, and such a regulation as the Parliament shall see needful, may be legal, must be necessary, and cannot be dangerous: And to the King and Parliament we may with Satisfaction refer it. The Parliament will consent to no Force, but such as they shall judge safe and necessary; and the King will insist on no other Army than the Parliament consents to; and while they agree to it, why should we be concern'd. For while the King allows the disposal of the Army to the Vote of the Parliament, by which they may be either continued or dismissed, no future danger can appear; unless a Parliament shall part with that Power, which in this Reign is not likely to be desir'd of them.

The Conclusion

I Cannot pass over this Matter without a short Reflection upon the Persons and Designs of the Authors of this, and the like Pamphlets against the Government, and to enter a little into the History of their Practices for some years past.

His Majesty has found the influence of their more secret Actions, during the War, in their Delaying and Disappointing of Funds and Supplies, which, two Years together, prolong'd the War, and had like to have been fatal to the Army in *Flanders*, who went without Pay longer than any Army in the World (but themselves) would have done; and let his Majesty know, that they would not only Fight for him, but Starve for him, if there was occasion; and which his Majesty took great notice of in his Speeches at the opening of the next Parliament.

After this, they set up for Male-Contents, and always went about Town, complaining of mis-management, ill Officers, State Ministers, and the like: Angry that they were not preferr'd, and envying all that were; crying out, we must have Peace, and we should be ruin'd by the War; magnifying the Power of the *French*, which now they Undervalue so much; and saying, we should be subdued by the Power of *France*, if we did not save our selves by a Peace; and the like.

At last, the King, contrary to their Expectations, and false Prophesies, brought the *French* to Terms safe and honourable; and a Peace has been obtain'd as good as was not only expected, but desired.

This was no sooner done, but they strike at the Root; and now for fear of his hurting us, we must disarm the King, and leave him no more Weapons than should be trusted to a Child, or a Mad Man: And in order to secure us from a Tyrant, the whole Nation must be disarm'd, our Confederates deserted, and all the Leagues and Treaties (made for mutual Defence and Security) be broken, and the King left unable to perform the Postulata's of his own part. In order to this, they appear in Print; and setting up as Champions of the Peoples Liberty, form'd themselves into a Club, and appear openly both in Print, and publick Discourses; and being all of them maintainers of the most infamous Heresie of *Socinus*, they bid defiance to the Son of God on one hand, and to the King and Government on the other.

And that their Blasphemy might go hand in hand with their Politicks, they Publish'd two *Socinian* Books,[21] and two Books against the Army, almost together.

Much about the same time, from the same people, came out into the World, two Volumes of *Ludlow's Memoires;*[22] in all which, the Conduct of the Parliament against the King is exceedingly magnified; the Government of a single Person opposed covertly, under the Person of O. C.[23] but in general, of any single Person whatever; and all the Common-Wealth-Principles advanced and defended.

And having much Work of this sort to do, and being under some Fears of a restraint, from an Act for Regulating the Press, they endeavoured to ward off that Blow by publishing a Book for the Liberty of the Press,[24] which they mannaged with such Artifice, that the Bill was not past, and so their Fears vanisht.

This was a Victory they knew how to make use of, and it was immediately followed by a publication of Coll. *Sidney's* Maxims of Government, writ against *Filmer*; for which the Author dyed a Martyr, and of which one of the Publishers had the impudence to say it was the best Book, the Bible excepted, that ever came abroad in the World. And that he went no farther, I'll assure you the Pen-men of the holy Scripture were very much beholding to him.[a]

And now from the same Forge is hammer'd out the *History of the Standing Armies*, in which all the Artifice in the World is made use of, to set things in a false light, to raise the Cry of Tyranny and Despotick Government, which has been so long abdicated; to decry state Ministers, ridicule our Settlement, banter the King, and terrifie the People. And to this I must add an impudent Libel to direct the Honourable House of Commons in chusing a Speaker.[b]

And that it might have its due force, to sow Dissention and Disagreement between the King and his People, both these attacks made against the Army were tim'd to appear just at the opening of the Parliament,[25] and so industriously handed about, that they have been seen in the remotest Countries of *England* before they were published in *London*.

'Tis hoped these Circumstances will a little open the Eyes of the World, and teach us to mark such as sow Divisions among us, and not to meddle with those who are given to Change.

But to leave the matter to the Parliament, who are proper Judges of the Fact, and have always been very careful both of our Liberty and our Safety.

The Original

POWER

OF THE

COLLECTIVE
BODY

OF THE

People of England,

Examined and Asserted.

LONDON,
Printed in the Year 1702.

TO THE KING.

SIR,

'TIS not the least of the Extraordinaries of Your Majesty's Character, That as you are King of Your People, so You are the Peoples King.

This Title, as it is the Most Glorious, so is it the Most Indisputable in the World.

God himself appointed, the Prophet proclaim'd, but the Peoples assent was the finishing the Royal Authority of the first King of *Israel*.

Your Majesty, among all the Blessings of Your Reign, has restor'd this, as the best of all our Enjoyments, the full Liberty of Original Right in its Actings and Exercise.

Former Reigns have Invaded it, and the last thought it totally supprest, but as Liberty revived under Your Majesty's just Authority, this was the first Flower she brought forth.

The Author of these Sheets humbly hopes, That what Your Majesty has so Gloriously Restor'd, what our Laws and Constitution have Declared and Setled, and what Truth and Justice openly appears for, he may be allow'd to Vindicate.

Your Majesty knows too well the Nature of Government, to think it at all the less Honourable, or the more Precarious, for being Devolv'd from and Center'd in the Consent of your People.

The pretence of Patriarchal Authority, had it really an uninterrupted Succession, can never be supported against the demonstrated Practice of all Nations; but being also Devested of the chief Support it might have had, if that Succession could have been prov'd: The Authority of Governours *Jure Divino* has sunk Ignominiously to the Ground, as a preposterous and inconsistent Forgery.

And yet, if *Vox Populi* be, as 'tis generally allow'd, *Vox Dei*, Your Majesty's Right to these Kingdoms *Jure Divino*, is more plain than any of Your Predecessors.

How happy are these Nations, after all the Oppressions and Tyranny of Arbitrary Rulers, to obtain a King who Reigns by the universal Voice of the People, and has the greatest share in their Affections that ever any Prince enjoy'd, Queen *Elizabeth* only excepted.

And how vain are the Attempts of a Neighbouring Prince, to Nurse up a *Contemptible Impostor*,[1] upon the pretence of Forming a Claim on the Foundation of but a pretended Succession, against the Consent of the general Suffrage of the Nation.

To what purpose shall all the Proofs of his Legitimacy be, *supposing it could be made out*, when the universal Voice of the People, already express'd in enacted Laws, shall answer, *We will not have this Man to Reign over us*.

May this Affection of Your Subjects continue to the latest Hour of Your Life, and may Your Satisfaction be such as may convince the World, *That the Chiefest Felicity of a Crown consists in the Affections, as the first Authority of it derive from the Consent of the People*.

TO THE
LORDS SPIRITUAL AND TEMPORAL,
AND THE
COMMONS OF ENGLAND.

My Lords and Gentlemen,

THE Vindication of the Original Right of all Men to the Government of themselves, is so far from a Derogation from, that it is a Confirmation of your Legal Authority.

Your Lordships, who are of the Nobility, have your Original Right, your Titles and Dignities from the Greatness of your Shares in the Freeholds of the Nation: If Merit has raised any of your Ancestors to distinguishing Honours; or, if the Royal Favours of Princes has Dignified Families, it has always been thought fit to bestow or to enable them to Purchase some Portion of the Freehold of England to be annexed to the said Titles, to make such Dignity rational, as well as to support the Succession of Honour.

From hence you are Vested with Sovereign Judicature, as being the properest to be trusted with the Distribution of Justice in that Country, of which you were supposed to have, and once had, the principal Propriety.

From hence you sit in Parliament as a Branch of our Constitution, being part of the Collective Body, representing no Body but your selves; and as a Testimony that the Original of all Power Centers in the whole.

The rest of the Freeholders have Originally a Right to sit there with you, but being too numerous a Body, they have long since agreed that whenever the King thinks fit to advise with his People, they will chuse a certain few out of their Great Body to meet together with your Lordships.

Here, in short, is the Original of Parliaments; and here, if Power at any time meet with a Cess,[2] if [a] Government, Bishops and Thrones become Vacant to this Original, all Power of Course returns. This is the happy Center in the great Circle of Politick Order.

From hence at the late Revolution, when the King deserted the Administration, and His present Majesty was in Arms in England, *Nature directed the People to have Recourse to your Lordships, and to desire your Appearance as the Heads of the great Collective Body;[3] and all the Champions for the great Arguments of Divine Right could not in that Exigence have Recourse to one President,[4] nor to One Rule of Proceeding, but what Nature would have dictated to the Meanest Judgement,* viz. That the Nation being left without a Governour, the Proprietors should meet to consider of another.

And you Gentlemen of the House of Commons, *who are the Representatives of your Country, you are this great Collective Body in Minature, you are an Abridgment of the many Volumes of the* English *Nation.*

To you they have trusted jointly with the King and the Lords, the Power of making Laws, raising Taxes, and Impeaching Criminals: But how? 'Tis in the Name of all the Commons of England, *whose Representatives you are.*

All your Power is yours, as you are a Full and Free Representative. I no where attempt to prove what Powers *you have not, possibly the Extent of your Legal Authority was never fully understood, nor have you ever thought fit to Explain it. But this I may be bold to advance, That whatever* Powers *you have, or may have, you cannot Exercise but in the Name of the* Commons of England, *and you enjoy them as their Representative, and for their Use.*

All this is not said to lessen your Authority; Nor can it be the Interest of any English Freeholder *to lessen the Authority of the* Commons *assembled in* Parliament.

You are the Conservators of our Liberties, the Expositors of our Laws, the Levyers of our Taxes, and the Redressors of our Grievances, the King's best Councellors, and the Peoples last Refuge.

But if you are Dissolved, for you are not Immortal; or if you are Deceived, for you are not Infallible; 'twas never yet supposed, till very lately, that all Power *dies with you.*

You may Die, but the People remain; you may be Dissolved, and all immediate Right may cease; Power may have its Intervals, and Crowns their Interregnum; *but Original Power endures to the same Eternity the World endures to: And while there is People, there may be a Legal Authority Delegated, though all Succession of Substituted Power were at an End.*

Nor have I advanced any new Doctrine, nothing but what is as ancient as Nature, and born into the World with our Reason: And I think it would be a Sin against the Parliament of England, *to suggest that they would be offended either with the Doctrine or with the Author, since 'tis what their own Authority is built upon, and what the* Laws of England *have given their assent unto by confirming the Acts of the last* Collective Body of the People, *from whence the present Settlement of the Nation does derive.*

Wherefore I make no Apology for Protection or Favour as to the Fact; as to Language[a] *I am ready to ask Pardon if I offend, declaring my Intention is neither for nor against either Person or Party. As there is but* One Interest *in the Nation, I wish there were but* One Party, *and that Party would adhere to Unbyas'd Justice, and pursue the Honour and Interest of the* Protestant Religion, *and the* English Liberty.

THE ORIGINAL RIGHT[5]
OF THE PEOPLE OF ENGLAND,
EXAMINED AND ASSERTED.

I Have observ'd, when Interest obliges any Person or Party to defend the Cause they have Espous'd, they please themselves with fancying they conceal their Private Designs, by covering their Discourses with Gay Titles.

Like a late Act of Parliament, which in the Preamble calls it self, *An Act for the Relief of Creditors*, but in its Effect was really *an Act for the Relief of Debtors*.

Thus some Gentlemen place fine specious Titles on their books, as *Jure Populi Anglicanis*,[6] *A Vindication of the Rights of the Commons of* England,[7] and a *Vindication of the Rights of the Lords*,[8] and the like; and with large and high Encomiums upon the Excellency of our Constitution, treat the levity of some Peoples Judgments with fine Notions; whereas the true End and Design is defending the Interest and Party they have Espous'd.

The Defence of the Rights of the Representative Body of the People, understood by the Name of the Commons of *England* in Parliament, *is a great Point*; and so plain are their Rights, that 'tis no extraordinary Task to defend them: But for any Man to advance, that they are so August an Assembly that no Objection ought to be made to their Actions, nor no Reflection upon their Conduct, though the Fact be true; and that it is not to be examin'd whether the Thing said be true, but what Authority the Person speaking has to say it, *is a Doctrine wholly new*, and seems to me to be a Badge of more Slavery to our own Representative than ever the People of *England* owes them, or than ever they themselves expected.

This therefore, together with some Invasions of the Peoples Rights made publick by several Modern Authors, are the Reasons why I have adventur'd, *being wholly Disinterested and Unconcerned either for Persons or Parties*, to make a short Essay at declaring the Rights of the People of *England*, not Representatively but Collectively considered.

And with due Defference to the Representative Body of the Nation, I hope I may say, *it can be no Diminution of their Rights*, to assert the Rights of that Body from whom they derive the Powers and Priviledges of their House, and which are the very Foundation of their Being. For if the Original Right of the People be overthrown, the Power of the Representative, which is subsequent and subordinate, must dye of it self.

And because I have to do rather with Reason and the Nature of the Thing, than with Laws and Precedents, I shall make but very little use of Authors, and Quotations of Statutes, since Fundamentals and Principles both in Law and Argument, are superiour to Laws or Examples.

To come directly to what I design in the following Papers, 'tis necessary to lay down some Maxims, other than what a late *Author has furnish'd us with. *Sir H. M. Vindication of the Commons.*

1. That *Salus Populi suprema Lex,*[9] all Government, and consequently our whole Constitution, was originally design'd, and is maintain'd, for the support of the Peoples Property, who are the Governed.

2. That all the Members of Government, whether King, Lords or Commons, if they Invert the Great End of their Institution, the Publick Good cease to be in the same Publick Capacity,

And Power retreats to its Original.[a 10]

3. That no Collective or Representative Body of Men whatsoever, in Matters of Politicks any more than Religion, *are or ever have been Infallible.*

4. That Reason is the Test and Touch-stone of Laws, and that all Law or Power that is Contradictory to Reason, is *ipso facto* void in it self, and ought not to be obeyed.

These four Generals run through the whole following Discourse.

Some other Maxims less General are the Consequence of these; as,

First, That such Laws as are agreeable to Reason and Justice being once made, are binding both to King, Lords and Commons, either separately, or conjunctively, till they are actually Repealed in due Form.

That if either of the Three Powers do Dispense with, Suspend, or otherwise Break any of the known Laws so made, they Injure the Constitution; and the Power so acting ought to be restrained by the other Powers not concurring according to what is lately allowed, *That every Branch of Power is designed as a Check upon each other.* Sir H. M. Vindication of the Commons.

But if all the Three Powers should joyn in such an Irregular Action, the Constitution suffers a Convulsion, Dies, and is Dissolved of Course.

Nor does it suffice to say, That King, Lords and Commons can do no Wrong, since *the mutual Consent of Parties*, on which that foolish Maxim[11] is grounded, does not extend to every Action King, Lords and Commons are capable of doing.

There are Laws which respect the Common Rights of the People, as they are the Parties to be Governed, and with respect to these the King can do no Wrong, but all is laid upon his Ministers – who are accountable.

And there are Laws which particularly respect the Constitution; the King, Lords and Commons, as they are the Parties governing: In this regard each Branch, may Wrong and Oppress the other, or all together, may do Wrong to the People they are made to Govern.

The King may Invade the Peoples Properties, and if the Lords and Commons omit to defend and protect them, *they all do Wrong* by a tacit approving those Abuses they ought to oppose.

The Commons may extend their Power to an exorbitant Degree, in Imprisoning the subjects, Dispensing with the *Habeas Corpus* Act, giving unlimited Power to their Sergeant to Oppress the People in his Custody, withholding Writs of Election from Burroughs and Towns, and several other ways; which if they are not Check'd either by the King or the Lords, *they are altogether Parties to the Wrong*, and the Subject is apparently injured.

The Lords may Err in Judicature, and deny Justice to the Commons, or delay it upon Punctillioes and studied Occasions, and if neither the King nor the Commons take care to prevent it, Delinquents are excused, and Criminals encouraged, *and all are Guilty of the Breach of Common Justice.*

That to prevent this, it is absolutely necessary that in Matters of dispute the Single Powers should be Governed by the Joint, and that nothing should so be insisted upon as to break the Correspondence.

That[a] the Three should be directed by the Law; and where that is silent, by Reason.

That every Person concern'd in the Law is in his Measure a judge of the Reason, and therefore in his proper place ought *to be allowed to give his Reason in Case of Dissent.*

That every Single Power has an absolute Negative upon the Acts of the Other; and if the People, who are without Doors, find Reason to Object, *they may do it by Petition.*[12]

But because under pretence of Petitioning, Seditious and Turbulent People may foment Disturbances, Tumults and Disorders: The Subjects Right of Petitioning being yet recogniz'd and preserv'd, the Circumstances of such Petitions are regulated by Laws, as to the Numbers and Qualities of the Persons Petitioning.

But the Laws have no where prescrib'd the Petitioners to any Form of Words, and therefore no pretence of Indecency of Expression can be so Criminal as to be destructive of the Constitution; because, though it may deserve the Resentment of the Petitioned, yet it is not an illegal Act, nor a Breach of any Law.

And yet the Representative Body of the People ought not to be Banter'd[13] or Affronted neither, at the Will and Pleasure of any private Person without Doors, who finds Cause to Petition them.

But if any Expression be offensive to the House, it seems Reasonable that the Persons who are concerned therein should be requir'd to explain themselves: And if upon such Explanation the House find no Satisfaction as to the particular Affront, they are at Liberty to proceed as the Law directs; but no otherwise.

And to me, the Silence of the Law in that Case seems to imply, that rejecting the Petition is a Contempt due to any Indecency of that Nature, and as much Resentment as the Nature of the Thing requires: But as to breaking in upon Personal Liberty, which is a Thing the Law is so tender of, and has made so strong a Fence about, I dare not affirm 'tis a justifiable Procedure; no, not in the House of Commons.

It is alledged, That it has been practiced by all Parliaments; which is to me far from an Argument to prove the Legality of it.

I think it may pass for a Maxim, That a Man cannot be Legally punish'd for a Crime which there is no Law to prosecute. Now since there is no Law to prosecute a man for Indecency of Expression in a Petition to the House of Commons, it remains a Doubt with me how they can Legally punish'd.

Precedents are of Use to the Houses of Parliament where the Laws are silent, in Things relating to themselves, and are doubtless a sufficient Authority to act from. But whether any Precedent, Usage or Custom, of any Body of Men whatever, can make a Thing Lawful which the Laws have expressly forbid, remains a Doubt with me.

It were to be wish'd some of our Parliaments would think fit, at one Time or another, to clear up the Point of the Authority of the House of Commons, in Case of Imprisoning such as are not of their House, that having the Matter stated by those who are the onely Expositors of our Laws, we might be troubled with no more *Legion Libels*,[14] to tell them what is, or is not, Legal in their Proceedings.

The Good of the People Governed is the End of all Government, and the Reason and Original of Governours; and upon this Foundation it is that it has been the Practice of all Nations, and of this in particular, That if the Male-Administration of Governours have extended to Tyranny and Oppression, to Destruction of Right and Justice, over-throwing the Constitution, and abusing the People, the People have thought it Lawful to Reassume the Right of Government into their own Hands, and to reduce their Governours to Reason.

The present Happy Restoring of our Liberty and Constitution is owing to this Fundamental Maxim, according to a late Author,

> That Kings when they descend to Tyranny,
> Dissolve the Bond, and leave the Subject free.[a][15]

If the People are Justifiable in this Procedure against the King, I hope I shall not be Censur'd if I say, *That if any one should ask me, whether they have not the same Right, in the same Cases, against any of the Three Heads of the Constitution*, I dare not answer in the Negative.

I may be allow'd to suppose any Thing which is possible; and I will therefore venture to suppose, That in the late King's Reign the House of Commons, then sitting, had Voted the Restoration of Popery in *England*, in Compliance with the King's Inclination.

I doubt not but it had been Lawful for the *Grand Juries, Justices of the Peace*, and *Free-holders of any County*, or of every County, to have Petition'd the House of Commons not to proceed in giving up their Religion and Laws.

And in Case of Refusal there, they might Petition the House of Lords not to have Pass'd such a Bill.

And in Case of Refusal there, they might Petition the King, and put Him in Mind of His Coronation Engagement.

And in Case of Refusal to that Petition, they might Petition the King again to Dissolve the Parliament, or otherwise to protect their Liberties and Religion.

And if all these Peaceable Applications fail'd, I doubt not but they might Associate for their Mutual Defence against any Invasion of their Liberties and Religion, and apply themselves to any Neighbouring Power or Potentate for Assistance and Protection.

If this be not true, I can give but a slender Account of our late

Revolution; which nevertheless I think to be founded upon the exact Principles of Reason and Justice.

Nor will the Pretence of Indecency of Expression be any Argument to bar the Subject of his Right of Petitioning, or justifie the ill Treatment of such Petitioners: For the Case exceedingly differs from the supposed Case of the Lord Chancellor, and the Complaint which a late Author brings,[16] in desiring the Lord Chancellor *to turn his plausible Speeches into Righteous Decrees.*

First of all, The Freeholders of England stand in a different Capacity to the Members of the House, who are their *Trustees*, their *Attorneys*, their *Representatives*, from that of a Complainant in *Chancery* to the Judge of that Court.

Secondly, The Lord Chancellor has a Right by Law to Commit for personal Affronts offered in Court: Whether the House of Commons have the same Right by Law I know not, nor will not undertake to determine; but I do not find that Worthy Member has yet attempted to prove they have.

Thirdly; This is Arguing from the Inferiour Court to the Parliament of *England*, which is directly against Sir *H. M.*'s late Position, *Fol.* 4. where he had, as I suppose, forgot that he had laid us down this Rule.

'*When there is Occasion to Debate concerning these Superiour Powers of King, Lords and Commons, we must not argue like Lawyers in* Westminster-Hall, *from the narrow Foundation of private Causes of* Meum *and* Tuum; *but like Statesmen and Senators, from the Large and Noble Foundation of Government, and the general Good of the King and People.*'

Fourthly, But I am also informed, that the Case is wrong too, and that even in that Instance: The Lord Chancellor had no Power to Commit to the *Fleet*,[17] unless it were an Affront, *Viva Voce*, in Court.

Nor would it be any Argument in the supposed Case I am upon, for any Body to say, That the Occasion must concern that part of the Country[18] from whence such Petition is brought: for the Introducing of Popery would certainly concern every County of *England*.

And suppose again, the People thought themselves in danger of an Invasion from *France*, and thereupon the Counties of *Kent* and *Sussex* should have Petitioned the House to take them into Consideration, who, in such Case, were like to be the Seat of the War, and first Exposed to the Enemy; Would any Body say, the Occasion did not arise in the County from whence such Petition did proceed.

In this *Universal Right of the People* consists Our general Safety: For notwithstanding all the Beauty of our Constitution, and the exact Symetry of its Parts, about which some have been so very Elegant, *this noble well-contrived System has been Overwhelmed*; the Government has been Inverted, the Peoples Liberties have been trampled on, and Parliaments have been rendred useless and insignificant: *And what has restored us?* The last Resort has been to the People; *Vox Dei has been found there*, not in the *Representatives*, but in their Original the *Represented*.

And what has been the Engine that has led the Nation to it? The Reason and Nature of the Thing. Reason governs Men when they are Masters of their Sences, as naturally as Fire flies upwards, or Water descends.

For what is it that King, Lords and Commons assemble? 'Tis to Reason together concerning the weighty Matters of the State, and to Act and Do for the Good of the People, what shall be agreeable to Reason and Justice.

I grant 'tis reasonable that every Branch should be vested with due Powers, and those Powers be equally distributed.

But if they must be vested with Power, some Body must vest them with it: If these Powers must be distributed, some Body must distribute them. So that

There must be some Power *Prior* to the Power of King, Lords and Commons, from which, as the Streams from the Fountain, the Power of King, Lords and Commons is derived.

And what are all the different Terms which Statesmen turn so often into fine Words to serve their Ends; as, *Reason of State, Publick Good*, the *Commonwealth*, the *English Constitution*, the *Government*, the *Laws of England*, the *Liberties of England*, the *Fleets*, the *Armies*, the *Militia of England*, the *Trade*, the *Manufactures of England*? All are but several Terms drawn from and reducible to the great Term, the *People of England*. That's the General, which contains all the Particulars, and which *had all Power before any of the Particulars had a Being*. And from this Consideration it is, that some who yet would be Opposers of this Doctrine, say, *when it serves their Turn*, that all of the Great Offices which have the Title of *England* annexed to them, ought to be Nominated and Approved by the People of *England*, as the High Chancellor of *England*, High Admiral of *England*, and the like.

That Power which is Original, is Superior; *God is the Fountain of all Power, and therefore is the Supreme*: And if we could suppose a Prior and Original of the Divine Power, *that Original would be God*, and be Superiour; for all subsequent Power must be subject and inferiour to the precedent.

The Power vested in the Three Heads of our Constitution is vested in them by the People of *England*, who were a People before there was such a thing as a Constitution.

And the Nature of the Thing, is the Reason of the Thing: It was vested in them by the People, because the People were the only Original of their Power, being the only Power Prior *to the Constitution.*

For the publick Good of these People, a Constitution and Government was Originally Formed; from the mutual Consent of these people the Powers and Authorities of this Constitution are derived: And for the preservation of this Constitution, and enabling it to answer the Ends of its Institution in the best manner possible, those Powers were divided.

The Second Maxim is a Rational Natural Consequence of the former, That at the *final, Casual, or any other* Determination[19] of this Constitution, the Powers are Dissolv'd, and all Authority must derive *de novo* from the first Fountain, Original and Cause of all Constitutions, *the Governed.*

Now it cannot be suppos'd this Original Fountain should give up all its Waters, but that it reserves a Power of supplying the Streams: Nor has the Streams any power to turn back upon the Fountain, and invert its own Original. All such Motions are Excentrick and Unnatural.

There must always remain a Supream Power in the Original to supply, in Case of the Dissolution of Delegated Power.

The People of *England* have Delegated all the Executive Power *in the King*, the Legislative in the *King, Lords and Commons*, the Soveraign Judicature *in the Lords*, the Remainder is reserv'd in themselves, and not committed, no not to their Representatives: All Powers Delegated are to one Great End and Purpose, and no other, and that is *the Publick Good*. If either or all the Branches to whom this Power is Delegated invert the Design, the end of their Power, the Right they have to that Power ceases; and they become Tyrants and Usurpers of a Power they have no Right to.

The Instance has been visible as to Kings in our Dayes; and History is full of Precedents in all Ages, and in all Nations; particularly in *Spain*, in *Portugal*, in *Swedeland*, in *France*, and in *Poland*.

But in *England*, the late Revolution is a particular Instance of the Exercise of this Power.

King *James* on the Approach of a Foreign Army, and the general recourse of the People to Arms, fled out of the Kingdom. What must the People of *England* do? They had no Reason to run after him to be Govern'd there; there was no Body to call a Parliament, so the Constitution was entirely Dissolv'd.

The Original of Power, *the People*, Assembled in Convention, to consider of Delegating New Powers for their future Government, and accordingly made a New Settlement of the Crown, a New Declaration of Right, and a New Representative of the People; *and what if I should say*ª *they ought to have given a New Sanction to all precedent Laws.*

It remains to argue from hence, But what Course must the People of *England* take, if their Representatives exercise the Power intrusted with them, to the Ruine of the Constitution?

It has been advanced, That every Man must submit, and not presume to argue against it upon any Supposition of Mismanagement.

I can see no Reason given to confirm such a Position; for unless we will place the Original of Power in the persons Representing, not in the persons Represented, it cannot be made out that there ought to be no Complaint upon the score of Mismanagement.

It is not the Design of this Discourse to lessen the Authority of Parliament: But all Power must Centre some where. If it is in the Three Branches of the Constitution, 'tis there inherently and originally, or it is there by Deputation. If it be there by Deputation, then there must be a Power Deputing, and that must be both *Prior*, and consequently Superiour to the Deputed, *as before.*

If we will come off of this, we must fly to the old weak Refuge of a Power *Jure Divino*, a Doctrine which the most famed Pretenders to, have lived to be ashamed of; and whose Foundation is so weak, that 'tis not worth while to Expose it.

I should therefore have been very glad, that for the Perfecting the Defence of the *English* Constitution, the Gentlemen who have begun so well, would have gone forward to Recognize the Power of the People of *England*, and their undoubted Right to judge of the Infractions made in their Constitution, by either Parties abusing the particular Powers vested in them; and inverting them, by turning them against the People they are designed to defend.

That they would have stated fairly what the People of *England* are to do, if their Representatives shall hereafter betray the Liberties or Religion of the People they are intrusted with the Defence of.

What by the Laws of Nature and Reason is to be expected, and what by the Laws of our Constitution are allowed.

To say, It cannot be supposed the House of Commons can ever betray their Trust, is a Compliment: No Man is bound to make them, *Humanum est Errare.*[20] We have seen Parliaments Err, and do what succeeding

Parliaments have thought fit to undoe: *And as that which has been may be, so that may be which never has been before.*

We have seen Parliaments comply with Kings to the Ruine of the Nation; and we have seen Parliaments Quarrel with Kings, to the Over-turning of the Constitution, Dissolving the House of Lords, and Suppressing the Monarchy.

We have seen Parliaments concur so with the Fate and Fortunes of Princes, as to comply backward and forward, in Deposing and Reinthron-ing alternately two Kings as often as Victory put power into their Hands, I mean *Henry* the Sixth, and *Edward* the Fourth, who were Kings and Prisoners five or six times, and always the Parliament complied with the Conquerors.

We have seen a Parliament of *England* confirm the Usurpation of *Richard* the Third, the greatest Tyrant and most bloody Man that ever *England* brought forth.

We have seen a *Parliament* confirm *Henry* the Seventh, who really had no Right at all by Succession, and Rescind all the precedent *Parliament* had done.

Afterwards, in Matters of Religion, King *Henry* the Eighth made a *Popish Parliament* pull down the Supremacy of *Rome*, and set up the King's; and afterwards suppress all the Religious Houses in the Nation. His Son pulled up Popery by the Roots, and planted the Reformation, *still the Parliament complied.* Queen *Mary* Re-established Popery, and unravelled both the Reformation of King *Edward*, and all the Acts both of Church and State relating to her Mother's Divorce, *and still the Parliament consented.* One *Parliament* Voted Queen *Mary* Legitimate, and Queen *Elizabeth* a Bastard: Another *Parliament* Legitimated Queen *Elizabeth*, and Repudiated Queen *Mary.* Queen *Elizabeth* undid all her Sister had done, and suppress'd all the proceedings of Popery; and *all was by Authority of Parliament.*

So that this Parliamentary Branch of Power is no more Infallible than the Kingly.

Had Sir *H. M.* gone on to have Recogniz'd the Peoples Right, to preserve their own Liberties in case of failure in any, or in all the Branches of the Constituted Power, he had compleated his *Vindication of the Commons of England*, which no man could have done better than himself.

If then upon the Subversion of the Laws, and Interruption of Common Justice, the Center of Power is in the People, *a Fortiori* the People are also concerned in every Degree of such a Subversion.

And 'tis the most reasonable thing in the World, that those who upon a total Subversion are the Sufferers, and have a Right to the Re-establishment, should have a Right to take Cognisance of any Degree of Invasion made upon their Right, and which tends to that general Subversion.

'Twould be Nonsence to suppose, that which has all the Greater Powers should not have the Less.

Can the Peoples Good be the main and only End of Government, and the Peoples Power be the last Resort when Government is Overwhelmed by the Errors of Governors? and have these People no Right, not so much as to be sensible of the Ruine of their Liberties, till it is absolutely compleated? 'Twould be ridiculous.

The truth is in right Reasoning, the first Invasion made upon Justice, either by the tacit or actual Assent of the three Heads of our Constitution, is an actual Dissolution of the Constitution; and, for ought I can see, the People have a right to dispossess the Incumbent, and commit the Trust of Government, *de Novo*, upon that first Act.

But I chuse rather to put the Argument upon total Subversions of right Order and Defence, and I am sure no Body will dispute it with me there.

And here, if I have any foresight, lies an absolute Security for us against that Bug-bear, which so many pretend to be frighted at *a Commonwealth*.

The *Genius* of this Nation has always appear'd to tend to a Monarchy, a legal limited Monarchy; and having had in the late Revolution a full and uninterrupted Liberty, to Cast themselves into what Form of Government they pleas'd: There was not discovered the least Inclination in any Party towards a *Commonwealth*, tho' the Treatment they met with from their last two Kings, had all in it that could be, to put them out of Love with Monarchy.

A Commonwealth can never be introduc'd, but by such Invasions of Right as must make our present Constituted Government impracticable: The Reason is, because Men never willingly change for the Worst; and the People of *England* enjoy more Freedom in our Regal, than any People in the World can do in a Popular Government.

The People of *England* can never chuse a Commonwealth Government, till they come to desire less Liberty than they now enjoy; that is, till they come to be blind to their own Interest. 'Tis true, Example is no Argument; but I might freely Appeal to the Friends of the Last Republick in *England* to answer this Question.

Whether the People of *England*, during the short Government of Parliament in *England*, which was erroneously called a Commonwealth, did, or whether they can under any Commonwealth Government, founded never so wisely, enjoy greater Privileges and Advantages than under the present Constitution in its full and free Exercise, uninterrupted by the Excesses of Kings evil Councellors, Parties and Passions.

If any shall pretend that the late Parliament [21] is aimed at in this, I hope I may have as much liberty to suppose they are Mistaken; *for the Days of Judging by* Inuendo *are at an end.*

If any thing seem to lie that way, the Error must be theirs who have so mean thoughts of them, as to think the Coat will fit them; *if it does, they are welcome to wear it.* For my part, I declare my self to intend only the bringing things to such a right Understanding, as may preserve the Ballance of Power; and, I hope, I cannot offend any Free Representative of the People of *England*, in saying, that *What Power they have they receive from the People they represent; and, That some Powers do still remain with the People, which they never neither divested themselves of, nor committed to them.*

Nor can I be sensible of offending if I say, that *'Tis possible for even a House of Commons to be in the Wrong.* 'Tis possible for a House of Commons to be misled by Factions and Parties. 'Tis possible for them to be Brib'd by Pensions and Places, and by either of these Extreams to betray their Trust, and abuse the People who entrust them: And if the People should have no Redress in such a Case, then were the Nation in the hazard of being ruined by their own Representatives. And 'tis a wonder to find it asserted in a certain Treatise,[22] *That it is not to be supposed that ever the House of Commons can Injure the People who intrust them.* There can be no better way to demonstrate the possibility of a thing, than by proving that it has been already.

And we need go no farther back than to the Reign of King *Charles* the Second, in which we have seen Lists of 180 Members who received private Pensions from the Court; and if any Body shall ask whether that Parliament preserv'd the Ballance of Power in the three Branches of our Constitution, in the due distribution some have mentioned, *I am not afraid to answer in the Negative.*

And why even to this day are Gentlemen so fond of spending their Estates to sit in that House, that Ten thousand Pounds has been spent at a time to be Chosen, and now that way of procuring Elections is at an end, *private Briberies* and Clandestine Contrivances are made use of to get into the House. *No Man would give a Groat to sit where he cannot get a Groat honestly for sitting, unless there were either Parties to gratifie, Profits to be made, or Interest to support.*

If then these things are possible, it seems to me not so improper for the People, who are the Original and End of the Constitution, and have the main Concern in it, to be very sollicitous that the due Ballance of Power be preserv'd, and decently; and, according to Law, always to shew their Dislike and Resentment at any publick Encroachment, which either Branch of the Constitution, shall make on each other, or on the whole, be it by their own Representatives or any where else.

If it is expected, that I should descend to particular Matters, debated between the two Houses in the last Session of this present Parliament, such Expectants will be deceived: I shall not meddle with a Case which appears so difficult to be decided, that the two Houses of Parliament could not agree about.

And since, as I said before, every Person who takes upon him to speak to or of the Parliament, ought to have liberty to Explain himself; so I have taken that Liberty in the Preface to this Book, to which I refer. But this in General I may say, for I am upon Generals, and shall keep to them without any relation to particular Cases.

It cannot be that the *People of England*, who have so much Concern in the good Agreement of their Governors, can see the Two Houses of Parliament at any time Clash with one another, or with the King, or the King with them; or Encroach upon the Rights and Liberties of the Subjects, and be Unconcern'd and not express their Fears.

If any Fellow Subject be Impeach'd, to see the Disputes between the Two Houses about Punctilioes of Form, interrupt the due and ordinary Course of Justice; so that a Criminal cannot be Detected, nor an Innocent Man be Justified, but such Impeachments shall lie as a Brand upon the Reputation of an Innocent Person, *which is a Punishment worse than his Crime deserv'd, if he were Guilty*: These are Injuries to the Subject in general, and they cannot be easie to see them.

We have a great Cry against an Evil Ministry, the noise of which is so great, as it drowns the Complaints of the People; but I dare say none of the People of *England* would be against having due Resentments shown, and legal Punishments inflicted with impartial Justice, where the Persons appear Guilty: But if Enquiry after Disorders at Home should delay taking care of our Safety Abroad; if private Clashings and Disputes between Parties and Interests should take up the Hours which are due to the Emergency of Foreign Affairs, the People of *England* will be very ill serv'd; and the Persons, whoever they are concerned, will be able to give but a sorry account to the Country that employ'd them of the Trust they had committed to them: Not that Delinquents should not be Punish'd, or Evil Ministers Impeach'd, but, as our Saviour says in another Case, *These things ye ought to have done,*[23] *and not have the other left undone.*

What shall we then say to the manner of fixing Guilt upon a Person or a Party by Vote. That the Lords denying a free Conference was a Delay of Justice, and tended to destroy the good Correspondence, *&c.** and refusing to proceed to the Tryal of one Impeach'd Lord, because another Lord, not Impeach'd, had affronted the House.[24]

Truly I shall venture to say nothing of it but this, That the Clashings and Disagreement between the two Houses are things our Enemies rejoyc'd at, and the People of *England* were very sorry for. Who are in the right of it Sir *H. M.* must answer for me, who says, *It is not to be imagin'd that a Majority of so numerous a Body of Gentlemen can be influ-enc'd against Reason and Justice.* But at the same time[†] supposes the Lords may, by receiving Articles of Impeachment to Day, and appointing to Try them Forty Years hence, or else tomorrow Morning at *Truro*[25] in *Cornwall.*

If he means that it is not probable, I readily allow it; but if he means that 'tis not possible, I cannot agree, for the Reasons and Examples afore-said: And if it be but possible, 'tis not reasonable the Liberty and Safety of *England* should be exposed even to a possibility of a Disaster; and therefore Reason and Justice allows, that when all Delegated Powers fail or expire, when Governours devour the People they should protect; And when Parliaments, *if ever that unhappy time shall come again*, should be either destroy'd, or, which is as bad, be Corrupted, and betray the People they Represent, the People themselves, who are the Original of all Delegated Power, have an undoubted Right to defend their Lives, Liberties, Properties, Religion and Laws, against all manner of Invasion or Treachery, be it Foreign or Domestick; the Constitution is Dissolv'd, and the Laws of Nature and Reason act of Course, according to the late Author quoted before.

> The Government's ungirt when Justice dies,
> And Constitutions are *non Entities*:
> The Nation's all a Mob; there's no such thing
> As Lords and Commons, Parliament or King.
> A great promiscuous Croud the *Hydra* lies,

---

* *This refers to Impeaching Lord* Hallifax, *etc., but refusing to try him, till the Commons had Justice done them, for Words spoken by the Lord* Haversham.[a]

† *Sir* Humphrey's *Defence of the Rights of the Commons of* England, *Fol.* 7.[b]

> Till Laws revive and mutual Contract ties.
> A *Chaos* free to chuse for their own share
> What Case of Government they please to wear.
> If to a King they do the Reins commit,
> All Men are bound in Conscience to submit.
> But then that King must by his Oath assent
> To *Postulata*'s of the Government:
> Which if he breaks he cuts off the Intail,
> And Power retreats to its Original.[a][26]

It may be Objected; But who are these People to whom Power must thus Retreat? And who have the Original Right in their Hands? It must be the whole People. If there be one Negative, every one having an equal Right, the real Claim of Power is Imperfect: And since there can be no general Collective Meeting of the whole Community, there can be no Execution of their Power; and therefore this does not justifie a few of that Body in the name of the rest, to Execute any part of that Power.

This may be Answer'd; though upon a Dissolution of Government all the People collectively cannot be enquired of as to what they will have done, yet one Negative ought not to Interrupt the whole.

I'll suppose a general Dissolution of Government in any Country, such as was seen in this Nation at the last Revolution.

The People assembled in a Universal Mob to take the Right of Government upon themselves, are not to be supposed to give their personal Suffrages to every Article, but they may agree to a Convention of such Persons as they think fit to Intrust, to Constitute *de Novo*,[27] and may Delegate their Power, or part of it to such a Convention; and in such Case a general Concurrence is to be suppos'd, unless there be a publick Dissent.

Now suppose the general Collective Body of the People should not unanimously agree, 'tis own'd the Power could not be universally Delegated, and there a Division would follow; but in such Case, those who Dissented from such an Agreement, must declare their Dissent, and agree to any other Form of Government for themselves, and so divide from the other Body, and if they do not divide, they in effect do not Dissent.

But then this Division must be before any Members are Delegated by them to Convene.

For Example:

Suppose the Freeholders in *Cornwall* in such a Case should say, We do not approve of your deputing Men to meet and consult of a new

Government and Constitution, we are resolved to be govern'd by *such a Man* of our own Country.

This Resolution being against no Law, and that County having sent no Members to represent them, and to join with the rest of the Body, they cannot be legally disturb'd, or punish'd, or forc'd to Unite with the rest of the Nation.

Such a Division might be look'd upon as a Misfortune to the General Body, and unkind in the County or part dividing from the self, but in the nature of the thing it could not be Unjust.

Because[a] any Body of Men are at Liberty, upon the Dissolution of former Contracts, to be Governed by such Laws and Persons, and in such manner as they shall think fit.

Yet is there no fear of such a Division in a Country so depending on its several Parts as this is, because the rest would render them so uneasie, that Interest would compel them to comply.

Note, I[b] do not place this Right upon the Inhabitants, but upon the *Freeholders*; the *Freeholders* are the proper Owners of the Country: It is their own, and the other Inhabitants are but Sojourners, like Lodgers in a House, and ought to be subject to such Laws as the Freeholders impose upon them, or else they must remove; because the Freeholders having a Right to the Land, the other have no right to live there but upon sufferance.

In former Days the Freehold gave a Right of Government to the Freeholder, and Vassalage and Villinage was deriv'd from this Right, that every Man who will live in my Land shall be my Servant; if he wont, let him go about his Business, and live somewhere else: And 'tis the same still in right reasoning.

And I make no question but that Property of Land is the best Title to Government in the World; and if the King was universal Landlord, he ought to be Universal Governour of Right, and the People so living on his Lands ought to obey him, or go off of his Premises.

And if any single Man in *England* should at any time come to be Landlord of the whole Freehold of *England*, he could indeed have no Right to Dispossess the King, till the present Legal Settlement of the Crown fail'd, because it was settled by those that had then a Right to settle it.

But he would immediately be the full Representative of all the Counties in *England*, and might Elect himself Knight of the Shire for every County, and the Sheriff of every County must Return him accordingly.

He would have all the Baronies and Titles of Honour which are entail'd upon Estates devolv'd upon him, and upon any Expiration of the Settlement would be King by natural Right.

And he would be King upon larger Terms than ever any Man was legally King of *England*; for he would be King by inherent Right of Property.

When therefore I am speaking of the Right of the People, I would be understood of the Freeholders, for all the other Inhabitants live upon Sufferance, and either are the Freeholders Servants, or having Money to pay Rent live upon Conditions, and have no Title to their living in England, other than as Servants, but what they must pay for.

Upon this foot it is that to this Day our Law suffers not a Foreigner to Purchase any of the Freeholds of *England*: For if a Foreigner might Purchase, your Neighbours (having Money to spare) might come and buy you out of your own Country, and take Possession by a legal and indisputable Right.

This Original Right was the first Foundation of the several Tenures of Land in *England*; some held of the King, some of the Lord, some by Knight Service, Soccage,[28] and the like, and some were called Freeholds. The Lords of Mannors had their Homages and their Services from their Tenants, as an Acknowledgment that the Right of the Land gave a certain Right of Government to the Possessor over all the Tenants and Inhabitants.

But he that possess'd the least Freehold, was as much Lord of himself, and of that Freehold, as the greatest Noble-man in the Nation, he ow'd no Homage or Service, no, not to the King, other than as limited by Laws of his own making, that is as he was represented in Parliament.[a]

And as a thing which will put this Argument out of all question, The Right to Lands, Mannors, and Lordships was not Originally a Right granted by Patents from Kings or Acts of Parliament, but a natural Right of Possession handed down by Custom and ancient Usage, as the Inheritance from the still more ancient Possessors, and Prescription, as the Lawyers call it, or Usage time out of mind, is to this Day allow'd to be a sufficient Title in several Cases, where Conveyances, Deeds, Charters, and Writings of Estates are silent, especially as to Buttings and Boundings of Land, Highways, Footpaths, Water Courses, Bridges, and the like.

This Right, as all Right Originally, is Founded upon Reason. For it would be highly Unreasonable, that those People who have no share of the House should live in it whether he that built it will or no. No Person has any Right to live in *England*, but they to whom *England* belongs; the Freeholders of *England* have it in possession; *England* is their own, and no Body has any thing to do here but themselves.

If they permit other People to live here, well and good, but no Man but a Freeholder lives here upon any Terms but *permissu Superiorum*,[29] and he pays Rent for his Licence to live here.

Thus the Liberties and Privileges of Towns and Corporations are founded upon Acts of Parliament to confirm Charters or Grants from the Crown, by which the Freeholders give their Consent that such and such Bodies of Men living in such Towns, shall enjoy certain Privileges in Consideration of their being so considerably serviceable to the Nation, by paying Taxes, maintaining the poor, by Manufactures, Trade, and the like, notwithstanding they are not possess'd of any part of the Freehold.

And 'tis observable, the King cannot give this Privilege, so as to enable any of these Corporations to send Representatives to Parliament. None but the Freeholders of *England* (and such Towns in Conjunction) to whom the Freeholders have already granted such Privilege, can give a Qualification of such a Nature, as is a receiving them into an equal state of Privilege with a Freeholder.

Every Man's Land is his own Property; and 'tis a Trespass in the Law for another Man to come upon his Ground without his Consent. If the Freeholders should all agree, That such a Man shall not come upon their Land; That they will not Lett him a House for his Money; That whose Land soever he sets his Foot on, the Owner shall Indict him for a Trespass, as by Law he may, the Man must fly the Nation of Course.

Thus the Freeholders having a Right to the Possession of *England*, the Reason must be good that they must have the same Right to the Government of themselves, that they have to the Government of the rest of the Inhabitants; and *that there can be no Legal Power in* England, *but what has its Original in the Possessors; for Property is the Foundation of Power.*

I am not undertaking to find fault with our Constitution, tho' I do not grant neither, that it is capable of no Amendment; but I would endeavour to make way, by retreating to Originals, for every Member to perform its proper Function, in order to put the general Body into its regular Motion.

For as in the natural Body, if any Member, either by Contraction of the Organ, Dislocation, or other Accident, fails in the performance of its proper Duty, the Locomotive Faculty is either interrupted, and the Body distorted, or at least the regularity of Natural Motion is invaded:

So in the Body Politick, if one Branch of the general Union err, and that Error is not Corrected, the whole Constitution suffers a shock, and there is an Infraction of the general Order.

The Excellency of our Constitution consists of the *Symitry of Parts*; *and the Ballance of Power*; and if this Ballance be broken, one Part grows too great for the other, and the whole is put into Confusion.

To give some Instances of this, 'twill be needful to enter a little into History, and we need not go far to inform our selves, that there has been a Time when the weakness of our Constitution has appeared.

Our Constitution, when all the fine things in the World have been said of it, is not impregnable, when Power has been thrown wholly into one Scale, the other has always been trampled under Foot, and overthrown by it.

The Regal Power under King *Charles* the First, over-Ballanc'd the Lords and Commons, to the invading the Right of Levying Taxes vested wholly in the Parliament, and to the discontinuing Parliaments for fourteen Years, and the many Convulsions the Constitution felt in that time, is too melancholy a Subject to reflect upon.

The House of Commons in the next Settlement over-Ballanc'd the Lords; and Power being added to one side, toss'd the Upper House quite out of the Scale, absolutely Annihilated the very being of the Peers *as a House*,[30] and voted them out of the Constitution.

By the Restoration the Constitution return'd to its Original, and the Ballance was pois'd again: What attempts have since been made to overthrow it, are needless to be insisted upon, but the nature of the thing leads me to make one Remark, That if the King can do no Wrong, nor is not punishable or blamable by our Constitution, but the Ministery, as a late Author[31] has very clearly set down, Then we have acted strangely in the late Revolution, in which the King who must be innocent only suffered; and the Ministry, who must be Guilty, not only were excused, but intrusted and employed.[a]

Not that I am of some Peoples Opinion neither, who think the late King had hard measure in being Depos'd, when he was really not accountable. For I presume I may affirm, That the Deposing King *James* was founded upon his Deserting the Nation, not his Male-administration; for had he continued in *England* you might possibly have subdu'd him, and took him Prisoner, but there had been no room for Transposing the Crown while he had been alive.

And 'tis allow'd by all, that those Persons who advised him to quit the Kingdom by flying out of it, either wilfully betray'd him, or very ignorantly gave him the only Council which could compleat his Ruine.

How then it comes to pass that those evil Ministers have arriv'd to Impunity for what was past, and again to be trusted both in the Court and in the Parliament with the Peoples Liberties, is *a Mystery past our reaches.*

If I had no Name my self, I would set down theirs; or if I had a Press in the Clouds to Print their Practices, the World should not be Ignorant; but since 'tis not so, I shall only say as our Saviour said of some Body else, *By their Works ye shall know them.*[32]

These are the Men who Cry loudest against the present Ministery, and on all Occasions make use of the pretence of *Liberty* to animate the Nation against not only the present, but against every Ministery by which the publick Affairs shall be manag'd, and against the King himself. The same Men who in former Days Cried up a Popish Army in a profound Peace, the very same now Cried down a Protestant Army in time of Danger. The very same Men who could digest the absolute Power of ruining our Liberty and Religion, being vested in a Popish King, were the first and forwardest that durst not trust a Protestant King with Forces enough to defend us till Peace was better Establish'd, but have by that means, according to their Hearts desire, laid us and all *Europe* under a necessity of Arming again to maintain that Peace, which 'twas then in our power to have maintain'd.

For I am free to say 'twas not the Treaty of Partition[33] which so much run the *Spaniards* upon giving themselves up to the *French*, as it was the despicable Figure the *English* Forces were reduced to, which made the *French* King bold to take possession of the *Spanish* Monarchy, which had some, I do not say all our Forces been continued but a year or two longer, he would not have ventur'd to have done.

And yet all these Forces might have been subjected so absolutely to Parliamentary Power, as if they had been their own; for the King never denied them any Security they desired, and so they might have been Disbanded as easily now as then.

Nor do I think that in this Discourse I can be supposed to favour that Party, *if there be such a Party, which indeed I question*, who would Govern this Nation by the help of a Standing Army; but I must be allowed to lay down this for a Maxim, That any Force as shall be agreed to by Consent of Parliament is Legal, and some Force may at some particular times be necessary, of which the Parliament are the only Judges.

Still I allow that of this Power so derived from Property, the *House of Commons* are the Abridgment; they are *the Freeholders of* England *in*

Minature; to them all needful Powers and Privileges are committed, to make them capable of acting for the People they Represent; *and, Extremities excepted, they are our last Resort*: But if they employ those Privileges and Powers against the People, the reason of those Powers is destroy'd, the End is inverted, and the Power cease of course.

From hence 'tis reasonable to give them Instructions; and though they are not conditionally Chosen as to their Instructions, yet they ought in Honour to think themselves under equal Obligation to stand by those Instructions.

Instructions to Members are like the Power given to an Arbitrator, in which though he is left fully and freely to act, yet 'tis in Confidence of his Honour that he will think himself bound by the Directions he receives from the Person for whom he acts.

If an Arbitrator Inverts the Design of his Principal, he destroys the end of his Election, and is sure never to be entrusted again.

The *House of Commons* are our Sanctuary against the Oppression of Princes, the Nations Treasurers, and the Defenders of their Liberties; but all these Titles signifie, that at the same time they are the Nations Servants.

The *House of Commons* also are Mortal, as a House; a King may Dissolve them, they may die and be extinct; but the Power of the People has a kind of Eternity with respect to Politick Duration: Parliaments may cease, but the People remain; for them they were originally made, by them they are continued and renewed, from them they receive their Power, and to them in reason they ought to be accountable.

The Conclusion.

THE Dissolution of the last Parliament[34] has been subsequent to the Writing these Sheets, and two Observations fall out so naturally on this occasion, that I cannot but conclude this Subject with them.

That both His Majesty and the whole Nation have very happily given their Approbation to the Positions here laid down.

It cannot be doubted but that the Language of the Addresses of the People presented to his Majesty, upon the Indignity offer'd him by the *French* King,[35] has in general a Dislike included in them of the Management of their late Representatives; and tho' it is a new thing, yet it is plain that their Proceedings in general have been Disobliging to the Nation.

There was no need to express in words at length, *before also His Majesty's Intentions were known*, that they desire him to Dissolve the present Parliament. Good Manners required, that they should not so plainly lead His Majesty in what he was to be the Author of; besides, the Parliament was in Being, and the illegal Arbitrary Usage of the *Kentish* Gentlemen[36] fresh in the Memory of the People. But what is the meaning of the following Expressions in the Addresses?* *If Your Majesty please to entrust us with the Choice of a new Parliament; When Your Majesty shall be graciously pleased to call a new Parliament; In conjunction with a Parliament;* and the like. What would the Addressors have us, or have the King to understand by these Expressions, but that the People finding themselves Injur'd by the Proceedings of their Representatives, and the Nation in danger of being abused and betray'd to the Invasions of the *French*, by the Illegal and Arbitrary Designs of a Party in the House, have recourse to his Majesty, to depose *for them* a Power which they saw going to be misapplied to the Ruine of those from whom and for whom it was appointed.

Nor was this any thing but what was seen and known before; all those Addresses are the Legitimate Off-spring of the *Kentish* Petition; and had not the Freeholders been aw'd by the ill usage of the *Kentish* Gentlemen, the whole Nation had then as unanimously Petition'd the House; as they have now Address'd His Majesty.

This is evident from the Tenour, and yet undiscovered Original of the *Legion Paper*; the Contents of which had so much plain Truth of Fact, and Truth of Law, that the House stood Convicted in the plain Consternation the Contents of it threw them in; *and which I could give a better History of, if it were needful* by which they gave a full assent to the Right of the People.

But beyond all this is His Majesty's Proclamation, wherein, according to Truth, Reason, and the Nature of the Thing, His Majesty has graciously given a Sanction to the natural Right of his People, proclaiming from the *English* Throne, of which he is the most Rightful Possessor by the Voice of the People, that ever sat on it.

That when the People of *England* do universally express their Resolution to do what should or ought to be desired of good *English-Men* and Protestants,[†] *It is reasonable to give them an Opportunity to chuse such Persons to represent them in Parliament, as they may judge most likely to bring to effect their just and pious Purposes.*

[†] See his Majesty's Proclamation for Dissolving the Parliament.[a]

---

* Vide. *The Addresses in the* Gazettes, *No. —*.[b]

The Words need no Comment, they contain in them a glorious Recognition from the late Restorer of *English* Liberty, an unexampled Testimony to the reasonableness of those just Rights, which, *though former Kings, blinded by Ambition, have indeavour'd to suppress*, His present Majesty, according to his first Declaration and continued Practice, has accounted it his Chief Honour to preserve, and which we doubt not he will hand down unbroken to Posterity.[a]

SOME

REMARKS

On the First Chapter in

Dr. *DAVENANT*'s

ESSAYS.

LONDON:
Printed and Sold by *A. Baldwin*, near the *Oxford-*
Arms in *Warwick Lane*. MDCCIV.

SOME REMARKS
ON THE FIRST CHAPTER IN
DR. DAVENANT'S ESSAYS.

Concerning Appeals to the People from their Representatives.

'TIS one of the most unhappy Methods can possibly be taken by an Author, to have the Title of his Book tell the World one thing, and the Book it self another: for as it savours of abundance of Insincerity in Principle, so it seems to bring some Scandal upon the very Design of the Book, as if it had occasion for a double Aspect.

I cannot think when I meet with such a Book, that I do the Author any wrong, by supposing that different Colours are put upon the Face of the Work, because for some reason or other, it is not fit to be seen in its Own.

Disguises are never used where nothing is to be concealed, and nothing is concealed, but what Shame, Fear, or Policy commands to be hid.

A Genuine Cause carrys its Native Colours always outermost, is never shy of its Face, nor fond of being concealed.

The application lies full against the Essays of a learned Author lately Published and Dedicated to her Majesty, which I cannot but say, had been Genuine enough, had the Title and Dedication not given us a wrong Idea of the Work; had the Title been, *An Essay against Peace at Home*; the Author whether he had discovered his Mind or no, I wont determine, had certainly made the Title and the Book correspond, the Doctrine had been suitable to the Text, and the Work all of a Piece.

Neither can I reconcile the Dedication of it to the Subject, much less to the time 'twas wrote in, for whereas the Author owns the time, the Tracts here pointed at were wrote in, to be a time of Provocation, Disgust, and ill Blood, and thinks there was good Reason for it too; the suiting it to a time when her Majesty makes a healing Proposal of Peace, makes a little more Incongruity than is usual to be seen in his more Polite Management of his Pen.

But this is not all, for I could easily have abated this Gentleman the Observation of ill Timeing one Piece, and he might be allowed to be very capable of such Alterations as might heal the Breach of Time between the Tract it self and the Queen's Speech.

But there seems to me such a contrariety of Circumstances, in the very Substantial Essential Part of her Majesties Speech, and that part of the Book which I have here taken in hand, that 'tis impossible to make a Symphony of such discording Parts.

This is to tell her Majesty, we joyn with her Proposal of Peace and Union,[1] and will endeavour to pursue it by devesting all her Subjects as a collective Body of their Native Original Power and Property, and overturning the very Center of the Monarchy.

How easy 'tis for Men of Wit to give any thing a fair Face, and by a happy turn of Language call things of contrary Subjects by the same Name; Dr. *Davenant* depriving the People of all Power, but what is Representative and giving the Delegated Power a Superiority over the Power Delegating. *Sir Humphrey Mackworth*[2] defending an Occasional Bill, and both presented to the World with the Equi-Vocal Title of *Peace at Home*, and dedicated to the Queen with high Strains of Eloquence, of which both are very Good Masters, complimenting her Majesty on the Head of Peace proposed in her Speech to the Parliament.

Certainly, Gentlemen, you must both of you mistake her Majesties Meaning, who without doubt is acting in the safe middle Way, between both your Extreams. If you are driving at *Peace at Home*, 'tis by some Antiperistasis, some contraries in Nature, and consequently the End you aim at is remote, and the Means tedious: It may be a Way to Peace for ought we know, but certainly 'tis not that Peace her Majesty means, 'tis not the Peace the Nations want, and therefore give me leave to make this just Distinction between her Majesties Proposal, and your projected Essay, as to the Nature of Peace.

Your Peace is a Peace of Subjection, her Majesties is a Peace of Conjunction, and this her Majesty has most explicitly directed us to understand by the immediate addition of a term Comprehensive of both, *Union*: you may be for Peace, but 'tis *Peace and Union* that these Nations want, and which her Majesty recommends to all her Subjects to promote.

The first Head of the learned Essays lately published, and which I fix on in these Remarks, is concerning *The Danger of appealing to the People from their Representatives in Parliament*.

The Author says, P. 22. *That some Doctrines have been spread abroad in an open manner pretending, that in reference to the Publick, the People and their Representatives may have distinct Rights.*

That the People have not devolved their whole Power in Government upon their Representatives.

That Parliaments are accountable to, and to be controlled in all their Proceedings by the People.

That 'tis always Lawful, and often expedient to Appeal from the House of Commons to the People.

That these things have been printed, Arraigning the whole Proceedings of the House of Commons, calling their undoubted Priviledges in question, and as it were appealing to the Rabble from all their Resolutions.

It were to be wished that these Quotations had been Mark'd with proper References to the respective Authors or Books, which have advanced the things alledg'd, that the Originals being examined, might be assisted to speak for themselves, and tho' the omitting such References, admits of Objection and some Reflection, yet I choose to omit all such Reflections as are not absolutely necessary to the Case in Hand, being willing to treat my Author with all the Civility and Respect his Worth Demands, and the Case will bear.

This premis'd, I take all he alledges for granted, as to quotation, and shall only proceed to examine not whether it be fairly proved by him, that such things are printed, but whether he has fairly confuted the thing it self, and proved what he alledges.

In order to this, 'tis necessary to examine what it is the Dr. offers in answer to these Tenets which he says have been so openly spread abroad.

That this appealing to the People is destructive to the Nature of the Constitution, that 'tis practicing all the Methods of Sedition with which she attacks a just Authority, exciting the People to overthrow the Priviledges of their own Representatives.

I wish the Author of this matter had been pleased to tell us what he calls Appeals to the People, and that he had distinguish'd between the just Right of the People, and those of the Representatives, and between those Authors who are for maintaining the due Currency of Right in every part of it, and those who are guilty, as he says, of giving Authority a Mortal Blow.

Doubtless there are those who do not believe that all Power is given to the Representative, and none left with the represented, and yet are not for over-throwing the Priviledges of their Representatives; and of these I profess my self to be one.

I wish the Commons of *England* in Parliament would be pleased to ascertain what was their undoubted Right, and what not; that they would let us know how far their Power extends, with respect to the People they represent.

The Rights of the Commons of *England*, with respect to the Crown, and the supreme Authority of their King, has been often discuss'd, sometimes with the Pen, and sometimes with the Sword; and however some have affected a Doctrine of Non-Resistance, the Representatives of the Nation have always thought fit to assume a Right to defend their Liberties, when they have found them invaded by Exorbitant Power.

But what the Right of the Commons in Parliament are, and how far they extend, with respect to those from whom they come there, has never yet been ascertained by Parliament.

* A Vind. of the Rights of the Commons of England, by Sir H. M.

Some *Essays have been made this way from the Press, and Sir H. M. gave us a Scheme[3] of parliamentary Power drawn to a higher Extreme than ever any House of Commons have thought fit to extend the Practice.

A subsequent Author[4] thought fit to advance some contrary Notions, which however they are in general Exploded by both these Authors, have never yet met with any fair Confutation.

The best way to answer an Author in such Case is, by granting what they themselves allow, and from the necessary Consequences of what they Grant prove the Absurdity of what they Deny.

And to me, it seems, this Author[5] has laid himself open in this very Case, for in his Introduction, he allows, P. 14. *That the Peoples Representatives ought never to give up Fundamentals: Nor can they do it, because as to Fundamentals, they are but the People's Trustees, and can do no Act that can bind their Principals to any thing that is to their Destruction.*

This is Fundamental Truth, and I should be exceeding glad to see it reconciled to what is asserted afterward, in the Chapter of appealing to the People where 'tis affirmed, that to say, *The People may have Distinct Right from their Representatives, and that the People have not devolved their whole Power upon their Representatives, is destructive to the Nature of the Constitution, P. 22, 23.*

I am not very regular in the Method, but I am very certain of the Groundwork of my Argument, of which this is the Abstract.

If the Representatives of the People may do any thing which is not binding to their Principals *the People*, then the People have a Right to contradict, and make void something their Representatives may do, and consequently have some Power which is not devolved upon the Representatives.

I conceive this Error might slip our Author's Memory, for want of laying down a proper Foundation for his Argument, and coming to a positive Determination what we are to understand by Appeals to the People. *The Danger of Appeals to the People*, is the Title to the Chapter, but we are no where in the Chapter told what these Appeals to the People are.

If he means, *P. 26. The People being stirred up to lop off a Branch of the Common-Wealth by trampling on the Rights and Priviledges of the House of Commons.* I grant there is Danger in this; But how are the People thus to be stirred up? as that learned Gentleman Sir *H. M.* in his Book, *Of the Rights of the Commons in Parliament*, Observes, It cannot be that so many worthy Gentlemen can act contrary to, or Destructive of the Liberties of their Native Country.

So it cannot be that the People of *England* can ever Design to lop off this Branch, and trample on the Rights and Priviledges of their Representatives; this would be to destroy themselves, and cut themselves off from the principal Vital part of the Constitution; an universal Frenzy must possess the Minds of Men whenever such a Thing is supposed to come to pass, the People must be all Lunatick, and the Nation be a *Bedlam*, not a Civil Government.

And as we are secur'd by the very Nature of the Thing, from the Danger of the People of *England* ever dethroning their Representatives, so there is no real Necessity to prevent such an Imaginary Fear by the People divesting themselves of their Original Right, and Vesting all Power in their Representatives.

But since Demonstration is the best way of Argument, and the Subject I am upon has great plenty of those Helps; let us see if it is not an unpardonable Absurdity, to say the People have no distinct Right which their Representatives have not:

For Example,

The People have a Right when the King Dissolves their Representative to chuse another, this Power their Representative has not; this is a Right Distinct from their Representative, a Power which was never devolved upon them, and which I suppose never will; If the People had no Power but what was devolv'd upon their Representatives, then having once chosen such a Representative, that Body should upon every Dissolution Nominate a Succession of Representatives.

But whenever the Crown Dissolves a Parliament, the People have the Power distinct from their Representations to choose anew, and if so, then all the Power of the People is not devolved upon the Representatives, but *these* have some right Distinct from *them*.

Nor can I see any thing in this, which tends to Confusion, or which is any way destructive to the Constitution; Thus far I must ask the Author's Pardon, for saying, *with all the Respect for him which the Case will bear*, that his Arguments run a little foul of one another.

I come next to observe, that which I think is not extraordinary just in the way of Arguing; when, Page 27, he is pleased to allow, *Kings may differ with Lords and Commons, and the Two Houses may differ among themselves, and yet the publick Peace not be disturbed, the People also may differ about Civil or Religious Matters, and have various Thoughts concerning Government, Parties may grow up, and mutual Heats arise, and yet the Common Wealth remain unwounded in its Vitals. But Discord is fatal, when a strong Faction is form'd against any part of the Constitution.*

This seems a little Equi-vocal, and it appears likely, that a Discord in the publick Members of the Constitution may be as Fatal as the other; Heats in the Houses against one another, Factions in the Houses against their Prince or Designs of Tyrany in the Prince against either or both Houses of Parliament, these are all certainly as dangerous things and as Destructive of the Constitution as appeals to the People, and yet such is the Force of Rethorick, as to put a shaddow of indifference on these and charge all the Fatallity on the Peoples falling out with their Representatives.

I confess if any Man should ask me, which of those things before mention'd are of worst Consequence to the Nations Peace, I should find it difficult to tell him, but sure every one seperately or Conjunctively is as bad as a difference between the People and their Representatives.

Then let us go on to Examine the Parralel, as in the differences mentioned above, the Peace may remain Unbroken, and the Common Wealth Unwounded in its Vitals; so may it in this Case, the People may be generally dissatisfied with their Representatives, they may be very Uneasy and make loud Complaints, but it does not follow that they must immediately rise in Tumults, and pull the House about their Ears.

We have seen a time when a certain H—se[6] behav'd so, that the general Cry of the People was to desolve them, and Multitudes of Addresses did in as plain Language as decency to the Crown would admit of present the Peoples desire to have them dissolv'd: But what did this general dislike of their actions lead the People to: Not to draw the Sword at their own Representatives, that had been to be *felo de se* and Murther themselves, but to apply themselves to the Sovereign to dissolve them, and upon this Application, the King did dissolve them; and a late Proclamation for dissolving the last Parliament of King *William*, acknowledges the People have a Right upon dislike of their Members proceeding to apply to the King to dissolve them. The Words of the Proclamation are, *We have thought it Reasonable in this Extraordinary Juncture, to give our Subjects the Opportunity of choosing such Persons to represent them in Parliament, as they may judge most likely to bring to effect their Just and Pious Purposes.* And in order thereto to Dissolve this present Parliament.

If so, If the People ought to have an Opportunity when they see cause to have a New Representative, *for that is the meaning*, then the People are in some Measure Judges of the Actions and Management of their Representatives, for else it could not be just to make them Judges of the Continuance, or Determination of their Being.

Where then is the Fatality of such an Appeal to the People, since when they have been something uneasy on that Head, it has amounted to no more than to address for a Dissolution; that if they don't like these they may have better, and the King from the Throne has declared, that 'tis reasonable they should be Gratified.

I do not hereby justify any of those things which are complained of by the Dr., P. 28: how innumerable Pamphlets accused the House of Commons in 1701, of not being mindful of the King's Honour, of being in the *French* Interest, wanting Affection to their Native Country, Zeal for its Religion, and as not intending to do what was needful to the Nations Safety; Nor do I say that Parliament were any ways guilty of that Charge, in all, or in any of these Branches. But I may be allowed to say this, and that is enough to my present Purpose; that if the Representative Body of the People were really Guilty of any, or of all of those Heads or Crimes, the People had certainly Reason to be dissatisfied with them, and could not do less than apply to the Sovereign to dismiss them, and give them an Opportunity to send better in their Room.

I believe I may venture to say, 'Tis impossible the People of *England*, call them by the worst Names you please, the *Rabble*, the *Mob*, the *Multitude*, or any thing; I say, 'tis impossible the People of *England* can ever, either by Inclination, or by Contrivance, be brought to a dislike of Parliaments as such; they may find reason to dislike this or that Set of Men, but that the People of *England* should ever attempt to destroy the Representative, *Qua Parliament*, 'Tis impossible.

I reckon that's properly said to be impossible as to Men, which they cannot do without forfeiting their Reason; and all the Claim they have to the Knowledge of their own Interest, Safety, Peace and Prosperity, which they cannot do without being Fools, and Mad-men; whatever Factions or Parties may be raised, 'tis against a Faction and a Party, not against the House it self; and therefore I remember in one of the worst of those numberless Pamphlets, which the Dr. takes notice of, among all the Gall against the Members of that House, it still appeared they had none against the Constitution, by this following Line.

For tho' we value Parliaments, we're out of love with you.[7]

If this be true, I'll examine no more what this Gentleman means by Appeals to the People from their Representatives, for let him mean what he will, there can be no danger in them; because 'tis impossible the People of *England* should ever be against a free Representative, *as such*; all the cries therefore of the Danger of Appeals of the People are Vain and Trifling.

Yet our Author is positive, *whether too positive or no, let others determine*; that nothing can be of more dangerous Consequence than to establish, that the People of *England* and their Representatives have distinct Rights; and yet I think with Submission, 'tis prov'd already, that nothing is more plain even from this Gentleman's own Book.

All the Rights and Priviledges of the House of Commons, says he, *are the Peoples Rights and Priviledges*; This I grant: But all the Peoples Rights and Priviledges are not the Rights and Priviledges of the House of Commons, The Rights of the Elected are transferred from the Electors, but 'tis plain they have not devolved all their Rights.

And tho' the Collective Body of the People are not a fourth Estate, yet they are the Center of the other three Estates, from whom constitution is derived, and for whom 'tis form'd.

Parliaments are neither Infallible nor Immortal, the Representative may die and be dissolved, but the Represented Body remains as the great Center of Power, the Fountain of Original Right, the last resort of Lives, Successions, and Governours.

To prove the Danger of the Appeals to the People, the Dr. brings in King *Charles* the 1st, in the Messages and Declarations he published; and the House of Commons in the Answer and Remonstrances, appealing to the People; *and that*, says he, *brought a Civil War*: This is a new way of arguing.

Had not the King appealed to his Standard at *Nottingham*, had not the Parliament appealed to the Earl of *Essex*'s Army, all their Printing and appealing to the People had done nothing. Proclamations and Remonstrances had not been fatal if both sides had not appealed to the Sword. A Pen and Ink War draws no Blood, and all their Printing of Declarations and Remonstrances, tended only to byass the People to this or that Party, and list in the War which both sides prepar'd for.

There are many better reasons to be given for the beginning of that War, than their Printed Papers, the Foundations of that War was laid in the grievances of Ship Money, Monopolies, discontinuing of Parliament, Clashing in Religion and the like; their Printing and Appeals to the People, were generally Recriminations of Partys, by which both sides Expos'd one another, but the ground of that War was lay'd too deep to pretend to be laid at that Door.

Those Gentlemen who place the Confusions of the Civil-War, on both sides appealing to the People, must either be very ill Read in our *English* History, which I am satisfyed this Gentlemen is not, or must be content to pass over the most Essential Points of Difference, between the King and Parliament, and place the whole upon a Subsequent Circumstance.

And yet in this very Case the Author is gone from his Title, which he calls, appealing to the People from their Representatives, and as an instance to Illustrate it, brings in the very Representatives appealing to them from themselves, and the King also doing the same.

From whence it Appears plain to me, that in all Cases of Extremity it has been the practice both of Kings, Partys, private Persons, and of Parliaments themselves to appeal to the People, when matters of Right, publick Oppressions, and Extraordinary Niceties of State come in Question.

And whereas this Learned Gentleman brings this matter into Dispute, 'tis worth observing, that he can give us no Instance, *in these latter Ages at least*, wherein all Partys have not in this manner Appealed to the People, of which we have not seen them yet Convinc'd of the Danger.

All the publick Declarations, and Manifesto's of Princes, are in this respect Appeals to the People. To go back no further than the Case of *Phillip* the Second of *Spain*; his Declaration and Proscription[8] of the Prince of *Orange*, was a Solemn Appeal to all the *Netherlands*; complaining of the Rebellions, Factions, Invasions, and as he calls them Ingratitudes of that Prince, and at last inviting all his Subjects to do him Justice upon the Traytor as he Terms him. *Fam. Strada*[9] *de Bello Belgico* Tom. I. p. 78.

Which very proscription was the cause which Incited *Balthazar Garrad*,[10] in an Impious and horrid manner, to Assasinate that Prince as he confest afterward, upon being Examin'd by Torture.

The Appology of that Prince was an Appeal to the People again, wherein he fully clears himself of all the Callumnies and Aspersions cast upon him, of Undutifulness and Ingratitude, and Recriminates upon the King, and yet neither of these were the Grounds of that Civil-War, *ibid.* p. 180.

The Catholick League,[11] *as it was call'd*, form'd by the House of *Guise* in *France* against *Henry* the 3d, in Conjunction with the *Spaniards*, published their several Manifesto's and Declarations, which in this Authors sence were Appeals to the People: *Henry* the III. return'd by a long Declaration, setting forth the Reasons of his coming in Arms to Besiege *Paris*; and of his joyning, with the King of *Navarr*, and accepting assistance of the *Hugonot* Armys against the Catholicks.

Yet in all these Cases the Appeals were not the Causes or Motives to a Civil-War, but the Consequences of it.

Thus far I thought fit to Examine Forreign History, to show that Appeals to the People have been practiced by other Nations, where matters have grown to Extremities between King and People, for indeed the People how much soever Contemn'd and Endeavoured to be supprest are the last Resort in all the Extremities of a Nation.

By the People here I would be understood Collectively, not Representatively Consider'd, and I confess my self at a Loss, to understand what a Gentleman means by the Collective Body of the People Assembled in Parliament; which to me seems an Inconsistent Collection of Words, put together without any Congruity of Signification.

But says our Author, *where ever the last resort is, there is the Soveraignity, and if among us the People have a Right to it, then we are a Democracy and not a Kingly Government.* P. 34.

Whether we have a Democracy or a Kingly Government, is not my business to Determine. Nor shall I pretend to enter into the Debate of it, but that the People of *England*, are the last Resort in *England*, admits of so much Demonstration both from the general practice of this Nation, the Tacit Consent of Kings and Parliaments, and from the nature of the thing, that I cannot but say it seems strange to me, an Authour of so much knowledge of Publick Affairs, should advance any thing so prejudical to the Character all Wise Men had of his Judgment.

This has been already offer'd to the World, in Answer to Sr. *H—M*'s

Vindication[12] of the Right of the Commons of *England*; and which that Learned Gentleman never thought fit to reply to.

'That Power which is Original, is Superior; *God is the Fountain of all Power, and therefore is the Supreme*: And if we could suppose a Prior and Original of the Divine Power, *that Original would be God*, and be Superiour; for all subsequent Power must be subject and inferiour to the precedent.

'The Power vested in the Three Heads of our Constitution is vested in them by the People of *England*, who were a People before there was such a thing as a Constitution.

'*And the Nature of the Thing, is the Reason of the Thing: It was vested in them by the People, because the People were the only Original of their Power, being the only Power* Prior *to the Constitution.*

'For the publick Good of the People, a Constitution and Government was Originally Formed; from the mutual Consent of these People the Powers and Authorities of this Constitution are derived: And for the preservation of this Constitution, and enabling it to answer the Ends of its Institution in the best manner possible, those Powers were devided.

'The second Maxim is a Natural Consequence of the former. That at the *final, Casual, or any other* Determination of this Constitution, the Powers are dissolv'd, and all Authority must derive *de novo* from the first Fountain, Original and Cause of all Constitutions, *the Governed*.

'Now it cannot be suppos'd this Original Fountain should give up all its Waters, but that it reserves a Power of supplying the Streams; Nor have the Streams any power to turn back upon the Fountain, and invert their own Original. All such Motions are Excentrick and Unnatural.

'There must always remain a Supream Power in the Original to supply, in Case of the Dissolution of Delegated Power.

'The People of *England* have Delegated all the Executive Power in *the King*, the Legislative in the *King, Lords, and Commons*, the Soveraign Judicature *in the Lords*, the Remainder is reserv'd in themselves, and not committed, no not to their Representatives: All Powers Delegated are to one great End and purpose, and no other, and that is *the Publick Good*. If either, or all the Branches to whom this Power is Delegated invert the Design, the End of their Power, the Right they have to that Power ceases; and they become Tyrants and Usurpers of a Power they have no Right to.

'The Instance has been visible as to Kings in our Days; and History is full of Precedents in all Ages, and in all Nations; particularly in *Spain*, in *Portugal*, in *Swedeland*, in *France*, and in *Poland*.

'But in *England*, the late Revolution is a particular Instance of the Exercise of this Power.

'King *James*, on the Approach of the Foreign Army, and the general recourse of the People to Arms, fled out of the Kingdom. What must the People of *England* do? They had no Reason to run after him; there was no Body to call a Parliament, so the Constitution was entirely Dissolv'd.

'The Original of Power, *the People*, Assembled in Convention, to consider of Delegating New Powers for their Future Government, and accordingly made a New Settlement of the Crown, a New Decleration of Right, and a New Representative of the People; *and what if I should say they ought to have given a New Sanction to all precedent Laws.*

'It remains to argue from hence, But what Course must the People of *England* take, if their Representatives exercise the Power intrusted with them, to the Ruin of the Constitution?

'It has been advanced, That every Man must submit, and not presume to argue against it upon any Supposition of Mismanagement.

'I can see no reason given to confirm such a Position; for unless we will place the Original of Power in the Persons Representing, not in the Persons Represented, it cannot be made out that there ought to be no complaint upon the score of our Mismanagement.

'It is not the Design of this Discourse to lessen the Authority of Parliament: But all Power must Centre some where. If it is in the Three Branches of the Constitution, 'tis there inherently and originally, or it is there by Deputation. If it be there by Deputation, then there must be a Power Deputing, and that must be both *Prior*, and consequently Superior to the Deputed, *as before.*

'If we will come off of this, we must fly to the old weak Refuge of a Power *Jure Divino*, a Doctrine which the most famed Pretenders to, have liv'd to be asham'd of, and whose Foundation is so weak, that 'tis not worth while to expose it.'

I hope I cannot offend in saying the Late Revolution is founded on a last Resort in the Collective Body of the People; the late Kings Declaration when Prince of *Orange* is a Solemn Appeal to the People in the manner of Our Author who acknowledges it to be so.

What was the Lords coming to a great Council at the *Guild-Hall* in the City of *London*, but a last Resort to the People? What was all the Appearance at *Bodon Down*[13] in *Lancashire*, the Declaration of the Gentlemen at *Nottingham*?[14] They were all the Resort to the People, or you must resolve them into Treasons, Insurrections and Rebellions.

Let any Man but put the Case to *January*, 1688:[15] the King was gone, there was no Representative power in Being, nor any power in being which had any Legal Authority, to call a Representative; the whole Machine of Government was Unhing'd, and the substance dissolv'd, all Delegated Power ceased, all Commissions determin'd, and none could grant more; there was no Officer no Magistrate could act, or any Power to make new ones. Authority was at an End; all Men had an Equallity of Power, Laws indeed were in Being, but no Man had any just Authority to put them in Execution.

Let any Man now tell me who had a just Title to frame a new Government: 'Tis plain the next of Blood to the Crown did not pretend to it, all retreated to the great Original of Power the People; *there was the last Resort*, first the Collective Body in several parts, without any Constituted Authority Assembl'd to advise with the Prince; the Lords dispose of Governments; and the City Addresss the Prince of *Orange* for his protection, the Prince Summonses the People to advise with him; they advise to call a *Convention*; which in English I take to mean a meeting of the Collective Body. They assemble, ask the Prince if he pleases to rule over them, present him with the Conditions of his Government, make a Declaration of Right; Claiming, that 'tis their natural Right, to be Governed so and no otherwise: he Accepts the Crown on these Terms, and so becomes a King, this is all the *jure Divino* which I can find in the Story of the present Settlement and if *Vox Populi* be *Vox Dei*, here is a plain Divine Right, and on this Foot her present Majesties Reign.

If this History, which all Men can remember to be true, be not a sufficient Proof, that the last resort is in the People of *England*, then I will undertake to give more Proofs, but I please my self with believing it cannot be contradicted. Whether the Gentleman I am concern'd with in this Case will infer from hence, that our Government is Democratick or not, I am not at all concern'd about, but that in our Government and indeed, in all Governments the Nature of the thing implyes, that when Successive or Representative Power ceases, the People Collectively considered have a Native Right to make Settlements and Constitutions, for the maintaining of Order and Justice, and for the Currency and Execution of the Laws; if not, Confusions and Inevitable Destruction, must be the Effect of the Demise of a Line of Kings, or the Cessation of a Delegated Power.

Let us come now to the express point, which I suppose our Author to mean, appealing from the Representatives to the People; and tho' I have the most hazardous point of the Argument in case by Inadvertancy

I should offend the Representatives of the Nation now sitting, yet as I resolve to say nothing but what is in it self true, and justified by infinite Precedents, I presume that honourable House never can resent that which comes in plain *English*, with Truth in its Company.

The House of Commons have always been very chary of the Priviledges and Honour of the People, whom they represent, and cannot be thought to be Usurping any Powers or Authorities over them, which by the Nature of the Thing, as well as by the design of their Election, is not committed to them; and therefore, as it is already noted: No House ever attempted to assume to themselves the Power of naming a successive Representative; but as it always lay in the Breast of the Sovereign to dissolve a Parliament in being, so it was always the Native inherent Right of the Freeholders of *England* to elect a New one.

This Power must be distinct from the Representatives; 'Twas never the Design of the People to delegate any Branch of this Power to their Representatives; nor did ever any Parliament pretend to invade this Right, or to assume it to themselves.

It might be supposed that on the Dissolution of a Parliament, and before the calling of another, a King should die; and being the last of his line, no Person had any Claim by Succession to the Crown, What must become of the Government? Must all the Confusions of Anarchy succeed a regular Government, or the Crown wait for who is strongest to lay hold on it.

The Laws of Nature make a plain Answer to all these Questions: Governments, and Constitutions, as they were originally derived from the People, must on all Occasions of a Dissolution, or total Interruption, be restored from, and rebuilt upon the Native Power and Original Authority of the People.

But as this seems to be a Mob Doctrine, and looks like setting up the Rabble above Law; Its proper to enquire who are these People, of whom this original Power is thus asserted.

Negatively, not all the Inhabitants but positively all the Freeholders, the Possessors of the Land have certainly a Right in the Government of it, and if these are called the People, to these there is a Case wherein an Appeal to them is absolutely necessary.

If I do quote the same Tract again for this, 'tis because no Man has ever yet thought fit to confront it either with Reason or History.

'I make no question but Property of Land is the best Title to Government in the World; and if the King was universal Landlord, he ought to be universal Governor of Right, and the People so living on his Lands ought to obey him, or go off of his Premises.

'And if any single Man in *England* should at any time come to be Landlord of the whole Freehold of *England*, he could indeed have no Right to Dispossess the King, till the present legal Settlement of the Crowd fail'd, because it was settled by those that had then a Right to settle it.

'But he would immediately be the full Representative of all the Countries in *England*, and might Elect himself Knight of the Shire for every County, and the Sheriff of every County must Return him accordingly.

'He would have all the Baronies and Titles of Honour which are entailed upon Estates devolv'd upon him, and upon any Expiration of the Settlement would be King by natural Right.

'And he would be King upon larger Terms than ever any Man was legally King of *England*; for he would be King by inherent Right of Property.

'When therefore I am speaking of the Right of the People, I would be understood of the Freeholders, for all the other Inhabitants live upon Sufferance, and either are the Freeholders Servants or having Money to pay Rent live upon Conditions, and have no Title to their living in *England*, other than as Servants, but what they must pay for.

'Upon this foot it is that to this Day our Law suffers not a Foreigner to Purchase any of the Freeholds of *England*: For if a Foreigner might Purchase, your Neighbours (having Mony to spare) might come and buy you out of your own Country, and take Possession by a legal and indisputable Right.

'This Original Right was the first Foundation of the several Tenures of Land in *England*; some held of the King, some of the Lord, some by Knight Service, Soccage, and the like, and some were called Freeholds. The Lords of Mannors had their Homages, and their Services from their Tenants, as an Acknowledgment that the Right of the Land gave a certain Right of Government to the Possessor over all the Tenants and Inhabitants.

'But he that possessed the least Freehold was as much Lord of himself and of that Freehold, as the greatest Noble man in the Nation, he ow'd no Homage or Service, no, not to the King, other than as limited by Laws of his own making that is as he was represented in Parliament.

'And as a thing which will put this Argument out of all question, The Right to Lands, Mannors and Lordships, was not originally a Right granted by Patents from Kings or Acts of Parliament, but a natural Right of Possession handed down by Custom, and ancient Usage, as the Inheritance from the still more ancient Possessors and Prescription, or Usage time out of Mind, is to this Day allowed to be a sufficient Title in several Cases, where Conveyances, Deeds, Charters, and Writing of Eases are silent, especially as to Buttings and Boundings of Land, Highways, Foot-paths, Water Courses, Bridges, and the like.

'This Right, as all Right Originally, is Founded upon Reason: For it would be highly unreasonable, that those People who have no share of the House should live in it whether he that built it will or no. No Person has any Right to live in *England*, but they to whom *England* belongs; the Freeholders of *England* have it in the possession; *England* is their own, and no Body has any thing to do here but themselves.

'If they permit other People to live here, well and good, but no Man but a Freeholder lives here upon any Terms but *permissu Superiorum*, and he pays Rent for his License to live here.

'Thus the Liberties and Priviledges of Towns and Corporations, are founded upon Acts of Parliament to confirm Charters of Grants from the Crown, by which the Freeholders give their consent that such and such Bodies of Men living in such Towns, shall enjoy certain Priviledges in Consideration of their being so considerably serviceable to the Nation, by paying Taxes, maintaining the Poor, by Manufactures, Trade, and the like, notwithstanding they are not possessed of any part of the Freehold.

'And 'tis observable, the King cannot give this Privilege, so as to enable any of these Corporations to send Representatives to Parliament. None, but the Freeholders of *England* (and such Towns in Conjunction) to whom the Freeholders have already granted such Privilege, can give a Qualification of such a Nature, as is a receiving them into an equal state of Priviledge with a Freeholder.

'Every Man's Land is his own Property; and 'tis a Trespass in the Law for another Man to come upon his Ground without his Consent. If the Freeholders should all agree, That such a Man shall not come upon their Land; That they will not Lett him a House for his Money; That whose Land soever he sets his Foot on, the Owner shall Indict him for a Trespass, as by Law he may, the Man must fly the Nation of Course.

'Thus the Freeholders having a Right to the Possession of *England*, the Reason must be good that they must have the same Right to the

Government of themselves, that they have to the Government of the rest of the Inhabitants; and *that there can be no Legal Power in* England, *but what has its Original in the Possessors; for Property is the Foundation of Power.*[16]

Nor is this Doctrine of Original Right any Derogation to the just and full Authority of Parliament, who may, notwithstanding this, exercise all their full and extended Priviledges in as ample a Manner as is agreeable to all the just Ends and Purposes for which they were first Designed and Intended.

If our Author would be understood in what he speaks of to mean, only the little publick Efforts of Private Persons, or Parties, who often express dissatisfaction at the Proceedings in Parliament, as they clash with their private Interests, and the Designs of enterprizing Men, these are not worth my defending, or his concern. I freely admit those People always Merit Pity or Punishment, and sometimes both, nor have our Parliaments often thought it worth while to take notice of such People.

The Liberty taken in Print, discovers sometimes the Malice of Authors, and not seldom pulls down Authority on their Heads, but as Truth has the least need of Advocates, so 'tis easy to defend her, and the Parliament has never thought fit to restrain the Press, because their Actions being generally squar'd by Truth and the Law, and design'd for the publick Good they have rather coveted to show them in the Light, than to limit the Enquiries of the World; choosing rather to suffer some Indecencies from ill govern'd Pens, than to give the World the least Shaddow of saying, They conceal their Actions from the publick Censure.

But take the People in the Sense I have before observed, and even Parliament themselves have always appealed to them, have been careful to print any remarkable thing which has been before them, that those who chose them to sit there, may see and be satisfied how careful they are of the general Good, and of discharging the Trust reposed in them.

What are the several Publications made by Parliament of the Controversy between the Houses, both upon Occasion of the late Impeachments, and on the occasional Bill, but Appeals to the People and Testimonials of the Candor of their Proceedings.

In all material Cases, the Representatives have thus appealed to the People, and why it should be so Criminal, or so Dangerous for any Man else to Appeal thither also, does not appear to me, since 'tis impossible it should ever be, that the Free-Holders of *England* can be reduced to such a Depravation of their Reason, as to demolish the Foundation on which they stand, and pull down their own House upon their Heads.

Neither is this appealing to the People, *which those Publications of Kings and Parliaments are called* any thing more or less, but the Vindication of the Proceedings of the Persons and Parties, and setting their Cases as far as they thought they required in a true Light, and no People who have had Truth and Honesty on their side, have ever thought it below them to appeal to all the World.

King *Charles* the IId, thus appealed to all the People in his Declaration, about the *Rye* Plot, King *William* in his Declaration,[17] at his coming over into *England*; and all the Kings of the World have used it as a constant Method to make publick Declarations, which in this Authors Sense are Appeals to the People upon every extraordinary Revolution of Affairs; the Declaration of the *French* King[18] at placing his Grandson on the Throne of *Spain*, the Manifesto's and Declaration of the Emperor at his sending Prince *Eugene* into *Italy*, and now again at the Transferring the Crown to the Duke of *Austria*,[19] are all Appeals to the People of *Spain*, to excite them to transfer their Obedience to, or from this, or that Party, as they may be prevailed upon by their Reasons, to believe this or that the most Rightful Successor.

But to come yet closer to the Point, the meaning, as I understand this Gentleman, is, that 'tis his Opinion that 'tis not in the Power of the People of *England* to Controul, Limit, or check their Representatives, and that such appealings as we have been speaking of, prompts the People to ruffle the Parliaments, and to question their Proceedings.

This is an Argument in which the Author has this Advantage of me, that what he advances has no danger in it, and what I ought to reply to it may, tho' it be really true, and under the restraint of this Circumstance, I cannot say that to it which I think the Case will bear.

But I am of the Opinion that there is a just Appeal from the Representative to the Collective Body of the People. In some particular extraordinary Case, and tho' I do not love to repeat things, I ask Pardon for it now, what else can the Doctor mean, when he says, *P.* 15. the Parliament, *Cannot touch Fundamentals, and that if they do anything to the Peoples Destruction, it cannot bind them*; what can be the meaning of this, but that there is an Appeal from them to the People, if they should attempt any thing to the Peoples Destruction.

To him that shall tell me the House of Commons can never do any thing to injure the People; I must reply as before, and with as good Authority, the People of *England* cannot act Destructive of their own Representative.

I do not speak it with a Design to lessen Parliaments in *England*, and I know them to be the Bulwark of the Peoples Liberties, but they are not infallible, they may err, and were it safe to speak all the Truth, perhaps I might say there has been a Time when they have been mistaken in many things.

Now if a Parliament should mistake, and that fatally too, shall the People of *England* have no Method to let them know it; then are they in worse Bondage to their Representative than to the Sovereign; what shall the People do, they may without doubt find out modest Methods to let them know they are in the wrong, and to inform them both that they see it and dislike it.

I could perhaps name the Time which the People have seen Reason to complain of some Steps their Representatives had made, but my Author can never name the time whenever the People of *England* attempted or discovered a Design to lop off this Branch of the Constitution, and demolish the just Authority of Parliament.

And after all, the Tendency this has to Peace and Union, is a Mystery past finding out, the Coherence this has with the Title of the Book is a Thing hid from Humane Understanding. To deprive the People of their just Right, and set up their Representative with an Authority they never pretended to themselves, may have a Title of Peace, but carries none in the Meaning. I could say something to the Doctor's pleasant Proposal of Peace in his Introduction, P. 17. *Implying, that the Resentments on all sides shou'd be laid by, and the weaker Party cajol'd into a Peace, till foreign Wars are over, and what then?* Then as you were.

But as I may examine some other Chapters of this Book, there cannot want Occasion for Reflections on that head.

Memorandum
to Robert Harley
[1704]

MEMORANDUM TO
ROBERT HARLEY.

I allow that in our constitution we admit of no supreme ministry;[1] that the nation is particularly jealous of favourites. These are the two chief obstructions in the way of a refined[2] and rising statesman, and these are the two reasons why we have had no capital men in the civil administration, no Richlieus,[3] Mazarines[4] or Colberts[5] in the state. But I must go back for a reason for these two principles, and must say: 1. It would be best to have a supreme ministry; 2. The nation may easily be reconciled to it. 'Twill be needless to prove the advantage of a chief ministry; our confusions in council, our errors in executing and unwariness in directing from the multitude and bad conduct of ministers make it too plain. To prove the nation may be easily reconciled to it, 'twill be needfull to go back for the reasons why former favourites have so ill pleased the nation, and how others have discharged themselves with honour. The Spencers, the Gavestones[6] of former reigns are too remote; the prime ministers of modern times have been principally the Earl of Leicester,[7] the [Dukes] of Somerset,[8] Buckingham,[9] etc. These all incurred the displeasure of the people by one crime: pursuing their private interest, enriching and aggrandizing themselves and families, and raising vast estates out of the spoils of the public, and by their Prince's favour heaping up honours and titles to themselves from mean originals. I need not search history for the particulars, the fact is too plain. The consequences of this spirit of covetousness were always extortions, oppressions, bribes, sale of public employments, intrenchments on the public moneys, exorbitant grants of royal bounty, and the like. If any man will show me the man that served the state abstracted from his own interest, I'll show them the man who was as much the people's favourite as the king's. Thomas Lord Cromwell[10] was such a one, and, though he fell, as who in the reign of that fickle, unconstant king could stand, he fell a sacrifice to the Protestant party, universally beloved and lamented of the people. Sir

Francis Walsingham,[11] though not a prime minister, yet, if we read his story, the ablest statesman and the longest employed, the most employed in difficult cases and the greatest master of intelligence in the age, [was such another]. Both these died poor, they spent their whole time in the service of their country, and no man would have repined at their enjoying their Prince's favour longer.

This premised I bring home the matter to the case in hand. How shall you make yourself Prime Minister of state, unenvied and unmolested, be neither addressed against by Parliament, intrigued against by parties, or murmured at by the mob? With submission 'tis very feasible with an accurate conduct. They say those designs require most policy which have least of honesty; this design must be honest, because it must be honest to serve our country. If it be objected, 'But I would not be Prime Minister,' I return, 'Then you can not be Secretary of State.' The Secretary's office well discharged makes a man Prime Minister of course;[12] and you must be Prime Minister with applause, or you will be Secretary with disgrace. Popular fame never thinks a man too high; popular hate never thinks him too low. A generous, free, noble, uncontracted conduct as effectually secures the affection of the people, as a narrow, covetous, craving spirit effectually engages their mortal aversion. 'Tis certainly a noble design to be popular from a principle of real merit. I observe when all our people clamoured at Dutchmen, and even the King could not please them, because he was a foreigner, no man ever had a bad word for Monsieur Overkirk.[13] Nothing wins this nation like generous, free, open-handed courtesy. The King of Sweden[14] in his German wars always employed trusty persons in the towns and cities he reduced, to inform themselves of any known case where one was oppressed, or any family that had the general pity; and unlooked for, unasked, he would send for, right, and relieve them. Sir, that noble soul is a rare pattern; he gained his very enemies by surprising acts of bounty. In your new post,[15] joined with the influence you have on the royal hand, you will have infinite opportunities to fix an invulnerable reputation. May not these heads be proper?

1. To keep a set of faithful emissaries selected by your own judgement; let them be your constant intelligencers of private affairs in the Court.

2. Set your friends by, if they are such they'll wait, but surprise your enemies, if you have any, with voluntary kindness.

3. Communicate your favours with unbiased hand, that all parties may court you.

4. You have estate enough, and honour enough. Let the world know you covet nothing; all men then will covet you.

Let no man under you make a profit of your favours. One Gehezai[16] in your attendants, will undo the merit of all your actions; he will get the money, and you the curse of the person that pays it. 'Tis absolutely necessary to be popular. The people's darling may be a few men's envy, but the people's hate is a statesman's ruin. This opinion of the people is easily gained at first, and if lost at first, never re-established. 'Tis gained by little acts of courtesy; one generous man obliged, one oppressed man relieved, does a man of trust more honour than twenty ill tongues can blot out. In order to this, your trusty servants will enquire you out occasions enough: a general forwarding and dispatch of petitions, and a thousand things which a man in such a post, with such a soul, never wants opportunity for. In the old Prince of Orange's[17] army a captain that had long served in the wars, talking to a friend, was heard to say he would give 10,000 guilders for such a regiment, the colonel being newly dead. 'Why do you not put in for it,' says his friend. 'Because,' says he, 'the Prince has no kindness for me, and I know he will deny me.' The Prince, knowing him to be a man of merit, sends the person who told him this story with orders to take his bond for the 10,000 guilders upon condition that he procured him the regiment, which he did accordingly. The next day the Prince sends for him, gives him the regiment, and as he was going out, 'Here,' says the Prince, 'and here's something for your equipage,' and threw him his bond. The man was so surprised with the generosity of it, he turned from a prejudiced person to the greatest admirer the Prince had.

Sir, this proposal of a generous bounty and courtesy is not directed because you want it, but because you have it. To suppose you want it would first be an insolence unpardonable, as it would propose your feigning it, and so make a virtue of hypocrisy; but, as I have more than ordinary proofs of your being master of the quality, I take the freedom to hint the uncommon advantage it gives you, to make yourself truly great and have all men pleased with it. Envy always goes with her mouth open, and you are not to expect that an advanced post will shut it; but there is a secret in management that checks it effectually, *viz.* a general, unaffected goodness of temper. Julius Caesar was remarkable for it, and conquered more enemies in the forum than in the field. A man can never be great that is not popular, especially in England. 'Tis absolutely necessary in the very nature of our constitution, where the people have so great a share in the government. Besides, the people here, in recovering their just rights, have usurped some that are not their due, *viz.* censuring their superiors. But the government is bound to submit to the grievance, because 'tis incurable. 'Tis true a wise man will slight popular reproach, but no wise man slights the general approbation, because nothing but virtue can obtain it. 'Tis therefore absolutely necessary for a statesman to be popular. A statesman once in the people's favour has a thousand opportunities to do with freedom what in a contrary circumstance he would not dare to attempt; for as the people often condemn hastily, they approve with more blindness than they censure, and yet, generally speaking, the common people have been always in the right. A statesman envied dares not attempt a thing which he knows is for the public service, lest the miscarriage falls upon himself. Cardinal Richlieu supplied the want of the people's favour by mere force and so ruined those that opposed him, as in the case of the Duke de Momorency[18] and a multitude of others. Though this would be impracticable here, it shows the absolute necessity of the king, *or of an equivalent.* And yet we find this Cardinal strove hard for the public voice and used a thousand artifices to obtain it; among which this was one, that he never appeared to his own resentments and, though a multitude of persons of all ranks were sacrificed to his politic interest, yet he never would be seen in a matter of punishment. If a pardon was to be granted, he took care the debt should be to the Cardinal, but, if justice was to be done, that was in the King. A popular statesman should have the obtaining all the favours and let others have the management of offences and the distribution of justice.

In your particular case, Sir, you have but one public misfortune, *viz.* that your friends for want of judgement are afraid of you, not afraid you'll hurt them but yourself. 'Twould be necessary to confirm them in the belief of all they hope to find.

No. 1. A particular step will absolutely effect it – of which by itself.

No. 2. A scheme of what I mean by popularity in your own particular, and how to be both obtained and improved for the public service, shall be drawn, if you please to admit it.

No. 3. Also a method to make the office of Secretary of State an inner cabinet, and execute necessary parts of private affairs without the intervention of the Privy Council, and yet have their concurrence as far as the law requires.

When a Prince is to act anything doubtful or anything likely to be disputed either at law or in Parliament, the Council is a necessary screen to the Secretaries of State. But in matters of war, treaties, embassies, private instructions, expeditions, how many such has the delay, the hesitations, the ignorance, or something worse, of Privy Councillors over-thrown! Matters maturely advised, deliberately concerted, and absolutely resolved require but two qualifications to legitimate their execution, (1) that they are legal, (2) really for the public good. Such need no Council table to screen them, fear no Parliamentary enquiry, and yet the authors are not answerable for the success. Cabinet Councils in England are modern and eccentric, and I question whether an action which is not justifiable unless transacted in Council is justified by being so in the Cabinet. But Cabinets of ten or fourteen are monsters and useless. If her Majesty leaves the course of things to follow the nature and custom of English Kings, her Privy Council should take cognisance of all needful affairs, but her Treasurer and Secretary of State should be all her Cabinet, unless she had a well qualified Chancellor to add to them. Six sorts of great officers are the moving springs of the state, and I cannot but own without flattery England was never capable of being better supplied, I do not say is fully supplied: a Lord Chancellor, a High Admiral, a Generalissimo, a Lord Treasurer, a Secretary of State, an Archbishop, who perhaps might expect to be put first, but not by me. Of these the first should be a good lawyer, the second a good sailor, the third a good soldier, the last a good divine. But the Treasurer and the Secretary ought to be good statesmen. The weight of all the public affairs lies on their shoulders – one for managing the revenues, providing needful funds, maintaining public credit, and regulating abuses and exactions, etc.; the other for foreign intelligences, correspondence with the courts abroad, managing settling and obtaining confederates, observing and suiting affairs with the circumstances and interest of princes.

Intelligence is the soul of all public business. I have heard that our Secretary's office is allowed 12,000 *l. per annum* for this weighty article, and I am credibly informed the King of France has paid 11 millions in one year for the same article, and 'tis allowed he never spares his money on that head, and thereby outdoes all the world in the knowledge of his neighbours. How much of the 12,000 *l.* allowed for intelligence is expended in our Secretary's office, I will not guess at; but this I presume, that, such a sum being so vastly disproportioned to the necessary expense, the work is not done, and consequently the money that is given for it is lost. Our statesmen have been so far from acquainting themselves with other countries that they are strangers to their own, a certain token that they have sought their private advantage not the public service. The Secretary's office should be an abridgement of all Europe. Her Majesty's Secretary of State ought to have tables of all the following particulars to refer to, stated so regularly that they might have recourse to any particular immediately. They ought to have, 1st, a perfect list of all the gentry and families of rank in England, their residences, characters, and interest in the respective counties; 2nd, of all the clergy of England, their benefices, their character and morals, and the like of the Dissenters; 3rd, of all the leading men in the cities and boroughs, with the parties they espouse. They ought to have a table of parties, and proper calculations of their strength in every respective part, which is to be had by having the copies of the polls sent up on all elections, and all the circumstances of such elections historically collected by faithfull hands and transmitted to the office. They should know the names of all the men of great personal estates, that they may know how and when to direct any occasional trust; they should have the special characters of all the justices of the peace and men of note in every county, to have recourse to on all occasions. Two trusty agents would easily direct all this, so if their hands are not too much tied up as to money, and yet the persons entrusted not know who they serve nor for what end. The Secretary of State should have a table of all the ministers of state, lists of the households, the privy councils, and favourites of every court in Europe, and their characters, with exact lists of their forces, names of the officers, state of their revenue, methods of government, etc., so just and authentic and regularly amended as alterations happen that by this he may duly estimate their strength, judge of their interests and proceeding, and treat with them accordingly. He should keep a correspondence of friendship in all courts with ministers of like quality, as far as may be honourably obtained and without prejudice carried on. Mr. Milton[19] kept a constant epistolary conversation with several foreign ministers of state and men of learning abstracted from affairs of state, but so woven with political observations that he found it as useful as any part of his foreign correspondence. A hundred thousand pounds *per annum* spent now for 3 year in foreign intelligences might be the best money ever this nation laid out, and I am persuaded I could name two articles where, if some money had been well applied, neither the insurrection in Hungary[20] nor the war in Poland[21] should have been so fatal to the confederacy as now they are. If it may be of service, I shall give a scheme for the speedy settling those two uneasy articles, and consequently bringing down such a force on the French as should in all probability turn the scale of the war on the Danube and the Po.

A settled intelligence in Scotland, a thing strangely neglected there, is without doubt the principal occasion of the present misunderstandings between the two kingdoms;[22] in the last reign it caused the King to have many ill things put upon him, and worse are very likely to follow. I beg leave to give a longer scheme of thoughts on that head than is proper here, and a method how the Scots may be brought to reason. There is a large article of spies abroad among the enemies. This I suppose to be settled, though by our defect of intelligence, methinks it should not; but it reminds me of a book in eight volumes published in London about 7 or 8 years ago called *Letters Writ by a Turkish Spy*.[23] The books I take as they are a mere romance, but the moral is good. A settled person of sense and penetration, of dexterity and courage, to reside constantly in Paris, though, as 'tis a dangerous post, he had a larger allowance than ordinary, might by one happy turn earn all the money and the charge be well bestowed. There are 3 towns in France where I would have the like, and they might all correspond, one at Thoulon, one at Brest, one at Dunkirk. They three might trade together as merchants, and the fourth also with them. As intelligence abroad is so considerable, it follows in proportion that the most useful thing at home is secrecy; for, as intelligence is the most useful to us, so keeping our enemies from intelligence among us is as valuable a head. I have been in the Secretary's office of a post night when, had I been a French spy, I could have put in my pocket my Lord N—m's[24] letters directed to Sir George Rook[25] and to the Duke of Marlbrough laid carelessly on a table for the doorkeeper to carry to the post. How many miscarriages have happened in England for want of silence and secrecy! Cardinal Richlieu was the greatest master of this virtue that ever I read of in the world, and, if history has not wronged him, has sacrificed many a faithful agent after he had done his duty, that he might be sure he should not be betrayed. He kept three offices for the dispatch of his affairs, and one was so private that none was admitted but in the dark, and up a pair of back remote stairs, which office being at the apartments of his niece made room for a censure passed upon her character, which the Cardinal chose to suffer, that he might have the liberty to transact affairs there of much more moment. This is a principal reason why I object against bringing all things before the Council, for I will not affirm that the minutes of our Privy Council have not been read in the Secretary's office at Versailles. 'Tis plain the French outdo us at these two things, secrecy and intelligence, and that we may match them in these points is the design of the proposal.

Further schemes as to trade funds for taxes, etc., relating to the Lord Treasurer's share in the public administration I omit, having taken up too much room with this.

No. 1 What I mean by a step to confirm your friends in the belief of what they hope for from you cannot be explained without filling your ears with some of those ill-natured things they take the freedom to say, *viz.* that you are a man wholly resolved to make your fortunes and to bring it to pass will sacrifice your judgement as well as your friends to your interest; that you gave proofs of this in embracing the party of those people who pleased themselves and strove to be popular at the expense of King William; that you forsook the king, who treated you kindly, and that his Majesty spoke of it in very moving terms, as what he was concerned for; that now you have forsaken the Dissenters and fallen in with their enemies and promoted the first Occasional Bill;[26] *cum multis aliis*, etc. Sir, it is not that I suppose the Dissenters ought to be deceived, or that you will deceive them, that I repeat it again, *they are to be pleased with words.* But, Sir, as good words are useful in their place, so when not spoken with design [they] are honourable in themselves. There is no immediate action by which you can demonstrate you will serve them. Only let some proper persons carefully inform them that on all occasions they may depend on your good offices with the Queen, and give them some notices by such hands as may be trusted that you are their friend. Particularly it may be very easy to possess the Dissenters that they owe the change of her Majesty's sentiments with relation to the Occasional Bill to your management and councils, and that her Majesty's changing sides was, together with the measures you prescribed, the only reason of the majority obtained in the House of Lords against the said Bill. To effect this a short paper shall be handed about among the Dissenters only, giving them a pretended view of the measures taken by some persons, naming none, to convince the Queen of the unreasonableness of this Bill. It cannot fail to open their eyes that you are their friend, and yet, if your affairs should require you to disown such a paper, it shall easily be true that you had no knowledge of it, for you may really know nothing of it. If my service in another case is accepted, I shall take care to make such a paper be read in all parts of the kingdom. I allow the particular steps mentioned in such a paper may not be fact, yet, if it [be] really fact that you have appeared against the Bill, that you have influenced and advised her Majesty in favour of the toleration, etc., the general is truth and therefore the design just. This is part of the particular step marked No. 1.

No. 2. Of popularity.

That which I call popularity may a little differ from the thing which goes by that name in the general opinion, and therefore 'tis needful to

distinguish the term. Popularity in general is the general esteem of the
people; but the popularity I mean must have an adjunct, *viz.* a general
esteem founded on good actions, truly meriting the love of the people.
'Tis true the people are not so apt to love as to hate, and therefore,
when the former is fixed on a person, it ought to imply some merit. But
this is not universally true, for the people sometimes love by antithesis,
and show a general affection for one person to show their dis-esteem of
his enemy, and this may be visible in the case of the Duke of Monmouth,
who really had not a great deal of personal merit. We say happiness
consists in being content; but I must deny it, unless the contentment be
fixed on a centre of virtue, for a vicious man may so be more happy than
a virtuous, and a mad man than both. So here a man may be popular
without merit, but that popularity will neither be useful nor serviceable:

> For though by wicked acts men gain applause,
> The reputation's rotten, like the cause.

A wise man is willing to be popular, and a wise statesman will be so, but
it is such a popular esteem as rises from acts of virtue, bounty, and noble
principles. 'Tis my opinion, Sir, as to yourself, and I speak it with the
same plainness as I do things less smooth, that I ought to use more arguments with you to persuade you to desire this popular esteem than to
deserve it. And therefore, Sir, I leave the philosophy of the argument
to your own speculation, and go on to the present case. The popularity
I mean now is – a political conduct of your self, between the Scylla
and the Charybdis[27] of parties, so as to obtain from them all a general
esteem. Though this part of conduct is called dissimulation, I am content
it shall be called what they will, but, as a lie does not consist in the indi-
rect position of words but in the design by false speaking to deceive and
injure my neighbour, so dissembling does not consist in putting a different
face upon our actions but in the further applying that concealment to
the prejudice of the person. For example, I come into a person's chamber
who on a surprize is apt to fall into dangerous convulsions; I come in
smiling and pleasant, and ask the person to rise and go abroad, or
any other such question, and press him to it till I prevail, whereas the
truth is I have discovered the house to be on fire, and I act thus for
fear of frighting him. Will any man tax me with hypocrisy and dissimulation? In your particular post, Sir, you may so govern as that every
party shall believe you their own. I think I may answer for one side, and
shall think very meanly of my own designs if I do not bring the Dissenters
to believe it firmly, if you please to give me leave to act as effectually

as I may convince you will be needful. The Dissenters, Sir, may be brought: 1, To believe better of past actions, of which I mean in the scheme no. 1; 2, They shall always believe you their friend with the Queen; 3, Take you for their advocate and apply to you on all occasions; 4, Freely acquaint you of all circumstances relating to what they desire or fear; 5, If ever you find occasion, you may be the head of the whole party, and consequently influence them as you please; 6, You will have the opportunity upon all occasions both to represent them right to the Queen, and the Queen right to them, the want of which has been injurious to both; 7, You will caution them against indiscretions, and anything that may be to their disadvantage; 8, You may at second hand acquaint them of the designs of a party against them, and have the honour of saving them from the mischief intended. The influence your office, as well as personal merit, gives you on the Queen will give you opportunities either to bring off many of the hot men on the other side or to discourage them that they may cease to disturb; and as to the moderatest of them, you will often by serving them oblige them to acknowlege you. Of the moderate men you are secure, and they cannot but both approve your conduct, as they see it moves towards the real happiness of us all. This is the dissimulation I recommend, which is not unlike what the Apostle says of himself becoming all things to all men, that he might gain some. This hypocrisy is a virtue, and by this conduct you shall make yourself popular, you shall be faithful and useful to the Sovereign and beloved by the people.

No. 3. Of making the Secretaries of State an inner cabinet to the Queen.

If the Secretaries of State have a right understanding and act entirely in concert, it will forward it exceedingly. The Secretaries should have a set of able heads, under a secret management, with whom to make general calculations, and from whom to receive such needful informations as by other agents under them may be obtained in all necessary or difficult cases, and yet these secret heads need not correspond. From this fund of advice all things needful to be concerted for the occasions of state may be formed into schemes and come out perfect. The proposals made by the Secretaries shall no more be embryos, and be brought before the Council to be argued and amended, but shall be born at once and come before them whole and complete, and the Council have little to do but to approve a thing as it is proposed. If all the proposals relating to public matters were thus digested, her Majesty would find there was a secret sufficiency somewhere in her Secretary's office that in time would bring both herself and Council to depend upon the Secretaries of State for all models of action, as well as the management, and thus, Sir, I have brought out what I affirmed at first, that the Secretary of State must of course be Prime Minister. An essay or two of this nature shall be made when you please.

I acknowlege the conjunction of the Lord Treasurer for the time being would make a complete conduct, because 'tis impossible but his Lordship must be furnished with such helps as may finish things with less difficulty. In this concert all the great actions of state, all orders given to admirals and generals, all foreign treaties, and foreign intelligences, would receive their last turns, be digested, and finished, and the Queen see herself mistress of the most capital part of her affairs before they come before the Council. All funds for taxes, ways and means, projects of trade, etc., shall be here formed into heads, and either be fitted for execution or laid aside as impracticable, and my Lord Treasurer be eased of the intolerable impertinence of fund makers and projectors. Secret matters relating to parties, to private persons, home management, etc., will here be settled, determined, and prepared for execution. Here all the business of the Crown, the affairs of law only excepted, will centre, and the Secretary's office be thus the only Cabinet. This would make our actions uniform, our councils secret, our orders regular and practicable, and the execution punctual. This would bring the Secretary's office, and above all the Secretary, into such reputation that orders issued would have more regard, since resentments of misconduct would lie in the breast of the Secretary and be very certain and severe. Here would be a Prime Ministry without a grievance, the people pleased, the government served, envy ashamed, intrigues fruitless, enterprises successful, and all our measures be both better directed and better executed. At home parties would be suppressed, furious tempers on all sides checked and discountenanced, peace promoted and union obtained. All the leading men of all sides would be influenced here, by a rare and secret management; they should never stir nor speak as a party but it should be known. Not a Mayor or an Alderman in an corporation, not a Sheriff of a county, not a Member of Parliament or Convocation, could be elected, but the Government should know who to oppose and how to do it, if they saw fit. This would be the wheel of all public business, and all the other business must of course depend on the management of this office. [. . .]

REASONS

AGAINST THE

SUCCESSION

OF THE

House of *Hanover*,

WITH AN

ENQUIRY

How far the Abdication of
King *James*, supposing it to
be Legal, ought to affect the
Person of the

PRETENDER.

Si Populus vult Decipi, Decipiatur.[1]

LONDON:
Printed for *J. Baker*, at the *Black-Boy* in
Pater-Noster-Row. 1713. (Price 6*d.*)

REASONS AGAINST THE
SUCCESSION, &c.

WHAT Strife is here among you all? And what a Noise about who shall or shall not be King, *the Lord knows when*? Is it not a strange thing we can't be quiet with the Queen we have, but we must all fall into Confusion and Combustions about who shall come after? Why, pray Folks, How Old is the Queen, and when is she to Die, that here is this Pother made about it? I have heard wise People say the Queen is not Fifty Years Old, that she has no Distemper but the Gout, that is a Long-life Disease, which generally holds People out Twenty, or Thirty, or Forty Years; and let it go how it will, the Queen may well enough linger out Twenty or Thirty Years, and not be a Huge Old Wife neither. Now! What say the *People*, must we think of living Twenty or Thirty Years in this wrangling Condition we are now in? This would be a Torment worse than some of the *Ægyptian* Plagues, and would be intolerable to bear, tho' for fewer Years than that. The Animosities of this Nation, should they go on, as it seems they go on now, would by time be come to such a Height, that all Charity, Society, and Mutual Agreement among us, will be destroy'd. Christians shall we be call'd! No; Nothing of the People call'd Christians will be to be found among Us. Nothing of Christianity, or the Substance of Christianity, *viz.* Charity, will be found among Us! The Name Christian may be assum'd, but it will be all Hypocrisie and Delusion; the Being of Christianity must be lost in the Fog, and Smoke, and Stink, and Noise, and Rage, and Cruelty, of our Quarrel about a King. Is this Rational? Is it Agreeable to the true Interest of the Nation? What must become of Trade, of Religion, of Society, of Relation, of Families, of People? Why, hark ye, you Folk, that call your-selves Rational, and talk of having Souls, is this a Token of your having such things about you, or of thinking Rationally; if you have, pray what is it likely will become of you all? Why, the Strife is gotten into your Kitchens, your Parlours, your Shops, your Counting-houses, nay, into your very Beds. You Gentlefolks, if you please to listen to your Cook-maids and Footmen in your Kitchens, you shall hear them scolding, and swearing, and scratching, and fighting, among themselves; and when you think the Noise is about the Beef and the Pudding, the Dish water, or the Kitchen-stuff, alas you are mistaken, the Feud is about the more mighty Affairs of the Government, and who is for the Protestant Succession, and who for the Pretender. Here the poor despicable Scullions learn to cry, *High-Church, No Dutch Kings, No Hannover*, that they may do it dexterously when they come into the next Mob. Here their Antagonists of the Dripping-pan practise the other Side Clamour, *No French Peace, No Pretender, No Popery*. The thing is the very same up one Pair of Stairs, in the Shops and Warehouses the Prentices stand some on one Side of the Shop, and some on the other, (having Trade little enough,) and there they throw *High-Church* and *Low-Church* at one another's Heads like Battledore and Shuttlecock; instead of Posting their Books, they are Fighting and Railing at the *Pretender* and the House of *Hannover*; it were better for us certainly that these Things had never been heard of. If we go from the Shop one Story higher into our Family, the Ladies instead of their innocent Sports and Diversions, they are all falling out one among another; the Daughters and the Mother, the Mothers and the Daughters; the Children and the Servants; nay, the very little Sisters one among another. If the Chamber-maid is a Slattern, and does not please, hang her, she is a Jade; or I warrant she is a High-Flier; or, *on t'other Side*, I warrant she is a Whig; I never knew one of that sort good for any thing in my Life. Nay, go up to your very Bed-Chambers, and even in Bed, the Man and Wife shall quarrel about it. People! People! What will become of you at this rate? If ye cannot set Man and Wife together, nor your Sons and Daughters together, nay, nor your Servants together, how will ye set your Horses together, think ye? And how shall they stand together Twenty or Thirty Years, think ye, if the Queen should live so long? Before that time comes if you are not reduc'd to your Wits, you will be stark Mad; so that unless you can find in your Hearts to agree about this Matter beforehand, the Condition you are in, and by that time will in all likelihood be in, will Ruin us all; and this is one sufficient Reason why we should say Nothing, and do Nothing, about the Succession, but just let it rest where it is, and endeavour to be quiet; for it is impossible to live thus: Further, if *Hannover* should come while we are in such a Condition, we shall Ruin him, or he us, that is most certain. It remains to enquire what will be the Issue of Things. Why, (1.) If ye will preserve the Succession, and keep it right, you must settle the Peace of the Nation; we are not in a Condition to stand by the Succession now, and if we go on we shall be worse able to do so; in his own Strength *Hannover* does not pretend to come, and if he did he must miscarry; if not in his own, in whose then but the People of *Britain*? And if the People be a weaken'd, divided and deluded, People, and see not your own Safety to lye in your Agreement among yourselves, how shall such weak Folk assist him, especially against a strong Enemy; so that it will be your Destruction to attempt to bring in the House of *Hannover*, unless you can stand by and defend him when he is come; this will make you all like *Monmouth*'s Men in the *West*,[2] and you will find yourselves lifted up to Halters and Gibbets, not to Places and Preferments. Unless you reconcile yourselves to one another, and bring things to some better Pass among the Common People, it will be but to banter yourselves to talk of the Protestant Succession; for you neither will be in a Condition to bring over your Protestant Successor, or to support him on the Throne when you have brought him; and it will not be denied, but to make the Attempt, and not succeed in it, is to ruin yourselves; and this I think a very good reason against the Succession of the House of *Hannover*.

Another Argument relates something to the Family of *Hannover* itself. Here the Folk are continually fighting and quarrelling with one another to such a Degree as must infallibly weaken and disable the whole Body of the Nation, and expose them to any Enemy, Foreign or Domestick. What Prince, think you, will venture his Person with a Party or a Faction, and that a Party crush'd, and under the Power of their Enemy; a Party who have not been able to support themselves or their Cause, how shall they support and defend him when he comes? And if they cannot be in a Posture to Defend and Maintain him when they have him, how shall he be encourag'd to venture himself among them? To come over and make the Attempt here according to his just Claim and the Laws of the Land would be indeed his Advantage, if there was a Probability that he should succeed, otherwise the Example of the King of *Poland*[3] is suffi-cient to warn him against venturing while the Nation is divided, and together by the Ears, as they are here. The whole Kingdom of *Poland*, we see, could not defend King *Augustus* against the *Swedes* and their Pretender; but tho' he had the Majority, and was receiv'd as King over the whole Kingdom, yet it being a Kingdom divided into Factions and Parties, and those Parties raging with bitter Envy and Fury one against another, even just as ours do here, what came of it but the Ruin of King *Augustus*, who was as it were a Prisoner in his own Court, and was brought to the Necessity of Abdicating the Crown of *Poland*, and of acknowledging the Title of the Pretender to that Crown. Now what can the Elector of *Hannover* expect if he should make the Attempt here while we are in this divided factious Condition, while the Pretender, back'd by his Party at Home, shall also have the whole Power of *France* to support him, and place him upon the Throne?

Let us but look back to a Time when the very same Case almost fell out in this Nation; the same many Ways it was, that is, in the Case of the Queen *Mary* I. your Bloody Papist Persecuting Queen *Mary* and the Lady *Jane*[4] *Dudley*, or *Gray*. The late King *Edward* VI. had settled the Protestant Succession upon the Lady *Jane*; it was receiv'd universally as the Protestant Succession is now. The Reasons which mov'd the People to receive it were the same, *i. e.* the Safety of the Protestant Religion, and the Liberties and Properties of the People, all the Great Men of King *Edward*'s Court and Council came readily into this Succession, and gave their Oaths, or what was in those Days, (whatsoever it may be now,) thought equal to an Oath, (*viz.* their Honour,) for the standing by the Successor in her taking Possession of her said just Right. *Mary*, Daughter of *Catherine* of *Spain*, was the Pretender; her Mother was Abdicated, (so we call it in this Age,) Repudiated, they call'd it, or Divorc'd. Her Daughter was adjudg'd Illegitimate or Spurious, because the Marriage of her Mother was esteem'd Unlawful; just as our Pretender is by this Nation suggested Spurious, by Reason of the yet unfolded Mysteries of his Birth. Again, that Pretender had the whole Power of *Spain*, which was then the most dreaded of any in the World, and was just what the *French* are now, *viz.* the Terror of *Europe*. If Queen *Mary* was to have the Crown, it was allow'd by all that *England* was to be govern'd by *Spanish* Councils and *Spanish* Maxims, *Spanish* Money and *Spanish* Cruelty. Just as we say now of the Pretender, that if he was to come in we shall be all govern'd by *French* Maxims, *French* Councils, *French* Money, and *French* Tyranny. In these Things the Pretender (*Mary*) at that Time was the Parallel to our Pretender Now, and that with but very little Difference. Besides all this, she was a Papist, which was directly contrary to the Pious Design of King *Edward* in propagating the Reformation. Exactly agreeing these Things were with our Succession, our Pretender, our King *William*, and his Design, by settling the Succession for the propagating the Revolution, which is the Reformation of this Day, as the Reformation was the Revolution of that Day. After this formal settling of the Succession the King (as Kings and Queens must) dies, and the Lords of the Council, suppose Lords Justices, as our Law calls them, *they were the same thing*, they Meet and Proclaim their Protestant Successor, as they were oblig'd to do; and what follow'd? Had they been Unanimous, had they stuck to one another, had they not divided into Parties, High and Low, they had kept their Protestant Successor in spight of all the Power of *Spain*, but they fell out with one another; High Protestants against Low Protestants; and what was the Consequence? One Side to ruin the other brought in the Pretender upon them, and so *Spanish* Power, as it was predicted, came in upon them, and devoured them all. Popery came in, as they fear'd, and all went to Ruin; and what came of the Protestant Successor? Truly they brought Her to Ruin. For first bringing her in, and then, by Reason of their own Strife and Divisions, not being able to maintain Her in the Possession of that Crown, which at their Request She had taken, She fell into Her Enemies Hand, was made a Sacrifice to their Fury, and brought to the Block. What can be a more lively Representation of our Case now before us? He must have small Sense of the State of our Case, I think, who in our present Circumstances can desire the *Hannover* Succession should take Place. What! Would you bring over the Family of *Hannover* to have them Murther'd? No, no, those that have a true Value for the House of *Hannover*, would by no Means desire them to come hither, or desire you to bring them on such Terms; first let the World see you are in a Condition to Support and Defend them, that the Pretender, and his Power and Alliances of any kind, shall not Disperse and Ruin him and you together; first unite and put yourselves into a Posture that you may defend the Succession, and then you may have it; but as it stands now, good Folks, consider with yourselves what Prince in *Europe* will venture among Us, and who that has any Respect or Value for the House of *Hannover* can desire them to come hither.

These are some good Reasons why the Succession of the House of *Hannover* should not be our present View. Another Reason may be taken from the Example of the good People in the Days of King *Edward* VI. They were very Good Religious People, (that must be allow'd by all Sides,) and who had very great Zeal for the Protestant Religion and the Reformation, as it was then newly establish'd among them; and this Zeal of theirs appear'd plainly in a Degree we can scarce hope for among the Protestants of this Age, *viz.* in their Burning for it afterwards; yet such was their Zeal for the Hereditary Right of their Royal Family, that they chose to fall into the Hands of *Spanish* Tyranny, and of *Spanish* Popery, and let the Protestant Religion and the Hopes of its Establishment go to the D—l, rather than not have the Right Line of their Princes kept up, and the Eldest Daughter of their late King *Henry* come to the Crown.

Upon this Principle they forsook their good Reforming King *Edward*'s Scheme, Rejected the Protestant Succession, and they themselves, Protestants, sincere Protestants, such as afterwards died at a Stake for their Religion, the Protestant Religion; yet they brought in the Pretender according to their Principles, and run the Risque of what could follow thereupon. Why should we think it strange then that Protestant now in this Age, and Church of *England* Protestants too, should be for a Papish Pretender? No doubt but they may be as good Protestants as the *Suffolk* Men[5] in Queen *Mary*'s Time were, and if they are brought to it, will go as far, and die at a Stake for the Protestant Religion, and in doing this, no doubt but it is their real Prospect to die at a Stake, *or they would not do it to be sure*. Now the Protestant Religion, the whole Work of Reformation, the Safety of the Nation, both as to their Liberties and Religion, the keeping out *French* or *Spanish* Popery, the dying at a Stake, and the like, being always esteem'd Things of much less Value than the faithful adhering to the Divine Rule of keeping the Crown in the Right Line, let any true Protestant tell me, how can we pretend to be for the *Hannover* Succession? It is evident that the Divine Hereditary Right of our Crown is the Main Great Article now in Debate. You call such a Man the Pretender, but is he not the Son of our King? And if so, what is the Protestant Religion to us? Had we not much better be Papists than Traytors? Had we not much better deny our God, our Baptism, our Religion and our Lives, than deny our lawful Prince, our next Male in a Right Line? If Popery comes, Passive Obedience is still our Friend; we are Protestants; we can Die, we can Burn, we can do any Thing but Rebel; and this being our first Duty, (*viz*) to Recognize our Rightful Sovereign, are we not to do that first? And if Popery or Slavery follow we must act as becomes us. This being then Orthodox Doctrine, is equally a Substantial Reason why we should be against the *Hannover* Succession.

There may be sundry other Reasons given why we should not be for this New Establishment of the Succession, which tho' perhaps they may not seem so Cogent in themselves, have yet a due Force, as they stand related to other Circumstances, which this Nation is at present involv'd in, and therefore are only left to the Consideration of the People of these Times. No Question but every Honest *Britain*[6] is for a peaceable Succession: Now if the Pretender comes, and is quietly Establish'd on the Throne, why then you know there is an End of all our Fears of the Great and Formidable Power of *France*; we have no more need to fear an Invasion, or the Effects of leaving *France* in a Condition by the Peace to act against Us, and put the Pretender upon us; and therefore Peace being of so much Consequence to this Nation, after so long and so cruel a War, none can think of entering upon a New War for the Succession without great Regret and Horror. Now it cannot be doubted but the Succession of *Hannover* would necessarily involve us again in a War against *France*, and that perhaps when we may be in no good Case to undertake it for these Reasons. (1.) Perhaps some Princes and States in the World by that Time, seeing the great Encrease and Growth of *French* Power, may think fit to change their Sentiments, and rather come over to that Interest for want of being supported before, than be willing to Embark against *France*, and so it may not be possible to obtain a New Confederacy in the Degree and Extent of it, which we have seen it in, or in any Degree suitable to the Power of *France*; and if so, there may be but small Hopes of Success in Case of a new Rupture; and any War had better be let alone than be carried on to Loss, which often ends in the Overthrow of the Party or Nation who undertake it, and fails in the carrying it on. (2.) *France* itself, as well by the Acquisition of those Princes who may have chang'd Sides, as above, as by a Time for taking Breath after the Losses they have receiv'd, may be rais'd to a Condition of Superiour Strength, and may be too much an Over-match for us to venture upon; and if he thinks fit to send us the Person we call the Pretender, and order us to take him for our King, and this when we are in no Condition to withstand him, Prudence will guide as to accept of him; for all People comply with what they cannot avoid; and if we are not in a Condition to keep him out, there wants very little Consultation upon the Question, whether we shall take him in? or no? Like this is a Man, who being condemn'd to be Hang'd, and is in Irons in the Dungeon at *Newgate*, when he sees no[a] Possibility either of Pardon from the Queen, or Escape out of Prison, what does he resolve upon next? What! Why he resolves to die. What should he resolve on? Every Body submits to what they cannot escape. People! People! If ye cannot resist the *French* King, ye must submit to a *French* Pretender. There is no more to be said about that. (3.) Then some Allies, who it might be thought would be able to lend you some Help in such a Case as this is, may pretend to be disgusted at former Usage, and say they were abandon'd and forsaken in their Occasion by us, and they will not hazard for a Nation who disoblig'd them so much before, and from whom they have not receiv'd suitable Returns for the Debt of the Revolution. And if these Nations should take Things so ill as to refuse their Aid and Assistance in a Case of so much Necessity as that of the Succession, how shall we be able to maintain that Attempt? And (as before) an Attempt of that, or any other Kind like that, is better unmade than Ineffectually made. (4.) Others add a yet farther Reason of our Probable Inability in such a Case, *viz.* That the Enemies of *Britain* have so misrepresented Things to some of the Neighbouring Nations, our good Friends and Allies, as if we *Britains* had betray'd the Protestant Interest, and not acted faithfully to our Confederacies and Alliances, in which our Reputation, it is pretended, has suffer'd so much, as not to merit to be trusted again in like Cases, or that it should be safe to depend upon our most Solemn Engagements. This, tho' it is Invidious and Harsh, yet if there may be any Truth in it, as we hope there is not, may be added as a very good Reason, why, after this War is over, we may be in no good Case at all to Undertake or to Carry on a New War in Defence of the New Protestant Succession, when it may come to be necessary so to do. Since then the Succession of *Hannover* will necessarily involve us in a New War against *France*, and for the Reasons above, if they are allowed to be good Reasons, we may not be in a Condition to carry on that War: Is not this a good Reason why we should not in our present Circumstances be for that Succession? *Other* Reasons may be taken from the present Occasion the Nation may lye under of preserving and securing the best Administration of Things that ever this Nation was under in many Ages; and if this be found to be inconsistent with the Succession of *Hanover*, as some feign, it is hoped none will say but we ought to consider what we do: If the Succession of *Hanover* is not consistent with these Things, what Reason have we to be for the said Succession, till that Posture of Things be arrived when that Inconsistency may be removed? And now, People of *Britain*! Be your own Judges upon what Terms you can think it Reasonable to insist any longer upon this Succession. I do not contend that it is not a Lawful Succession, a Reasonable Succession, an Established Succession, nay, a Sworn Succession; but if it be not a Practicable Succession, and cannot be a Peaceable Succession; if Peace will not bring him in, and War cannot, what must we do? It were much better not to have it at all, than to have it and ruin the Kingdom, and ruin those that claim it at the same Time.

But yet I have other Reasons than these, and more Cogent ones; Learned Men say, some Diseases in Nature are Cured by Antipathies, and some by Sympathies; that the Enemies of Nature are the best Preservatives of Nature; that Bodies are brought down by the Skill of the Physician that they may the better be brought up, made Sick to be made Well, and carried to the Brink of the Grave in order to be kept from the Grave; for these Reasons, and in order to these Things, Poisons are administred for Physick; or Amputations in Surgery, the Flesh is cut that it may heal; an Arm laid open that it may close with Safety; and these Methods of Cure are said to be the most certain as well as most necessary in those particular Cases, from whence it is become a Proverbial Saying in Physick, *Desperate Diseases must have Desperate Remedies.* Now it is very proper to enquire in this Case whether the Nation is not in such a State of Health at this Time, that the Coming of the Pretender may not be of absolute Necessity, by Way of Cure of such National Distempers which now afflict us, and that an Effectual Cure can be wrought no other Way? If upon due Enquiry it should appear that we are not fit to receive such a Prince as the Successor of the House of *Hanover* is, that we should maltreat and abuse him if he were here, and that there is no Way for us to learn the true Value of a Protestant Successor so well as by tasting a little what a Popish Pretender is, and feeling something of the great Advantages that may accrue to us by the Superiority of a Jacobite Party; if the Disease of Stupidity has so far seiz'd us that we are to be Cured only by Poisons and Fermentations; if the Wound is Mortified, and nothing but Deep Incisions, Amputations, and Desperate Remedies, must be used; if it should be necessary thus to teach us the Worth of Things by the Want of them; and there is no other Way to bring the Nation to its Senses; why, what can be then said against the Pretender? Even let him come that we may see what Slavery means, and may enquire how the Chains of *French* Gallies[7] hang about us, and how easie Wooden Shoes are to walk in; for no Experience teaches so well as that we buy Dearest, and pay for with the most Smart.

I think this may pass for a very good Reason against the Protestant Succession: Nothing is surer than that the Management of King *Cha.* II. and his late Brother, were the best Ways the Nation could ever have taken to bring to pass the Happy Revolution; yet these Afflictions to the Island were not Joyous, but Grievous, for the Time they remain'd, and the Poor Kingdoms suffered great Convulsions; but what weighs that if these Convulsions are found to be necessary to a Cure? If the Physicians prescribe a Vomit for the Cure of any particular Distemper, will the Patient complain of being made Sick? No, no; when you begin to be Sick, then we say, Oh, that is Right, and then the Vomit begins to work; and how shall the Island of *Britain* spue out all the Dregs and Filth the Publick Digesture[8] has contracted, if it be not made Sick with some *French* Physick? If you give good Nourishing Food upon a foul Stomach, you cause that wholsome Food to turn into Filth, and instead of Nourishing the Man, it Nourishes Diseases in the Man, till those Diseases prove his Destruction, and bring him to the Grave. In like Manner if you will bring the Protestant Successor into the Government before that Government have taken some Physick to cleanse it from the ill Digesture it may have been under, how do we know but the Diseases which are already begun in the Constitution may not be nourished and kept up, till they may hereafter break out in the Days of our Posterity, and prove Mortal to the Nation. Wherefore should we desire the Protestant Successor to come in upon a Foot of High-flying Menage,[9] and be beholding for their Establishment to those who are the Enemies of the Constitution? Would not this be to have in Time to come the Successors of that House be the same Thing as the Ages past have already been made Sick of, and made to spue out of the Government? Are not any of these Considerations enough to make any of us averse to the Protestant Succession? No, no; let us take a *French* Vomit first, and make us Sick, that we may be well, and may afterwards more effectually have our Health established.

The Pretender will no doubt bring us good Medicines, and Cure us of all our Hypochondriack Vapours that now make us so giddy: But say some, he will bring Popery in upon us; Popery, say you! Alas! It is true, Popery is a sad Thing, and that say some Folk ought to have been thought on before now; but suppose then this Thing called Popery! How will it come in? Why, say the Honest Folk, the Pretender is a Papist, and if a Popish Prince come upon the Throne we shall have Popery come in upon us without fail: Well, well, and what Hurt will this be to you? May not Popery be very good in its Kind? What if this Popery, like the Vomit made of Poison, be the only Physick that can cure you? If this Vomit make you spue out your Filth, your Tory Filth, your Idolatrous Filth, your Tyrannick Filth, and restore you to your Health, shall it not be good for you? Where pray observe in the Allegory of Physick; you heard before when you take a Vomit, the Physick given you to vomit is always something contrary to Nature, something that if taken in Quantity would destroy; but how does it operate? It attacks Nature, and puts her upon a Ferment to cast out what offends her: But remark it, I pray, when the Patient vomits, he always vomits up the Physick and the Filth together: So, if the Nation should take a Vomit of Popery, as when the Pretender comes, most certain it is that this will be the Consequence, they will vomit up the Physick and the Filth together; the Popery and the Pretender will come all up again, and all the Popish, Arbitrary, Tyrannical Filth, which has offended the Stomach of the Nation so long, and ruined its Digesture, it will all come up together: One Vomit of Popery will do us all a great deal of Good, for the Stomach of the Constitution is Marvellous Foul. Observe, People! This is no New Application; the Nation has taken a Vomit of this Kind before now, as in Queen *Mary* I. Time; the Reformation was not well chewed, and being taken down whole, did not rightly digest, but left too much Crudity in the Stomach, from whence proceeded ill Nourishment, bad Blood, and a very ill Habit of Body in the Constitution; Witness the Distemper which seized the Gospellers in *Suffolk*, who being struck with an Epilepsie or Dead Palsie in the better half of their Understanding, to wit, the Religious and Zealous Part, took up Arms for a Popish Pretender, against the Protestant Successor, upon the wild headed Whimsie of the *Right Line* being *Jure Divino*: Well, what followed, I pray? Why, they took a Vomit of Popery; the Potion indeed was given in a double Vehicle, (*viz.*) of Faggots a little inflamed, and this work'd so effectually, that the Nation having vomited, brought up all the Filth of the Stomach, and the Foolish Notion of Hereditary Right spued out Popery also along with it. Thus was Popery and Fire and Faggot the most effectual Remedy to cure the Nation of all its simple Diseases, and to settle and establish the Protestant Reformation; and why then should we be so terrified with the Apprehensions of Popery? Nay, why should we not open our Eyes and see how much to our Advantage it may be in the next Reign to have Popery brought in, and to that End the Pretender set up, that he may help us to this most useful Dose of Physick? These are some other of my Reasons against the Protestant Succession; I think they cannot be mended: It may perhaps be thought hard of that we should thus seem to make light of so terrible a Thing as Popery, and should jest with the Affair of the Protestants: No, People! No; this is no Jest, taking Physick is no Jest at all; for it is useful many Ways, and there is no keeping the Body in Health without it; for the Corruption of Politick Constitutions are as Gross and as Fatal as those of Human Bodies, and require as immediate Application of Medicines. And why should you People of this Country be so alarmed, and seem so afraid of this Thing called Popery, when it is spoken of in Intelligible Terms, since you are not afraid alternately to put your Hands to those Things which as naturally tend in themselves to bring it upon you, as Clouds tend to Rain, or Smoke to Fire; what does all your scandalous Divisions, your unchristian Quarrellings, your heaping up Reproaches, and loading each other with Infamy, and with abominable Forgeries, what do these tend to but to Popery? If it should be asked how have these any such Reference? The Question is most Natural from the Premises: If Divisions weaken the Nation; if Whig and Tory, even united, are, and have been, weak enough to keep out Popery; surely then Widening the unnatural Breaches, and Enflaming Things between them to implacable and irreconcilable Breaches, must tend to overthrow the Protestant Kingdom, which, as our Everblessed Saviour said, when *divided against itself cannot stand.* Besides, are not your Breaches come up to that Height already as to let any Impartial By-stander see that Popery must be the Consequences? Do not one Party say openly they had rather be Papists than Presbyterians, that they would rather go to Mass than to a Meeting-house, and are they not to that Purpose, all of them who are of that Height, openly joined with the Jacobites in the Cause of Popery? On the other Hand, are not the Presbyterians in *Scotland* so exasperated at having the Abjuration Oath[10] impos'd upon them, contrary, as they tell us, to their Principles, that they care not if he, or any else, would come now, and free them from that Yoke? What is all this but telling us plainly that the whole Nation is running into Popery and the Pretender? Why then, while you are Obliquely, and by Consequences, joining your Hands to bring in Popery, why, O distracted Folk! should you think it amiss to have me talk of doing it Openly and Avowedly? Better is open Enmity than secret Guile; better is it to talk openly, and profess openly, for Popery, that you may see the Shape and real Picture of it, than pretend strong Opposition of it, and be all at the same Time putting your Hands to the Work, and pulling it down upon yourselves with all your Might.

But here comes an Objection in our Way, which, however weighty, we must endeavour to get over, and this is, What becomes of the Abjuration? If the Pretender comes in we are all perjured, and we ought to be all Unanimous for the House of *Hanover*, because we are all perjured if we are for the Pretender: *Perjur'd, say ye!* Ha! Why, do not all these People say we are all perjur'd already? Nay, One, Two, Three, or Four Times? What signifie Oaths and Abjurations in a Nation where the Parliament can make an Oath to Day, and punish a Man for keeping it to Morrow! Besides, taking Oaths without Examination, and breaking them without Consideration, hath been so much a Practice, and the Date of its Original is so far back, that none, or but very few, know where to look for it; nay, have we not been called in the Vulgar Dialect of Foreign Countries the *Swearing Nation*? Note, we do not say the Forsworn Nation; for whatever other Countries say of us, it is not meet we should say so of ourselves: But as to Swearing and Forswearing, Associating and Abjuring, there are very few without Sin to throw the first Stone, and therefore we may be the less Careful to answer in this Matter: It's evident that the Friends of the Pretender cannot blame us; for have not the most profest Jacobites all over the Nation taken this Abjuration? Nay, when even in their Hearts they have all the while resolved to be for the Pretender? Not to instance in the Swearing in all Ages to and against Governments, just as they were, or were not, in Condition to protect us, or keep others out of Possession: But we have a much better Way to come off this than that, and we doubt not to clear the Nation of Perjury, by declaring the Design, true Intent and Meaning, of the Thing itself; for the Good or Evil of every Action is said to lye in the Intention; if then we can prove the bringing in the Pretender to be done with a Real Intention and Sincere Design to keep him out; or, as before, to spue him out; if we bring in Popery with an Intention and a Sincere Design to establish the Protestant Religion; if we bring in a Popish Prince with a single Design the firmer and better to fix and introduce the Protestant *Hanover* Succession, if I say these Things are the true Intent and Meaning, and are at the Bottom of all our Actions in this Matter, pray how shall we be said to be Perjured, or to break in upon the Abjuration, whose Meaning we keep whatever becomes of the Literal Part of it. Thus we are abundantly defended from the Guilt of Perjury, because we preserve the Design and Intention upright and entire for the House of *Hanover*; tho' as the best Means to bring it to pass we think fit to bring in Popery and the Pretender; but yet farther, to justifie the Lawfulness and Usefulness of such Kind of Methods, we may go back to former Experiments of the same Case, or like Cases, for Nothing can illustrate such a Thing so aptly, as the Example of Eminent Men who have practised the very same Things in the same or like Cases, and more especially when that Practice has been made use of by Honest Men in an Honest Cause, and the End been crowned with Success. This Eminent Example was first put in Practice by the late Famous E. of *Sunderland* [11] in the Time of King *James* II. and that too in the Case of bringing Popery into *England*, which is the very Individual Article before us: This Famous Politician, if Fame lyes not, turn'd Papist himself, went publickly to Mass, advised and directed all the forward rash Steps that King *James* afterwards took, towards the introducing of Popery into the Nation: If he is not slander'd, it was he advised the Setting up of Popish Chapels and Mass-houses in the City of *London*, and in the several Principal Towns of this Nation; the Invading the Right of Corporations, Courts of Justice, Universities, and, at last, the Erecting the High Commission Court, to sap the Foundations of the Church; and many more of the Arbitrary Steps which that Monarch took for the Ruin of the Protestant

Religion, as he thought, were brought about by this Politick Earl, purely with Design, and as the only effectual Means, to ruin the Popish Schemes, and bring about the Establishment of the Protestant Religion by the Revolution; and, as Experience after made it good, he alone was in the Right, and it was the only Way left, the only Step that could be taken, tho' at first it made us all of the Opinion the Man was going the ready Way to ruin his Country, and that he was Selling us to Popery and *Rome*. This was exactly our Case; the Nation being Sick of a Deadly, and otherwise Incurable, Disease, this Wise Physician knew that nothing but a Medicine made up of Deadly Poison, that should put the whole Body into Convulsions, and make it cast up the Dregs of the Malady, would have any Effect; and so he applied himself accordingly to such a Cure; he brought on Popery to the very Door; he caused the Nation to swallow as much of it as he thought was enough to make her as Sick as a Horse, and then he foresaw she would spue up the Disease and the Medicine together; the Potion of Popery he saw would come up with it, and so it did: If this be our Case now, then it may be true that bringing the Pretender is the only Way to establish the Protestant Succession; and upon such Terms, and such only, I declare myself for the Pretender: If any Sort of People are against the Succession of the House of *Hanover* on any other Accounts, and for other Reasons, it may not be amiss to know some of them, and a little to recommend them to those who have a Mind to be for him, but well know not wherefore or why they are so inclined. 1. Some being instructed to have an Aversion to all Foreign Princes or Families are against the Succession of the Princes of *Hanover*, because, as they are taught to say, they are *Dutchmen*; now tho' it might as well be said of the Pretender that he is a *Frenchman*, yet that having upon many Accounts been made more familiar to them of late, and the Name of a *Dutch* King having a peculiar Odium left upon it, by the Grievances of the late King *William*'s Reign, they can by no Means think of another *Dutch* Succession without Abhorrence; nay, the Aversion is so much greater than their Aversions to Popery, that they can with much more Satisfaction entertain the Notion of a Popish *French* Pretender than of the best Protestant in the World, if he hath any Thing belonging to him that sounds like a *Dutchman*: And this is some Peoples Reason against the *Hanover* Succession; a Reason which has produced various Effects in the World since the Death of that Prince, even to creating National Antipathies in some People to the whole People of *Holland*, and to wish us involved in a War with the *Dutch*, without any Foundation of a Quarrel with them, or any Reason for those Aversions; but these Things opening a Scene which relates to Things farther back than the Subject we are now upon, we omit them here for Brevity Sake, and to keep more closely to the Thing in Hand at this Time. Others have Aversions to the *Hanover* Succession as it is the Effect of the Revolution, and as it may reasonably be supposed to favour such Principles as the Revolution was brought about by, and has been the Support of, (*viz.*) Principles of Liberty, Justice, Rights of Parliaments, the Peoples Liberties, Free Possession of Property, and such like; these Doctrines, a certain Party in this Nation, have always to their utmost opposed, and have given us Reason to believe they hate and abhor them, and for this Reason they cannot be supposed to appear forward for the *Hanover* Succession; to these Principles have been opposed the more Famous Doctrines of Passive Obedience, Absolute Will, Indefeasible Right, the *Jus Divinum* of the Line of Princes, Hereditary Right, and such like; these, as preach'd up by that *Eminent Divine*, Dr. *Henry Sacheverell*, are so much preferrable to the Pretences of Liberty and Constitution, the Old Republican Notions of the Whigs, that they cannot but fill these People with Hatred against all those that would pretend to maintain the Foundation we now stand upon, (*viz.*) the Revolution; and this is their Reason against the *Hanover* Succession, which they know would endeavour to do so.

Come we in the Conclusion of this great Matter to one Great and Main Reason which they say prevails with a great Part of the Nation at this Time to be for the Pretender, and which many Subtle Heads and Industrious Hands are now busily employed all over the Kingdom to improve in the Minds of the Common People, this is the Opinion of the Legitimacy of the Birth of the Pretender; it seems, say these Men, that the Poor Commons of *Britain* have been all along impos'd upon to believe that the Person called the Pretender was a Spurious Birth, a Child fostered upon the Nation by the late King and Queen; this Delusion was carried on, say they, by the Whigs in King *William*'s Time, and a mighty Stir was made of it to possess the Rabbles in Favour of the Revolution, but nothing was ever made of it: King *William*, say they, promised in his Declaration to have it referred to the Decision of the *English* Parliament, but when he obtained the Crown he never did any Thing that Way more than encourage the People to spread the Delusion by Scurrilous Pamphlets to amuse[12] the poor Commons; have them take a Thing for granted which could have no other Thing made of it; and so the judging of it in Parliament was made a Sham only; and the People drinking in the Delusion, as they who were in the Plot desired, it has past ever since as if the Thing had been sufficiently proved. Now upon a more sedate Considering the Matter, say they, the Case is clear that this Person is the real Son of King *James*, and the Favourers of the Revolution go now upon another Foundation, (*viz*) the Powers of Parliaments to limit the Succession; and that Succession being limited upon King *James*'s Abdication, which they call Voluntary: So that now, say they, the Question about the Legitimacy of the Person called the Pretender is over, and nothing now is to be said of it: That he is the Son of King *James*, there is, say they, no more Room to doubt, and therefore the Doctrine of Hereditary Right taking Place, as the Ancient professed Doctrine of the Church of *England*, there can be no Objection against his being our Lawful King; and it is contrary to the said Church of *England* Doctrine to deny it. This then is the present Reason which the poor ignorant People are taught to give why they are against the Protestant Succession, and why they are easily persuaded to come into the New Scheme of a Popish Pretender, tho' at the same Time they are all heartily against Popery as much as ever.

It becomes necessary now to explain this Case a little to the Understanding of the Common People, and let them know upon what Foundation the Right of these Two Parties is founded, and if this be done with Plainness and Clearness, as by the Rights and Laws of *Englishmen* and *Britains* appertaineth, the said Commons of *Britain* may soon discover whether the Succession of the House of *Hanover*, or the Claim of the Person called the Pretender, is founded best, and which they ought to adhere unto. The First Thing it seems to be made clear to the Common People is, Whether the Pretender was the Lawful Son of King *James*, Yea, or No? And why the contrary to this was not made appear, according to the Promises which, they say, tho' falsly, were made by the late King *William*? In the first Place is to be considered, that the Declaration of the said King, when P. of O.[13] putting the said Case in the modestest Manner possible, had this Expression, *That there were violent Suspicions that the said Person was not Born of the Queen's Body, and that the Prince resolved to leave the same to the Free Parliament, to which throughout the said Declaration the said Prince declared Himself ready to refer all the Grievances which he came over to redress.* I shall give you this in the Words of a late Learned Author upon that Head.

That before a Free Parliament could be obtained, King James *withdrew himself, and carried away his Pretended Son into the Hands of the Ancient Enemies of this Nation, and of our Religion,* (viz) *the* French, *there to be Educated in the Principles of Enmity to this his Native Countrey.*

By which Action he not only declined to refer the Legitimacy of his said Son to the Examination of the Parliament, as the Prince of Orange *had offered in his said Declaration, but made such Examination altogether Useless and Impracticable, he himself (King* James) *not owning it to be a Legal Parliament, and therefore not consenting to stand by such Examination.*

By the said Abdication, and carrying away his said pretended Son into the Hands of the French *to be Educated in Popery, &c. he gave the Parliament of* England *and* Scotland *abundant Reason for ever to exclude the said King* James *and his said Pretended Son from the Government of these Realms, or from the Succession to the same, and made it absolutely Necessary for them to do so, if they would secure the Protestant Religion to themselves and their Posterity; and this without any Regard to the Doubt, whether he was the Lawful Son of King* James, *or no, since it is inconsistent with the Constitution of this Protestant Nation to be Governed by a Popish Prince.*

The Proof of the Legitimacy being thus stated, and all the violent Suspicions of his not being Born of the Queen being thus confirmed by the Abdication of King *James*, come we next to examine how far this Abdication could forfeit for this Pretender, supposing him to be the real Son of King *James*. This returns upon the Right of the Parliament to limit the Succession, supposing King *James* had had no Son at all; if the Abdication be granted a lawfully making the Throne vacant, it will be very hard to assign a Cause why the Parliament might not name a Successor while the Father was alive, whose Right had no violent Suspicions attending it, and not why they might not name a Successor tho' the Son was living: That the Father's Abdication forfeited for the Son is no Part of the Question before us; for the Father is not said to forfeit his Right at all; no one ever questioned his Right to Reign, nor, had he thought fit to have staid, could the Parliament have named a Successor, unless, as in the Case of *Richard* the Second, he had made a Voluntary Resignation or Renunciation of the Crown, and of his Peoples Allegiance; but the King having voluntarily abdicated the Throne, this was as Effectual a Releasing his Subjects from their Allegiance to him, as if he had read an Instrument of Resignation, just as King *Richard* did; all the Articles of such a Resignation were naturally contained in the said Abdication, except the naming the Successor, as effectually as if they had been at large repeated; and since the Resigning the Crown has been formerly practiced in *England*, and there is so eminent an Example in our *English* History of the same, it will questionless be of Use to the Reader of these Sheets to have the Particulars of it before his Eyes, which for that Purpose is here set down at large, as it was done in the Presence of a great Number of *English* Peers, who attended the King for that Purpose, and is as follows.

In the Name of God, Amen. *I* Richard, *by the Grace of God, King of* England *and* France, *and Lord of* Ireland, *do hereby acquit and discharge all Archbishops, Bishops, Dukes, Marquisses, and Earls, Barons, Lords, and all other my Subjects, both Spiritual and Secular, of what Degree soever, from their Oath of Fealty and Homage, and all other Bonds of Allegiance, to me due from them and their Heirs, and do hereby release them from the said Oath and Allegiance, so far as they concern my Person, for ever.*

    I also resign all my Kingly Majesty and Dignity, with all the Rights and Privileges thereunto belonging, and do renounce all the Title and Claim which I ever had, or have, to them. I also renounce the Government of the said Kingdom, and the Name and Royal Highness thereunto belonging, freely and wholly, and swearing upon the Evangelists that I will never oppose this my Voluntary Resignation, nor suffer it to be opposed, as judging myself not unworthily deposed from my Regal Dignity for my Deserts.

    This Resignation being read again in Parliament, they grounded the Deposing King *Richard* upon it, and declared him accordingly Deposed, that is, declared the Throne Vacant; and immediately, by Vertue of their own undoubted Right of Limiting the Succession, named the Successor. See the Form in the History of that Time thus.

    That the Throne was vacant by the Voluntary Cession and Just Deposition of King Richard *the Second, and that therefore according to their undoubted Power and Right so to do, they ought forthwith to the Naming a Successor to fill the said Throne, which they forthwith did, by Naming and Proclaiming* Henry, *Duke of* Lancaster, *to be King, &c.*

        See the History of the Kings of *England*, Vol. Fol. 287.[14]

    This was the same Thing with King *James*'s Abdication, and King *James*'s Abdication was no less or more than an Effectual Resignation in Form; now the Parliament, upon the Resignation of the Crown by the King, having a manifold and manifest Right to supply the Throne so become vacant, had no Obligation to regard the Posterity of the Abdicated Prince, so far as any of them are concerned in, or involved by, the said Abdication, and therefore considered of Establishing and Limiting the Succession, without mentioning the Reasons of the Descent, having the Reason in themselves: But suppose the Son of King *James* had been allowed Legitimate, yet as the Father had involved him in the same Circumstances with himself, by first carrying him out of the Kingdom, and afterwards educating him in the *Popish* Religion, he became abdicated also with his Father: Neither doth the being Voluntary or not Voluntary alter the Case in the least, since in the Laws of *England* a Father is allowed to be able to forfeit for himself and for his Children, and much more may he make a Resignation for himself and his Children, as is daily practiced and allowed in Law in the Cutting off Intails and Remainders, even when the Heir Intail is in Being, and under Age. The People of *Britain* ought not then to suffer themselves to be impos'd upon in such a Case; for tho' the Pretender were to be own'd for the Lawful Son of King *James*, yet the Abdication of King *James*, his Father, and especially his own Passive Abdication, was as Effectual an Abdication in him as if he had been of Age, and done it Voluntarily himself, and shall be allowed to be as binding in all respects in Law as an Heir in Possession Cutting of an Heir Intail. If this is not so, then was the Settlement of the Crown upon King *William* and Queen *Mary* Unrighteous, and those Two Famous Princes must be recorded in History for Parricides and Usurpers; nor will it end there, for the Black Charge must reach our most Gracious Sovereign, who must be charg'd with the Horrible Crimes of Robbery and Usurpation; and not the Parliament or Convention of the Estates at the Revolution only shall be charged as Rebels and Traytors to their Sovereign, and Breakers of the great Command, of rendring to *Cæsar* the Things that are *Cæsar*'s, but even every Parliament since, especially those who have had any Hand in placing the Intail of the Crown upon the Person of the Queen, and in confirming her Majesty's Possession thereof since her Happy Accession; and every Act of Parliament settling the Succession on the House of *Hanover* must have likewise been Guilty of Treason and Rebellion in a most unnatural Manner. This is a Heavy Charge upon her Majesty, and very Inconsistent with the great Zeal and Affection with which all the People of *Britain* at this Time pay their Duty and Allegiance to her Majesty's Person, and acknowledge her Happy Government: This may indeed be thought hard, but it is evident nothing less can be the Case, and therefore those People who are so forward to plead the Pretender's Cause, on Account of his being King *James*'s Lawful Son, can do it upon no other Terms than these, (*viz.*) To declare that the Queen is herself an Illegal Governour, an Usurper of another's Right, and therefore ought to be Deposed: Or, that the Hereditary Right of Princes is no Indefeasible Thing, but is subjected to the Power of the Limitations by Parliament. Thus I think the great

Difficulty of the Pretender's being the Rightful Son of the late King *James* is over, and at an End; that it is no Part of the needful Enquiry relating to the Succession, since his Father involved him in the Fate of his Abdication, and many Ways rendered him incapable to Reign, and out of Condition to have any Claim; since the Power of limiting the Succession to the Crown is an Undoubted Right of the Parliaments of *England* and of *Scotland* respectively. Moreover, his being Educated a Papist in *France*, and continuing so, was a Just Reason why the People of *England* rejected him, and why they ought to reject him, since according to that Famous Vote of the Commons in the Convention Parliament, so often Printed, and so often on many Accounts Quoted, it is declared, *That it is Inconsistent with the Constitution of this Protestant Kingdom to be Govern'd by a Popish Prince.* Vid. *Votes of the Convention, Feb.* 2. 1688.[15] This Vote was carried up by Mr. *Hambden* to the House of Lords the same Day, as the Resolution of all the Commons of *England*. Now this Prince being Popish, not only so in his Infancy, but continuing so even now, when all the Acts of Parliament in *Britain* have been made to exclude him, his Turning Protestant now, which his Emissaries promise for him, tho' perhaps without his Consent, will not answer at all; for the Acts of Parliament, or some of them, having been past while he, tho' of Age, remained a Papist, and gave no Room to expect any other, his Turning Protestant cannot alter those Laws, suppose he should do so; nor is it reasonable that a Nation should alter an Established Succession to their Crown whenever he shall think fit to alter or change his Religion: If to engage the People of *Britain* to settle the Succession upon him, and receive him as Heir, he had thought fit to turn Protestant, why did he not declare himself ready to do so before the said Succession was settled by so many Laws, especially by that Irrevocable Law of the Union of the Two Kingdoms, and that Engagement of the Abjuration, of which no Human Power can absolve us, no Act of Parliament can repeal it, nor no Man break it without Wilful Perjury.

What then is the Signification to the People of *Britain* whether the Person called the Pretender be Legitimate, or no? The Son of King *James*, or the Son of a Cinder-woman? The Case is settled by the Queen, by the Legislative Authority, and we cannot go back from it; and those who go about as Emissaries to persuade the Commons of *Great-Britain* of the Pretender's having a Right, go about at the same Time trayterously to tell the Queen's good Subjects that her Majesty is not our Rightful Queen, but an Usurper.

AND

What if the 𝔓𝔯𝔢𝔱𝔢𝔫𝔡𝔢𝔯 should come?

OR, SOME

CONSIDERATIONS

OF THE

ADVANTAGES

AND

Real Consequences

OF THE

PRETENDER's

Possessing the

CROWN

OF

Great-Britain.

London: Printed, and Sold by *J. Baker*, at the *Black Boy* in *Pater-noster-row.* 1713 (Price 6*d*.)

AND WHAT IF THE PRETENDER SHOULD COME? OR, SOME CONSIDERATIONS, &c.

IF the Danger of the Pretender is really so great as the Noise which some make about it seems to suppose, if the Hopes of his Coming are so well grounded, as some of his Friends seem to boast, it behoves us who are to be the Subjects of the Approaching Revolution, which his Success must necessarily bring with it, to apply ourselves seriously to examine what our Part will be in the Play, that so we may prepare ourselves to act as becomes us, both with Respect to the Government we are now under, and with Respect to the Government we may be under, when the success he promises himself shall (if ever it shall) answer his Expectation.

In order to this it is necessary to state, with what Plainness the Circumstances of the Case will admit, the several Appearances of the Thing itself. (1.) *As they are* offered to us by the respective Parties who are for or against it. (2.) *As they* really appear by an Impartial Deduction from them both, without the least Byass either to one Side or other; that so the People of *Britain* may settle and compose their Thoughts a little in this Great, and at present Popular Debate, and may neither be terrified or affrighted with Mischiefs, which have no Reason or Foundation in them, and which give no Ground for their Apprehensions; and on the other Hand, may not promise to themselves greater Things from the Pretender, if he should come hither, than he will be able to perform for them; in order to this we are to consider the Pretender in his Person, and in his Circumstances. (1.) The Person who we call the Pretender: It has been so much debated, and such strong Parties have been made on both Sides to prove or disprove the Legitimacy of his Birth, that it seems needless here to enter into that Dispute; the Author of the *Review*, one of the most Furious Opposers of the Name and Interest of the

Pretender, openly grants his Legitimacy,[1] and pretends to argue against
his Admission from Principles and Foundations of his own Forming;
we shall let alone his Principles and Foundations here, as we do his
Arguments, and only take him by the Handle which he fairly gives us,
(*viz.*) that he grants *the Person of the Pretender Legitimate*; if this be so, if
the Person we contend about be the Lawful true Son of King *James*'s
Queen, the Dispute whether he be the Real Son of the King will be
quite out of the Question; because by the Laws of *Great-Britain*, and
of the whole World, a Child Born in Wedlock shall inherit, as Heir of
the Mother's Husband, whether Begotten by him, as his Real Father,
or not. Now to come at the true Design of this Work, the Business is,
to hear (as above) what either Side have to say to this Point. The Friends
of his Birth and Succession argue upon it thus, if the Person be lawfully
Begotten, *that is*, if Born really of the Body of the Queen *Dowager*,
during the Life of King *James*, he was without any Exception his Lawful
Son; if he was his Lawful Son, he was his Lawful Heir; if he was his
Lawful Heir, why is he not our Lawful King? *Since* Hereditary Right
is Indefeasible, and is lately acknowledged to be so; and that the Doctrine
of Hereditary Right being Indefeasible, is a Church of *England* Doctrine
ever received by the Church, and inseparable from the true Members
of the Church, the contrary being the stigmatizing character of Republicans, King-killers, Enemies to Monarchy, Presbyterians, and Phanaticks.
The Enemies of the Birth and Succession of the Person called the
Pretender argue upon it thus, *That* he is the Lawfully Begotten, or
Son Born really of the Body of the Queen *Dowager* of the late King
James, they doubt; and they are justified in doubting of it, because no
sufficient Steps were taken in the proper Season of it, *either before his
Birth*, to convince such Persons as were more immediately concerned
to know the Truth of it, that the Queen was really with Child, which
might have been done past all Contradiction at that Time, more than
ever after: *Or at his Birth*, to have such Persons as were more immediately concern'd, *such as Her Present Majesty*, &c. thoroughly convinc'd
of the Queen being really deliver'd of a Child, by being Present at
the Time of the Queen's Labour and Delivery. This being omitted,
which was the Affirmative, *say they*, which ought to have been proved,
we ought not to be concerned in the Proof of the Negative, which by
the Nature of the Thing could not be equally certain; and therefore we
might be justly permitted to conclude, that the Child was a Spurious,
Unfair Production, put upon the Nation; for which Reason we reject
him, and have now, by a Legal and Just Authority, deposed his Father

and him, and settled the Succession upon the House of *Hanover*, being Protestants.

The Matter of his Title standing thus, divides the Nation into Two Parties, one Side for, and the other against, the Succession, either of the Pretender, or the House of *Hanover*, and either Side calling the other the Pretender; so that if we were to use the Parties Language, we must say, one Side is for, and the other Side against, either of the *Pretenders*; what the Visible Probabilities of either of these Claims succeeding are, is not the Present Case; the Nation appears at this Time strangely agitated between the Fears of one Party, and the Hopes of the other, each extenuating and aggravating, as their several Parties and Affections guide them, by which the Publick Disorder is very much encreased; what either of them have to alledge is our present Work to enquire; but more particularly what are the real or pretended Advantages of the expected Reign of him, who we are allow'd to distinguish by the Name of the Pretender; for his Friends here would have very little to say to move us to receive him, if they were not able to lay before us such Prospects of National Advantages, and such Views of Prosperity, as would be sufficient to prevail with those who have their Eyes upon the Good of their Country, and of their Posterity after them.

That then a Case so Popular, and of so much Consequence as this is, may not want such due Supports as the Nature of the Thing will allow, and especially since the Advantages and good Consequences of the Thing itself are so many, and so easie to be seen as his Friends alledge; why should not the Good People of *Britain* be made easie, and their Fears be turned into Peaceable Satisfaction, by seeing that this Devil may not be so Black as he is Painted; and that the Noise made of the Pretender and the frightful Things said of his Coming, and of his being receiv'd here, may not be made greater Scarecrows to us, than they really are; and *after all that has been said*, it it should appear that the Advantages of the Pretender's Succession are really greater to us, and the Dangers less to us, than those of the Succession of *HANOVER*, then much of their Difficulties would be over, who standing Neuter as to Persons appear against the Pretender, only because they are made to believe strange and terrible Things of what shall befall the Nation in Case of his Coming in, *such as* Popery, Slavery, *French* Power, destroying of our Credit, and devouring our Funds, (as that Scandalous Scribler, the *Review*, has been labouring to suggest,) with many other Things which we shall endeavour to expose to you, as they deserve. If we say it should appear then that the Dangers and Disadvantages of the Pretender's Succession are less than those of the House of *HANOVER*, who, because of an Act of Parliament, you know must not be called *Pretenders*; then there will remain nothing more to be said on that Score, but the Debate must be of the Reasonableness and Justice on either Side, for their Admittance, and there we question not but the Side we are really pleading for will have the Advantage.

To begin then with that most Popular and Affrighting Argument now made Use of, as the Bugbear of the People, against several other Things besides Jacobitism, we mean 𝔉𝔯𝔢𝔫𝔠𝔥 𝔊𝔯𝔢𝔞𝔱𝔫𝔢𝔰𝔰: It is most evident that the Fear of this must, by the Nature of the Thing, be effectually removed upon our receiving *the Pretender*; the Grounds and Reasons why *French* Greatness is rendred Formidable to us, and so much Weight supposed to be in it, that like the Name of *Scanderberg*,[2] we fright our very Children with it, lye only in this, that we suggest the King of *France* being a profest Enemy to the Peace, and the Liberty of *Great-Britain*, will most certainly, as soon as he can a little recover himself, exercise all that Formidable Power to put the Pretender upon us, and not only to place him upon the Throne of *Great-Britain*, but to Maintain and Hold him up in it, against all the Opposition, either of the People of *Britain*, or the Confederate Princes Leagued with the Elector of *Hanover*, who are in the Interest of his Claim, or of his Party. Now it is evident, that upon a Peaceable admitting this Person, whom they call the Pretender, to Receive and Enjoy the Crown here, all that Formidable Power becomes your Friend, and *the being so* must necessarily take off from it every Thing that is called Terrible; forasmuch as the greater Terror and Amusement the Power we apprehend really carries with it, the greater is the Tranquility and Satisfaction which accrues to us, when we have the Friendship of that Power which was so Formidable to us before: The Power of *France* is represented at this Time very terrible, and the Writers who speak of it apply it warm to our Imaginations, as that from whence we ought justly to apprehend the Impossibility of keeping out the Pretender, and this, notwithstanding they allow themselves at the same Time to suppose all the Confederate Powers of *Europe* to be Engaged, as well by their own Interest, as by the New Treaties of Barrier and Guarantee,[3] to Support and to Assist the Claim of the Elector of *Hanover*, and his Party. Now if this Power be so Great, and so Formidable, as they alledge, will it not on the other Side add a Proportion of Encrease to our Satisfaction, that this Power will be wholly in Friendship and League with us; and engaged to concern itself for the quieting our Fears of other Foreign Invaders; forasmuch as having once concern'd itself to set the Person of the Pretender upon the Throne, it cannot be supposed but it shall be equally concern'd to Support and Maintain him in that Possession, as what will mightily conduce to the carrying on the other Projects of his Greatness and Glory with the rest of *Europe*; in which it will be very much his Interest to secure himself from any Opposition he might meet with from this Nation, or from such as might be rendred Powerful by our Assistance. An Eminent Instance we have of this in the Mighty Efforts the *French* Nation have made for Planting, and Preserving when Planted, a Grandson of *France* upon the Throne of *Spain*; and how Eminent are the Advantages to *France* from the Success of that Undertaking; of what less Consequence then would it be to the August Monarchy of *France*, to Secure and Engage to himself the constant Friendship and Assistance of the Power of *Great-Britain*, which he would necessarily do, by the placing this Person upon the Throne, who would thereby in Gratitude be engaged to contribute his utmost in Return to the King of *France*, for the carrying on his Glorious Designs in the rest of *Europe*. While then we become thus necessary to the King of *France*, Reason dictates that he would be our Fast Friend, our Constant Confederate, our Allie, firmly engaged to Secure our Sovereign, and Protect our People from the Insults and Attempts of all the World: Being thus engaged reciprocally with the King of *France*, there must necessarily be an End of all the Fears and Jealousies, of all the Apprehensions and Doubts, which now so Amuse us, and appear so Formidable to us from the Prospect of the Power and Greatness of *France*; then we shall on the contrary say to the World, the stronger the King of *France* is, the better for the King of *England*; and what is best for the King, must be so for his People; for it is a most unnatural Way of Arguing, to suppose the Interest of a King, and of his People, to be different from one another.

And is not this then an Advantage incomparably greater to *Britain*, when the Pretender shall be upon the Throne, than any we can propose to ourselves in the present uneasie Posture of Affairs, which it must be acknowledged we are in now, when we cannot sleep in Quiet, for the terrible Apprehensions of being over-run by the Formidable Power of *France*.

Let us also consider the many other Advantages which may accrue to this Nation, by a nearer Conjunction, and closer Union, with *France*, such as Encrease of Commerce, Encouragement of Manufactures, Ballance of Trade; every one knows how vast an Advantage we reaped by the *French* Trade in Former Times, and how many Hundred Thousand Pounds a Year we gain'd by it, when the Ballance of Trade between us and *France* run so many Millions of *Livres* Annually against the *French* by the vast Exportation of our Goods to them, and the small Import which we receiv'd from them again, and by the Constant Flux of Money in *Specie*, which we drew from them every Year, upon Court Occasions, to the inexpressible Benefit of the Nation, and Enriching of the Subject, of which we shall have Occasion to speak hereafter more fully.

In the mean Time it were to be wished that our People, who are so bugbear'd with Words, and terrified with the Name of *French*, *French Power*, *French Greatness*, and the like, as if *England* could not Subsist, and the Queen of *England* was not Able to keep upon Her Throne any longer than the King of *France* pleased, and that Her Majesty was going to be a meer Servant to the *French* King, would consider that this is an unanswerable Argument for the Coming of the Pretender, that we may make this so Formidable Prince our Friend, have all his Power engaged in our Interest, and see him going on Hand in Hand with us, in the securing us against all Sorts of Encroachments whatsoever: For if the King of *France* be such an Invincible Mighty Monarch, that we are nothing in his Eyes, or in his Hands; and that neither *Britain*, or all the Friends *Britain* can make, are able to deliver us from him; then it must be our great Advantage to have the Pretender be our King, that we may be out of the Danger of this Formidable *French* Power being our Enemy; and that on the other Hand, we may have so Potent, so Powerful, so Invincible, a Prince be our Friend. The Case is evidently laid down to every common Understanding, in the Example of *Spain*; *till now*, the *Spaniards* for many Ages have been over-run, and impoverished, by their continued Wars with the *French*, and it was not doubted but one Time or other they would have been entirely conquered by the King of *France*, and have become a meer Province of *France*; whereas now, having but consented to receive a King from the Hands of the invincible Monarch, they are made easie as to the former Danger they were always in, are now most safe under the Protection of *France*; and he who before was their Terror, is now their Safety, and being safe from him, it appears they are so from all the World.

Would it not then be the manifest Advantage of this Nation to be likewise secur'd from the dangerous Power of *France*, and make that Potentate our fast Friend, who it is so apparent we are not able to resist as an Enemy? This is reducing the *French* Power the softest Way, if not the best and shortest Way; for if it does not reduce the Power itself, it brings it into such a Circumstance, as that all the Terror of it is removed, and we embrace that as our Safety and Satisfaction, which really is, and ought to be, our Terror and Aversion; this must of Necessity be our great Advantage.

How strange is it that none of our People have yet thought of this Way of securing their Native Country from the Insults of *France?* Were but the Pretender once received as our King, we have no more Disputes with the King of *France*, he has no Pretence to Invade or Disturb us; what a quiet World would it be with us in such a Case, when the greatest Monarch in the Universe should be our fast Friend, and be in our Interest to prevent any of the Inconveniences which might happen to us from the Disgust of other Neighbours, who may be dissatisfied with us upon other Accounts. As to the terrible Things which some People fright us, and themselves with, from the Influence which *French* Councils may have upon us, and of *French* Methods of Government being introduced among us; these we ought to esteem only Clamours and Noise, raised by a Party to amuse and affright us; for pray let us enquire a little into them, and see if there be any Reason for us to be so terrified at them; suppose they were really what is alledged, which we hope they are not; *for Example*, the absolute Dominion of the King of *France* over his Subjects, is such, say our People, as makes them Miserable; well, but let us examine then, are we not already miserable for Want of this Absolute Dominion? Are we not miserably divided? Is not our Government miserably weak? Are we not miserably subjected to the Rabbles and Mob? Nay, is not the very Crown mobb'd here every now and then, into whatever our Soveraign Lord the People demand? whereas on the contrary, we see *France* entirely united as one Man; no virulent Scriblers there dare Affront the Government; no Impertinent P—ments there disturb the Monarch with their Addresses and Representations; no Superiority of Laws restrain the Administration; no Insolent Lawyers talk of the Sacred Constitution, in Opposition to the more Sacred Prerogative; but all with Harmony and General Consent agree to Support the Majesty of their Prince, and with their Lives and Fortunes (not in Complimenting Sham Addresses only, but in Reality, and effectually) Support the Glory of their Great Monarch. In doing this they are all united together so firmly, as if they had but one Heart, and one Mind, and that the King was the Soul of the Nation: What if they are *what we foolishly call* Slaves to the Absolute Will of their Prince? That Slavery to them is meer Liberty; they entertain no Notions of that foolish Thing 𝕷𝖎𝖇𝖊𝖗𝖙𝖞, which we make so much Noise about; nor have they any Occasion of it, or any Use for it if they had it; they are as Industrious in Trade, as Vigorous in Pursuit of their Affairs, go on with as much Courage, and are as well

satisfied when they have wrought hard 20 or 30 Years to get a little
Money for the King to take away, as we are to get it for our Wives and
Children; and as they plant Vines, and plow Lands, that the King and
his Great Men may eat the Fruit thereof, they think it as great a Felicity
as if they Eat it themselves. The Badge of their Poverty, which we make
such a Noise of, and Insult them about so much, (*viz.*) their Wooden
Shoes, their Peasants make nothing of it; they say they are as happy in
their Wooden Shoes, as our People are with their Luxury and Drunken-
ness; besides, do not our Poor People wear Iron Shoes, and Leather
Doublets, and where is the Odds between them? All the Business forsooth
is this Trifle we call Liberty, which rather than be plagued with so much
Strife and Dissention about it as we are, who would be troubled with?
Now it is evident the Peace and *Union* which we should enjoy under
the like Methods of Government here, which we hope for under the
Happy Government of the Pretender, must needs be a full Equivalent
for all the pretended Rights and Priviledges which we say we shall loose;
and how will our Rights and Privileges be lost? Will they not rather be
Centred in our Common Receptacle, (*viz.*) the Sovereign, who is
according to the King of *France*'s happy Government the Common
Magazine of Universal Privilege, communicating to it, and preserving it
for, the general Use of his Subjects, as their Safety and Happiness requires.
Thus he protects their Commerce, encourages their Foreign Settlements,
enlarges their Possessions Abroad, encreases their Manufactures, gives
them Room for spreading their numerous Race over the World; at Home
he rewards Arts and Sciences, cultivates Learning, employs innumerable
Hands in the Labours of the State, and the like; what if it be true that
all they Gain is at his Mercy? Does he take it away, except when needful,
for the Support of his Glory and Grandeur, which is their Protection?
Is it not apparent, that under all the Oppressions they talk so much of,
the *French* are the Nation the most Improved and Encreased in
Manufactures, in Navigation, in Commerce, within these 50 Years, of
any Nation in the World? And here we pretend Liberty, Property,
Constitutions, Rights of Subjects, and such Stuff as that, and with all
these fine Gewgaws, which we pretend propagate Trade, and encrease
the Wealth of the Nation, we are every Day Declining, and become
Poor; how long will this Nation be blinded by their own foolish Customs?
And when will they learn to know, that the Absolute Government of a
Vertuous Prince, who makes the Good of his People his Ultimate End,
and esteems their Prosperity his Glory, is the Best, and most Godlike,
Government in the World.

Let us then be no more rendred uneasie with the Notions, that with the Pretender we must entertain *French* Methods of Government, such as Tyranny and Arbitrary Power; Tyranny is no more Tyranny, when improv'd for the Subjects Advantage; perhaps when we have tried it we may find it as much for our Good many Ways, nay, and more too, than our present Exorbitant Liberties, especially unless we can make a better Use of them, and Enjoy them, without being always going by the Ears about them, as we see daily, not only with our Governours, but even with one another; a little *French Slavery*, though it be a frightful Word among us, *that is*, being made so by Custom, yet may do us a great deal of Good in the Main, as it may teach us not to *Over* (Under) *Value* our Liberties, when we have them, so much as sometimes we have done; and this is not one of the least Advantages which we shall gain by the Coming of the Pretender, and consequently one of the good Reasons why we should be very willing to receive him.

The next Thing which they fill us with Apprehensions of in the Coming of the Pretender, is the Influence of *French* Councils, which they Construe thus, (*viz.*) That the Pretender being restor'd here by the Assistance of *France*, will not only Rule us by *French* Methods, (*viz.*) by *French* Tyranny, but in Gratitude to his Restorer he will cause us to be always ready with *English* Blood and Treasure to Assist and Support the *French* Ambition in the Invasions he will ever be making upon *Europe*, and in the Oppressions of other Nations; till at last he obtain the Superiority over them all, and turn upon us too, devouring the Liberties of *Europe* in his so long purposed and resolved *Universal Monarchy.* As to the Gratitude of the Pretender to the King of *France*, why should you make that a Crime? Are not all People bound in Honour to retaliate Kindness? And would you have your Prince be ungrateful to him that brought him hither? By the same Rule you would expect he could be ungrateful to us that receive him; besides, if it be so great an Advantage to us to have him brought in, we shall be all concern'd also in Gratitude to the King of *France* for helping us to him; and sure we shall not decline making a suitable Return to him for the Kindness; and is this any Thing more than common? Did we not pay the *Dutch* Six Hundred Thousand Pound *Sterling* for assisting the Late King *William*? And did we not immediately Embark with them in the War against the King of *France*? And has not that Revolution cost the Nation One Hundred Millions of *British* Money to Support it? And shall we grutch to Support the Pretender, and his Benefactor, at the same Expence, if it should be needful, for carrying on the New Scheme of *French* Liberty, which when that Time comes may be in a likely and forward Way to prevail over the whole World, to the General Happiness of *Europe?*

There seems to be but one Thing more which those People, who make such a Clamour at the Fears of the Pretender, take hold of, and this is Religion; and they tell us, that not only *French* Government, and *French* Influence, but *French* Religion, that is to say, 𝔓𝔬𝔭𝔢𝔯𝔶, will come upon us; but these People know not what they talk of, for it is evident that they shall be so far from being loaden with Religion, that they will rather obtain that so long desired Happiness, of having no Religion at all. This we may easily make appear has been the Advantage which has been long labour'd for in this Nation; and as the Attainments we are arriv'd to of that Kind are very considerable already, so we cannot doubt but that if once the Pretender were settled quietly among us, an Absolute Subjection, as well of Religious Principles, as Civil Liberties, to the Disposal of the Sovereign, would take Place. This is an Advantage so fruitful of several other manifest Improvements, that though we have not Room in this Place to enlarge upon the Particulars, we cannot doubt but it must be a most grateful Piece of News to a great Part of the Nation, who have long groan'd under the Oppressions and cruel Severities of the Clergy, occasion'd by their own strict Lives, and rigorous Virtue, and their imposing such Austerities and Restraints upon the People; and in this Particular the Clamour of Slavery will appear very scandalous in the Nation, for the Slavery of Religion being taken off, and an Universal Freedom of Vice being introduced, what greater Liberty can we enjoy.

But we have yet greater Advantages attending this Nation by the Coming of the Pretender than any we have yet taken Notice of; and though we have not Room in this short Tract to name them all, and enlarge upon them as the Case may require, yet we cannot omit such due Notice of them, as may serve to satisfie our Readers, and convince them, how much they ought to favour the Coming of the Pretender, as the great Benefit to the whole Nation; and therefore we shall begin with our Brethren of *Scotland*; and here we may tell them, that they, of all the Parts of this Island, shall receive the most evident Advantages, in that the setting the Pretender upon the Throne shall effectually set them free from the Bondage they now groan under, in their abhorr'd Subjection to *England* by the 𝔘nion, *which* may, no question, be declar'd Void, and Dissolv'd, as a Violence upon the *Scottish* Nation, as soon as ever the Pretender shall be Established upon the Throne; a few Words may serve to recommend this to the *Scots*, since we are very well satisfied we shall be sure to oblige every Side there, by it: The Opposition all Sides made to the Union at the Time of the Transaction of the Union in the Parliament there, cannot but give us Reason to think thus; and the present Scruple, even the Presbyterians themselves make, of taking the Abjuration,[4] if they do not, as some pretend, assure us that the said Presbyterian Nonjurers are in the Interest of the Pretender, yet they undeniably prove, and put it out of all question, that they are ill-pleased with the Yoke of the Union, and would embrace every just Occasion of being quietly and freely discharged from the Fetters which they believe they bear by the said Union. Now there is no Doubt to be made, but that upon the very first Appearance of the Pretender, the Antient Kingdom of *Scotland* should recover her former well-known Condition, we mean, of being perfectly free, and depending upon none but the King of *France*. How Inestimable an Advantage this will be to *Scotland* and how effectually he will Support and Defend the *Scots* against their Antient Enemies, the *English*, forasmuch as we have not Room to enlarge upon here, we may take Occasion to make out more particularly on another Occasion. But it may not be forgotten here, that the Union was not only justly Distasteful to the *Scots* themselves, but also to many Good Men, and Noble Patriots of the Church, some of whom entred their Protests against Passing and Confirming, or Ratifying the same, such as the late Lord *Hav—sham*, and the Right Wise, and Right Noble, E— of *Nott—*, whose Reasons for being against the said *Union, besides those they gave in the House of P—s,[5] which we do by no Means mean or reflect upon in the least in this Place*; we say, whose other Reasons for opposing the said Union were founded upon an Implacable Hatred to the *Scots* Kirk, which has been Established thereby. It may then not admit of any Question, but that they would think it a very great Advantage to be delivered from the same, as they would effectually be by the Coming of the Pretender; wherefore by the concurring Judgment of these Noble and Wise Persons who on that Account opposed the *Union*, the Coming of the Pretender must be an Inexpressible Advantage to this Nation; nor is the dissolving the Union so desirable a Thing, meerly as that Union was an Establishing among us a Wicked Schismatical Presbyterian Generation, and giving the Sanction of the Laws to their Odious Constitution, which we Esteem (you know) worse than Popery; but even on Civil Accounts, as particularly on Account of the P—s of *Scotland*, who many of them think themselves Egregiously maltreated, and robb'd of their Birthright,[6] as P—s, and have express'd themselves so in a something Publick Manner. Now we cannot think that any of these will be at all offended that all this New Establishment should be revoked; nay, we have heard it openly said, that the *Scots* are so little satisfied with the *Union* at this Time, that if it were now to be put to the Vote, as it was before, whether they should Unite with *England*, or no, there would not be one Man in Fifteen, throughout *Scotland*, that would Vote for it. *If then* it appears that the whole Nation thus seems to be averse to the Union, and by the Coming in of this most Glorious Pretender that Union will be in all Appearance dissolved, and the Nation freed from the Encumbrance of it, will any *Scots* Man, who is against the Union, refuse to be for the Pretender? Sure it cannot be. I know it is alledged, that they will lay aside their Discontent at the Union, and Unite together against the Pretender, because that is to Unite against Popery; we will not say what a few, who have their Eyes in their Heads, may do; but as the Generality of the People there are so well reconciled together, as such a Thing requires, it is not unlikely that such a Uniting may be prevented, if the Pretender's Friends there can but play the Game of dividing them farther, as they should do; to which End it cannot but be very serviceable to them to have the real Advantages of receiving the Pretender laid before them, which is the true Intent and Meaning of the Present Undertaking.

But we have more and greater Advantages of the Coming of the Pretender, and such as no question will invite you to receive him with great Satisfaction and Applause; and it cannot be unnecessary to inform you, for your Direction in other Cases, how the Matter, as to Real and Imaginary Advantage, stands with the Nation in this Affair; and *First*, The Coming of the Pretender will at once put us all out of Debt. These Abomination-Whigs, and these Bloody Wars, carried on so long for little or nothing, *have*, as is evident to our Senses *now*, (whatever it was all along,) brought a heavy Debt upon the Nation; so that if what a known Author lately Published is true, the Government pays now almost Six Millions a Year to the Common People for Interest of Money; that is to say, the Usurers Eat up the Nation, and Devour Six Millions Yearly; which is paid, and must be paid now for a long Time, if some *kind Turn*, such as this of the Coming of the Pretender, or such like, does not help us out of it; the Weight of this is not only Great, insuperably Great, but most of it is entailed for a terrible Time, not only for our Age, but beyond the Age of our Grand-children, even for Ninety-nine Years. By how much the Consideration of this Debt is Intolerable and Afflicting to the last Degree, by so much the greater must the Obligation be to the Person, who will Ease the Nation of such a Burthen, and therefore we place it among the Principal Advantages which we are to receive from the Admission of the Pretender, that he will not fail to rid us of this

Grievance, and by Methods peculiar to himself, deliver us from so great a Burthen as these Debts are now, and, unless he deliver us, are like to be to the Ages to come: Whether he will do this at once, by remitting most Graciously to the Nation the whole Payment, and consequently take off the Burthen, *Brevi Manu*, as with a Spunge wiping out the Infamous Score, leaving it to fall as Fate directs, or by prudent Degrees, we know not, nor is it our Business to determine it here; no Doubt the doing it with a Jerk, as we call it, *Comme une Coup de Grace*, must be the most expeditious Way; nay, and the kindest Way of putting the Nation out of its Pain; for lingering Deaths are counted cruel; and tho' *Une coup d'Eclat*[7] may make an Impression for the Present, yet the Astonishment is soonest over; besides, where is the Loss to the Nation in this Sense? Tho' the Money be stopt from the Subject on one Hand, if it be stopt to the Subjects on the other, the Nation Loses or Gains Nothing; we know it will be Answer'd, that it is unjust, and that Thousands of Families will be ruin'd, because they who Loose, will not be those who Gain. But what is this to the Purpose in a National Revolution; unjust! Alas! Is that an Argument? Go and ask the Pretender! Does not he say you have all done unjustly by him? And since the Nation in general loses Nothing, what Obligation has he to regard the particular Injury that some Families may sustain? And yet farther, is it not remarkable, that most Part of the Money[8] is paid by the Cursed Party of Whigs, who from the Beginning officiously appear'd to keep him from his Right? And what Obligation has he upon him to concern himself for doing them Right in Particular, more than other People? But to avoid the Scandal of Partiality, there is another Thought offers to our View, which the Nation is beholding to a Particular Author for putting us in Mind of; if it be unjust that we should suppose the Pretender shall stop the Payment on both Sides;[9] because it is doing the Whigs Wrong, since the Tories, who perhaps being chiefly Landed Men, pay the most Taxes; then, to keep up a just Ballance, he need only continue the Taxes to be paid in, and only stop the Annuities and Interest which are to be paid out. Thus both Sides having no Reason to Envy or Reproach one another with Hardships, or with suffering Unequally; they may every one lose their Proportion, and the Money may be laid up in the Hands of the New Sovereign, for the Good of the Nation.

This being thus happily proposed, we cannot pass over the great Advantages which would accrue to this Nation in such a Case, by having such a Mass of Money laid up in the *Exchequer* at the Absolute Command of a most Gracious *French* Sovereign. But as these Things are so Glorious, and so Great, as to admit of no compleat Explication in this short Tract, give us Leave, *O People* of *Great-Britain*, to lay before you a little Scetch of your future Felicity, under the Auspicious Reign of such a Glorious Prince, as we all hope, and believe, the Pretender to be. You are to allow, that by such a Just and Righteous shutting up of the *Exchequer* in about Seven Years Time, he may be supposed to have received about Forty Millions Sterling from his People, which not being to be found in *Specie* in the Kingdom, will, for the Benefit of Circulation, enable him to Treasure up Infinite Funds of Wealth in Foreign Banks, a prodigious Mass of Foreign Bullion, Gold, Jewels, and Plate, to be ready in the *Tower*, or elsewhere, to be issued upon Future Emergency, as Occasion may allow. This prodigious Wealth will necessarily have these happy Events, to the Infinite Satisfaction and Advantage of the whole Nation, and the Benefit of which I hope none will be so Unjust, or Ungrateful, to deny. It will for ever after deliver this Nation from the Burthen, the Expence, the Formality, and the Tyranny, of Parliaments. No one can perhaps at the first View be rightly sensible of the many Advantages of this Article, and from how many Mischiefs it will deliver this Nation. (1.) How the Countrey Gentlemen will be no longer harrass'd to come, at the Command of every Court Occasion, and upon every Summons by the Prince's Proclamation, from their Families, and other Occasions, whether they can be spared from their Wives, *&c.* or no, or whether they can trust their Wives behind them, or no; nay, whether they can spare Money or no for the Journey, or whether they must come *Carriage Paid* or no; *then* they will no more be unnecessarily exposed to Long and Hazardous Journeys, in the Depth of Winter, from the remotest Corners of the Island, to come to *London*, just to give away the Countrey's Money, and go Home again; all this will be dispenced with by the Kind and Gracious Management of the Pretender, when he, *God bless us*, shall be our more Gracious Sovereign. (2.) In the happy Consequence of the Demise of Parliaments, the Countrey will be eased of that intolerable Burthen of Travelling to Elections, sometimes in the Depth of Winter, sometimes in the Middle of their Harvest, whenever the Writs of Elections Arbitrarily Summons them. (3.) And with them the Poor Gentlemen will be eased of that abominable Grievance of the Nation, (*viz.*) the Expence of Elections, by which so many Gentlemen of Estates have been Ruin'd, so many innocent People, of honest Principles before, have been Debauched, and made Mercenary, Partial, Perjur'd, and been Blinded with Bribes, to Sell their Countrey and Liberties to who bids most. It is well known how often, and yet how in vain, this Distemper has been the constant Concern of Parliaments, for many Ages, to Cure, and to provide sufficient Remedies for. Now if ever the effectual Remedy for this is found out, to the inexpressible Advantage of the whole Nation; and this perhaps is the only Cure for it that the Nature of the Disease will admit of; what terrible Havock has this kind of Trade made among the Estates of the Gentry, and the Morals of the Common People? (4.) How also has it kept alive the Factions and Divisions of the Countrey People, keeping them in a Constant Agitation, and in Triennial Commotions? So that what with Forming New Interests, and Cultivating Old, the Heats and Animosities never cease among the People. But once set the Pretender upon the Throne, and let the Funds be but happily stopt, and paid into his Hands, that he may be in no more Need of a Parliament, and all these Distempers will be cur'd as effectually as a Feaver is cur'd by cutting off the Head, or as a Halter cures the Bleeding at the Nose. How Infatuated then is this Nation, that they should so obstinately refuse a Prince, by the Nature of whose Circumstances, and the avowed Principles of whose Party, we are sure to obtain such Glorious Things, such Inestimable Advantages, Things which no Age, no Prince, no Attempt of Parties, or Endeavour, though often aim'd at of Ministers of State, have ever been able to procure for us. This Amassing of Treasure, by the stopping the Funds on one Hand, and the receiving the Taxes on the other, will effectually enable the Pretender to set up, and effectually maintain, that Glorious, and so often-desir'd, Method of Government, *Au Coup de Cannon, Anglice,* a Standing Army. This we have the Authority of the Antient Borough of *Carlisle,*[10] that it is the Safety of the Prince, and the Glory of the Nation, as appears by their Renowned Address to King *James* II. Then we should see a new Face of our Nation, and *Britain* would no more be a naked Nation, as it has formerly been; then we should have Numerous and Gallant Armies surrounding a Martial Prince, ready to make the World, as well as his own Subjects, tremble; then our Inland Counties would appear full of Royal Fortifications, Citadels, Forts, and Strong Towns; the Beauty of the Kingdom, and Awe of Factious Rebels. It is a strange Thing that this Refractory People of ours could never be made sensible how much it is for the Glory and Safety of this Nation that we should be put into a Posture of Defence *against ourselves*: It has been often alledged, that *this Nation can never be ruin'd but with their own Consent*: If then we are our own Enemies, is it not highly requisite that we should be put in a Condition to have our Ruin prevented? And that since it is apparent we are no more fit to be trusted with our own Liberties, having a Natural and a National Propensity to destroy and undo ourselves, and may be brought to Consent to our own Ruin, we should have such Princes as for the future know how to restrain us, and how reasonable is it to allow them Forces *to do so*?

We might enlarge here upon the Great and Certain Advantages of this best of Governments, *a Standing Army*; we might go back to the *Persian*, *Grecian*, and *Roman* Empires, which had never arriv'd to such a Pitch of Glory if the People and Nations who they subdued had been able to Nose them[11] with such Trifles as what we call Constitution, National Right, Antient Privileges, *and the like*; we might descend also to particular Advantages of Government, which it is hoped we may attain to in *Britain* when the Pretender arrives, some of which are grown Obsolete, and out of Use, by Custom, and long Possession of those troublesome Things call'd Liberties; among these may be reckoned,

(1.) The whole Kingdom will be at once eased of that ridiculous Feather-caps Expence of Militia and Train'd-bands, which serve for little else but to justifie the Picking the Peoples Pockets, with an Annual Tax of Trophy-Money, and every now and then putting the City of *London*, and parts Adjacent, to Ten Thousand Pound Charge, to beat Drums, and shoot Muskets, for nothing; when on the contrary, you shall in the Blessed Revolution we now invite you to have all this done *Gratis*, by the Standing Troops kept constantly in Pay; and your Lieutenancy may lay down their Commissions among the rest of *Non-Significants* of the Nation.

(2.) You shall be for ever out of Danger of being ridden again by the Mob; your Meeting-houses shall no more be the Subject of the enraged Rabbles; nor shall the *Bank of England* desire the Drums to beat at Midnight to raise a Guard for *Grocer's-Hall*; your new Monarch will suffer none to Insult or Plunder the City *but himself*; and as the City itself shall never want Soldiers, *how should it, when the whole Kingdom shall become a Garrison?* The Money in the *Bank* shall always be defended by a strong Guard, who shall, whenever there is any Danger of its being too safe, convey it, for its Eminent Security, from *Grocer's-Alley* to the *Tower*, or to the *Exchequer*, where it shall not fail to be kept for the Advantage of the Publick.

(3.) Again, upon this happy Change we shall immediately be delivered from that most infamous Practice of Stock-jobbing, of which so much has been said to so little Purpose; for the Funds being turned all into One General Stock, and the Prince being himself your Security, you may even write upon all your Companies this General Phrase, (*viz.*) *No*

Transfer, as they do when the Books are shut up at the *Bank*, or *East-India* House; so as all the Rivers of Water are swallowed up in the Sea, as One Ocean, to which they are all tending, so all these petty Cheats will be Ingulph'd at once in the General Ocean of State Trick, and the *Exchange-Alley-Men* may justly be said to Buy the *Bear-Skin* ever after.

(4.) Then (which is a Blessing we fear we cannot hope for before) we may expect to be deliver'd from the Throng of Virulent and Contumatious Libels which now Infest our Streets; and the Libellers themselves being most exemplarily Punished, for a Terror to the rest, will not dare to affront the Government with Ballads and Balderdash; if an impudent Fellow dares lift up his Pen against the Authority and Power of his Prince, he shall instantly feel the Weight of that Power to crush him, which he ought before to have feared; and Pamphleteers shall then not be Whipped and Pillor'd, but Hang'd; and when Two or Three of them have suffered that Way, it is hoped those wholesome Severities may put an effectual stop to the Noise and Clamour they now make in the Nation; above all, the Hands of the Government will then be set free from the Fetters of Law; and it shall not be always necessary for the Ministers of State to proceed by all the Forms of the Courts of Justice, in such Cases, by which the Scriblers of the Age pretend to stand it out against the Government, and put their own Construction upon their Libels. But when these happy Days arrive, Juries and Judges shall find and determine in these, and all other Cases, bring Verdicts, and give Sentence, as the Prince in his Royal Justice shall direct.

We might enter here upon a long List of other happy Circumstances we shall all arrive to, and of great Advantages not here named, which the Coming in of the Pretender shall infallibly bring us to the Enjoyment of, particularly in Matters of Religion, Civil Right, Property and Commerce, but the needful Brevity of this Tract will not admit of it; we shall only add one Thing more, which gives Weight to all the rest, (*viz.*) That the Certainty of these Things, and of their being the Natural Consequences of the bringing in the Pretender, adds to the certain Felicity of that Reign. This Sums up the Happiness of the Pretender's Reign; we need not talk of Security,[12] as the *Review* has done, and pretend he is not able to give us Security for the Performance of any Thing he promises; every Man that has any Sense of the Principles, Honour, and Justice of the Pretender, his Zeal for the *Roman* Catholick Cause, his Gratitude to his Benefactor, the *French* King, and his Love to the Glory and Happiness of his Native Countrey, must rest satisfied of his punctually performing all these Great Things for us; to ask him Security, would be not to Affront him only, but to Affront the whole Nation; *No Man can doubt him*; the Nature of the Thing allows that he must do us all that Kindness; he cannot be true to his own Reason without it; wherefore this Treaty *executes itself*, and appears so rational to believe, that whoever doubts it may be supposed to doubt even the Veracity of *James* the Just.

What unaccountable Folly then must those People be Guilty of, who stand so much in the Way of their own and their Countrey's Happiness, as to oppose, or pretend to argue against, the receiving this Glorious Prince, and would be for having *Dutch* Men and Foreigners forsooth to come, and all under the Notion of their being *PROTESTANTS*? To avoid and detect which Fallacy, we shall in our next Essay enter into the Examination of the Religion and Orthodox Principles of the Person of the Pretender, and doubt not to make it out, for the Satisfaction of all Tender Consciences, that he is a true Protestant of the Church of *England*, Establish'd by Law, and that in very Natural Primitive Sense of that Phrase as it was used by His Royal Predecessor, of Famous and Pious Memory, *Charles* II. – and as such, no doubt, he will endeavour for the Recovery of the Crown, which Crown, if he obtains it, you see what Glorious Things he may do for himself, and us.

Quam si Non Tenuit Magnis Tamen Excidit Ansis.[13]

AN

ANSWER

TO A

QUESTION

That No Body thinks of,

VIZ.

But what if the QUEEN should die?

––––––––––––––––

LONDON:
Printed for *J. BAKER*, at the
Black Boy in *Pater-noster-Row.* 1713.
Price Six Pence.

AN ANSWER TO
A QUESTION, &c.

THAT we are to have a Peace, or, That the Peace is made, What sort of Peace, or How it has been brought about; these are Questions the World begins to have done with, have been so much, so often, and to so little purpose banded about, and toss'd like a Shuttlecock, from one Party to another; the Parties themselves begin to want Breath to rail and throw Scandal. *Roper and Ridpath*,[1] like two *Tom T—men*,[2] have thrown Night-Dirt at one another so long, and grop'd into so many Jakes's up to their Elbows to find it, that they stink now in the Nostrils of their own Party. They are become perfectly nauseous to read; the Nation is surfeited of them, and the People begin to be tired with ill using one another. Would any tolerable Face appear upon things, we might expect the People would be inclined to be easie; and were the Eyes of some Great Men open, they may see this was the Opportunity they never had before, to make the Nation easie, and themselves safe. The main thing which agitates the Minds of Men now, is the Protestant Succession and the Pretender. Much Pains have been taken on both sides to amuse the World about this remaining Dispute; one side to make us believe it is safe, and the other to convince us it is in Danger. Neither side hath been able to expatiate upon the Part they affirm. Those who say, the Protestant Succession is secure, have not yet shewn us any Step taken since these New Transactions, for its particular Security. Those who say it is in danger, have not so clearly determined even among themselves, from what particular Head of Publick Management that Danger chiefly proceeds. Both these Uncertainties serve to perplex us, and to leave the thing more undetermined than consists with the publick Ease of the Peoples Minds. To contribute something to that Ease, and bring those whose Place it is, to consider of Ways to make the People easie in this Case, this Work is made Publick. Possibly the Question propounded may not meet with a Categorical Answer. But this is certain, it shall shew you more Directly what is the chief Question which the substance of Things before us is like to turn upon; and to which all our Questions seem to Tend. Were the great Difficulty of the Succession brought to a narrow Compass, tho' we might spend fewer Words about it, we should sooner come to a direct Answer. Before I come to the Great and chief Question upon which this Affair so much seems to Turn, it seems needful to put the previous Question upon which so much Debate has been among us, and let that be Examined. This previous Question is this: Is there any real Danger of the Protestant Succession? Is there any Danger that the Pretender shall be brought in upon us? Is there any Danger of Popery, and Tyranny by Restoring the Son, *as they call him*, of Abdicated King *James*? This is the previous Question, as we may now call it. It is well known that there are some People among us, who are so far from allowing that there is any such Danger, as the said Question mentions, that they will have it be a Token of Disaffection to the Government to put the Question; and are for loading whoever shall offer to Start such a Question, with Characters, and Party-Marks odious to good Men; such as Incendiary, Promoter of Discontents, Raiser of Faction, Divider of the People, and the like: Names which the Writer of these Sheets, at the same time, both contemns and abhors. He cannot see that he is any Enemy to the Queen, in Inquiring as diligently as possible, whether there are any Attempts to Depose Her, or dangerous Prospects of bringing in the hated Rival of Her Glory and Dominion. It is so far from that, that it is apparently the Duty of every true Subject of Her Majesty, to Inquire seriously, whether the publick Peace, the Queen's Safety, Her Throne, or Her Person is in any Danger from the wicked Design of Her, and Her People's Enemies. Wherefore, and for the joint Concern every Protestant *Britain* has in this thing, I shall make no Difficulty, plainly and seriously to State, and to Answer this previous Question, (*viz.*) Whether there is any Danger of the Protestant Succession, from the present Measures, and from the present People concern'd? I am not ignorant of what has been said by some, to prove that the present Ministry cannot be suspected of having any View to the Pretender in any of their Measures. The best Reason which I have seen given upon that Subject, is, that it is not their Interest; and that as we have not found them Fools that are blind to their own Interest; that either do not understand, or pursue it. This we find handled sundry ways, by sundry Authors, and very much Insisted upon as a Foundation for us to build upon. We shall give our Thoughts upon it with plainness, and without Fear, or Favour. Good Manners requires we should speak of the

Ministry with all due regard to their Character and Persons. This is a Tract, design'd to Inquire seriously of a Weighty and Essential, not a trifling Thing, which requires but a trifling Examination; nor shall it be handled here with Satyr and Scurrility. We Approve neither of the Flatteries of one side, or the Insultings of the other. We shall readily and most willingly Joyn with those who are of Opinion, that it is not the Interest of the Ministry to be for the Pretender; and that the Ministry are not blind to, or careless of their own Interest; and Consequently, that the Ministry cannot be for the Pretender. This I hope may be called a direct Answer. When I say, *Cannot*, I must not be understood potentially, that they have no Moral Capacity; But they cannot without such Inconsistencies, Contradictions and Improbable things happening in, which render it highly Irrational, so much as to suppose it of them. To shut the Door against any possibility of Cavil, It may be needful also to take it with us as we go, what we mean by the Words *be for* the Pretender; and this can be no otherwise understood, than to have a Design however remote, and upon whatever Views to bring him in to possess the Throne of these Kingdoms. The matter then being laid down thus, as sincerely and plainly as possible; we come to the Question point-blank, and think it our Duty to say with the greatest Sincerity, that we do not believe the Ministry are in any Kind, or with any Prospect near, or remote, Acting for, or with a Design or View to bring in the Pretender. Having granted this, we must however, to prevent any Breaking in by way of Cavil on one Hand, or Triumph on the other; subjoyn immediately, that we do not in the least Grant by this, that the Protestant Succession is in no Danger, even from several of the Measures now taken in the World. It is far from any Reflection upon the Ministry, to say, that however they may Act upon a right sincere Principle for the Protestant Succession in all they do, which, as above we profess to believe. Yet that many of the Tools they make use of, are of another Make, and have no Edge to cut any other way; no Thoughts to move them towards any other End; no other Center, which they can have any Tendency to; that the Pretender's Interest is the Magnet, which draws them by its secret Influence, to point to him as their Pole; that they have their Aim at his Establishment here, and own it to be their Aim: And as they are not Shy to profess it among themselves; so their Conduct in many things makes it sufficiently publick. This is not meant as any Reflection upon the Ministry, for making use of such Men: The late Ministry did the same, and every Ministry will, and must Employ Men sometimes, not as they always Joyn with them in their politic Principles; but as either the Men are found useful in their several Employments, or as the Ministry may be under other Circumstances, which makes it Necessary to them to Employ them. Nor, as the *Review* well enough observ'd, does it follow that *because the Ministry have Employ'd, or Joyn'd with* Jacobites *in the publick Affairs, that therefore they must have done it with a* Jacobite *Principle.* But let the Ministry Employ these Men by what Necessity, or upon what Occasion they will, tho' it may not follow that the Ministry are therefore for *the Pretender*, yet it does not also follow that there is no Danger of the Protestant Succession from the Employing those sort of People: *For what if the Queen should Die?*

The Ministry, it is hoped, are Established in the Interest of their Queen and Country; and therefore it has been Argued, that supposing the Ministry had the Pretender in their Eye, yet that it is Irrational to suggest that they can have any such View during the Life of Her present Majesty. Nay, even those profest *Jacobites*, who we spoke of just now, cannot be so ungrateful to think of Deposing the Queen, who has been so Bountiful, so Kind, so exceeding Good to them, as in several Cases to suffer them to be brought into the Management of Her own Affairs, when by their Character they might have been thought Dangerous, even to Her Person; thus Winning and Engaging them by Her Bounty, and the Confidence that has been plac'd in them, not to Attempt any thing to Her prejudice, without the most Monstrous Ingratitude, without flying in the Face of all that Sense of Honour and Obligation, which it is possible for Men of common Sense to entertain. And it can hardly be thought that even Papists themselves under the highest possessions of their Religious Zeal, can Conquer the Native Aversions they must have to such abominable Ingratitude, or to think of bringing in the Pretender upon this Protestant Nation, even while the Queen shall be on the Throne. But tho' this may, *and some doubt that also*, tye up their Hands during the Queen's Life, yet they themselves give us but small Reason to expect any thing from them afterward; and it will be hard to find any body to Vouch for them then. These very *Jacobites, Papists,* and profest Enemies to the Revolution may be supposed upon these Pretentions to be Quiet, and offer no Violence to the present Establishment while Her Majesty has the Possession, and while that Life lasts, to which they are so much Indebted, for Her Royal Goodness and Clemency. *But what would they do, if the Queen should die?*

Come we next to the *French King.* We are told, that not the *French King* only, but even the whole *French Nation* are wonderfully forward to acknowledge the Obligation they are under, to the Justice and Favour which they have Received from Her Majesty, in the putting an End to the War; a War which lay Heavy upon them, and Threaten'd the very Name of the *French Nation* with Ruin, and much more Threatn'd the Glory of the French Court, and of their Great Monarch with an entire Overthrow, a total Eclipse. A War, which by their own Confession, it was Impossible for them long to have supported the Expences of, and which by the great Superiority of the *Allies*, became Dreadful to them, and that every Campaign more than other; a War which they were in such Pain to see the End of, that they tried all the Powers and Courts in Christendom, who were the least Neutral, to Engage a Mediation in order to a Treaty, and all in vain; and a War, which if Her Majesty had not Enclin'd to put an End to, must have Ended perhaps to the Disadvantage, and Confusion of both *France* and *Spain*, if not of all Christendom. The Obligations the *French* are under for the bringing this War to so just and Honourable a Conclusion, are not at all Concealed. Nay, the *French* themselves have not been backward to make them publick. The Declarations made by the *French King* of his Sincerity in the Overtures made for a General Peace, the Protestations of his being resolved to Enter into an entire Confidence, and a League Offensive and Defensive with the Queen's Majesty, for the Preservation of the Peace of Christendom, his Recognition of Her Majesty's just Right to the Crown, his entring into Articles to preserve the Union, acknowledging the Ninth Electorate[3] in favour of the House of *Hanover*, and joining in the Great Affair of the Protestant Succession. As these all convince the World of the Necessity his Affairs were reduced to, and the great Advantages accruing to him by a Peace; so they seem to be so many Arguments against our Fears of the *French* entring into any Engagements against the Crown of *Britain*, much less any against the Possession of the Queen during her Life. Not that the Honour and Sincerity of the King of *France* is a Foundation fit for her Majesty or her People to have any Dependance upon; and the Fraction of Former Treaties by that Court when the Glory of that Monarch, or his particular Views of things has dictated such Opportunity to him as he thought fit to close with, are due Cautions to us all not to have any Dependance of that kind. But the State of his Affairs, and the Condition the War has reduced him to, may give us some Ground to think our selves safe on that side. He knows what Power he has taken off from his Enemies in making Peace with Her Majesty; he knows very well with what loss he sits down, how his Affairs are weaken'd, and what need he has to take Breath after so terrible a War; besides the Flame such an Action would kindle again in *Europe*;

how it would Animate this whole *British* Nation against him, in such a manner, and Endanger bringing in a new War, and perhaps a new Confederacy upon him so violently, and that before he would be in a Condition to Match them; that no one can reasonably suppose the *French* King will run the hazard of it. And these things may Tend to make some People easier than ordinary in the Affair of the Succession; believing that the *French* King stands in too much need of the Favour of the Queen of *Great Britain*, whose Power it well behoves him to keep in Friendship with him, and whose Nation he will be very Cautious of provoking a third time, as he has already done twice to his fatal Experience. All these things, we say, may seem pretty well to assure us that nothing is to be feared on that side so long as Her Majesty lives to sit upon the *British* Throne. But all leaves our Grand Question unanswered; and tho' we may Argue strongly for the *French* King's Conduct while the present Reign continues, yet few will say, *What he will do if the Queen should die?*

Nay, we may even mention the *Pretender* himself, if he has any about him whose Councils are fit to be Depended upon, and can Direct him to make a Wise and prudent Judgment of his own Affairs; if he Acts by any Scope of Policy, and can take his Measures with any foresight; most easie it is for them to see that it must be in vain for him to think of making any Attempt in *Britain*, during the Life of the Queen; or to expect to Depose Her Majesty, and set himself up. The *French* Power, upon which he has already in vain Depended, as it has not hitherto been able to serve him, or his Father; but that their Exile has continued now above Twenty four Years. So much less can he be able to Assist him now while he has been brought as it were to Kneel to the *British* Court, to put an End for him to this cruel destructive War; The Reason is just spoken to, (*viz.*) that this would be to rekindle that Flame, which he has gotten so lately Quenched, and which Cost him so much Art, so much Management, so much submission to the *Allies* to Endeavour the Quenching of before. To Attack the Queen of *Great Britain* now in behalf of the *Pretender*, would not only be in the highest Degree Ungrateful, Perfidious, and Dishonourable; but would for ever make the *British* Court as well as the whole Nation, his Violent and Implacable Enemies; but would also Involve him again in a new War with all *Europe*, who would very gladly Fall in again with *Britain* to pull down more Effectually the *French* Power, which has so long been a Terror to its Neighbours. So that the *Pretender* can Expect no Help from the King of *France*. As to what the *Pope*, the *Spaniard*, and a few petty *Popish* Powers, who might pretend upon a Religious prospect to Assist him, and with whose Aid, and the Assistance of his Party here, he may think fit to hazard an Attempt here for the Crown; it is Evident, and his own Friends will agree in it, that while the Queen lives, it is Nonsence, and Ridiculous for them to Attempt it; that it would immediately Arm the whole Nation against them, as one Man; and in Humane probability, it would, like as his supposed Father was serv'd at the Revolution, be the Ruin of his whole Interest, and blow him at once quite out of the Nation. I believe that there are very few who Alarm themselves much with the Fears of the *Pretender*, from the Apprehension of his own strength from Abroad, or from his own Party and Friends at Home here, were they once sure that he should receive no Assistance from the King of *France*. If then the King of *France* cannot be reasonably supposed either to be Inclin'd, or be in a Condition to Appear for him, or Act in his behalf during the Life of the Queen; neither can the Pretender, *say some*, unless he is resolved to Ruin all his Friends, and at last to Ruin himself, make any Attempt of that Kind during Her Majesty's Life. *But what if the Queen should die?*

Having then View'd the several Points of the Nation's Compass, whence our Danger of *Jacobite* Plots, and Projects against the Protestant Succession may be expected to come; Let us now Enquire a little of the State of the Nation, that we make a right Estimate of our Condition, and may know what to trust to in Cases of Difficulty, as they lye before us. In doing this, as well to avoid giving offence to the People now in Power, as to the Entring into the Quarrels which Engage the present contending Parties in this Divided Nation; we shall allow, however some may think fit to Question it, the main Debate, and Grant this for the present as a fundamental, (*viz.*) *That we are in no Danger* of the Pretender, *during this Queen's Reign*, or *during this Ministry's Administration under Her Majesty*; and avoiding all Contention of that Kind, shall allow our Condition to be *SAFE* in every Article as we go along, *for so long as the Queen Lives*, referring the Observation of things in every Head, to those who can Answer the main Question in our Title, (*viz.*) *But what if the Queen should die?*

First of all, it may be Noticed, that the present Safety of this Nation, whether we respect Liberty, Religion, Property, or publick Safety and Prosperity, Depends upon this one Fundamental, (*viz.*) That *alluding reverently to that Text* [4] *of Scripture*, we are all built upon the Foundation of the late Revolution, *Establisht Law* and *Right*, being the *chief Corner-Stone*. By this it is, that Her Majesty is made our Queen, the Entail of the Crown being reserv'd in the remainder to Her Majesty in the Act of Settlement[5] made at the filling up the vacant Throne, and by all those subsequent Acts, which Her Majesty's Title was Confirm'd by, during the Life of the Late King. *This Revolution*, is that upon which the Liberties and Religion of this Nation, were Re-built after the Conflagration that was made of them in the Calamitous Times of King *Charles* II. and King *James* II. and from hence to the Love of Liberty, which is found almost to be Naturally plac'd in the Hearts of true *Britains*; and upon the View whereof they have acted all along in the Late War, and in all their Transactions at Home has obtained the Title of a *REVOLUTION PRIN-CIPLE*. Noting this then, as above, that Her Majesty is our Queen by vertue of the Revolution, and that during Her Reign, that Establishment alone must be the Foundation of all Her Administration; this must effectually Secure us against any Apprehension that the Persons acting under Her Majesty, can Act in behalf of the *Pretender*, during Her Majesty's Life; for that they must immediately Overthrow the Throne, Turn the Queen out of it, and Renounce the Revolution, upon which Her Majesty's Possession is Established. As the Revolution therefore is the Base upon which the Throne of Her Majesty's Possession is Established; so her Majesty, and all that Act under her, are obliged to Act upon the Foot of the said Revolution, even *Will* they, *Nil* they; or else they sink immediately out of rightful Power to Act at all; Her Majesty's Title would fall to the Ground, their own Commissions would from that Hour be Void; they must Declare their Royal Mistress and Benefactress, a Subject to the *Pretender*, and all Her Pretences of Rightful Possession, Injurious, and an Usurpation. These things, being so plain, that he that runs may read them, seem to stop all our Mouths from so much as any Suggestion, that any Body can Attempt to bring in the *Pretender* upon us during the Life of Her present Majesty. *But what if the Queen should die?*

Subsequent to the Revolution, many Essential things are form'd by our Parliaments and Government for the publick Good, on the Foundation of which much of the present Peace of the Nation is Founded; and while the said Revolution Foundation stands fast, there is good Ground to believe those Essential Points shall be preserved. If then we are satisfied that the Revolution Principle shall subsist as long as the Queen Lives, then for so long we may have good Ground to believe we shall Enjoy all those Advantages and Benefits which we received from the said Revolution. But still when we look back upon those dear Privileges, the obtaining of which has Cost so much Money, and the Maintaining of which has Cost so much Blood, we must with a deep

Sigh reflect upon the precarious Circumstances of the Nation, whose best Privileges hang uncertain upon the Nice and tender Thread of Royal Mortality, and say, we are happy while these last, and these may last while Her Majesty shall Live. *But what if the Queen should die?*

Let us Descend to some other Particulars of those Blessings which we do Enjoy purely as the Effect of the Revolution, and Examin in what Posture we stand, with respect to them, and what Assurance we have of their Continuance. And First, as to *TOLERATION*. This was the Greatest and first Blessing the Nation felt after the immediate Settlement of the Crown, which was Established by Vertue of the Revolution Engagement, mentioned in the Prince of *Orange's* Declaration. The Design of this Law, as it was to give Liberty for the Worship of God to such Dissenters as could not Conform to the Church of *England*, and to give Ease to tender Consciences, so as by the Law it self is expressed; it was to Ease the Minds of their Majesty's Subjects, and to give a general Quiet to the Nation, whose Peace had been frequently Disturbed by the violence of Persecution. We have seen frequent Assurances given of the Inviolable Preservation of this Toleration by Her Majesty from the Throne in Her Speeches to the Parliament; and during Her Majesty's Reign, we have great Reason to hope the Quiet of the poor People shall not be broken by either repealing that Law, or Invading the Intent and Meaning of it while it remains in Force; and there is a great many Reasons to hope that the present Ministry are so far Convinc'd of the Necessity of the said Toleration in order to preserve the Peace, and the common Neighbourhood of People, that they can have no Thought of Breaking in upon it, or any way making the People, who Enjoy it, uneasie. Nay, the rather we believe this, because the Ferment such a Breach would put the whole Nation into, is not the safest Condition the Government can be in upon any Account; And as the Ministry cannot be supposed to desire to give Uneasiness and Provocation to the Commons, but rather to keep them Easie and Quiet, and prevent the Enemies of the present Management from having any Handle to take hold of to some Distractions, and Disturbances among the People; It cannot be thought that they will push at the Toleration, so as to deprive the People of so Considerable a Thing. But after the present happy Establishment, shall have received such a fatal Blow, as that will be of the Queen's Death; and when Popish Pretenders, and *French* Influencies shall prevail, it may well be expected then, that not Toleration of Dissenters only, but even of the whole Protestant Religion may be in danger to be Lost; so that however secure we are of the free Enjoyment of Liberty of Religion during the Queen's Life, we may be very well allow'd to ask this Question with respect to not Toleration only, but the Church of *England* also, (*viz.*) what will become of them, *If the Queen should die*?

From Toleration in *England*, come we to the Constitution of Religious Affairs in *Scotland*; and here we have different Views from what the Case in *England* affords us; the powerful Interest of Jacobitism, if it may be said to be Formidable any where, is so there. The Enemies of the Revolution are all the Implacable Enemies of the Church Establishment there: Nay, many Thousands are the declared Enemies of the Revolution, and of the Queen's being upon the Throne, from a meer Implacable Aversion to the *Presbyterian Kirk*, which is Erected, and Established by that very Revolution which has set the Queen upon the Throne. The *Union*, which has yet farther Establish'd that *Presbyterian Kirk*, is for that Reason the Aversion of the same People, as it is the Aversion of the *Jacobites*, by being a further Confirmation of the *Hannover* Succession, and a further Fixing the Queen upon the Thone. Now as *it is sure*, that *as before*, while the Queen Lives, and the Revolution Influence carries its usual Force in the Kingdoms now United, the *Presbyterian Kirk* must and will remain, and all the little Encroachments[6] which have been made upon the *Kirk*, as it may be observed, tho' they have created Uneasiness enough, yet they still seem to suppose that the Establishment it self cannot be overthrown. The Union and the Revolution Settlement remain in *Scotland*, and must remain, as is said: While the Queen Lives we can have no Apprehensions of them; The Reasons are given above; and as we said before, we are to take them for granted in this Discourse, to avoid other Cavils. While then the Revolution, and the Union are to be the Foundation of the Administration in *Scotland*, the *Presbyterian* Establisht Church Government there must also remain as the only Legal *Kirk* Constitution, and so long we can Entertain no Fears of any thing on that Account. *But what if the Queen should die?*

From such Religious Concerns as effect *Presbyterians*, and other Sectaries, or *Dissenters*, as we call them; let us take a look at the remote Danger of the Church of *England*. We have had a great deal of Distraction in the time of the late Ministry, about the Danger of the Church; and as it appears by the *Memorial* of the Church of *England*,[7] published in those times, and Re-printed since; by the Sermons of Dr. *Sacheverell*, and the eminent Speeches at his Trial, that Danger was more especially Suggested to come from the Encrease of *Dissenters* here, the Ministry of the *Whiggs*, and the Establishing *Presbyterianism* in the North of *Britain*. These things being in a great Measure now overthrown by the late

Change of the Ministry, and the new Methods taken in the Management of the publick Affairs; the People, who were then supposed to Aim at overthrowing the Ministry of those *Whiggs* are pleased to assure us of the Safety and flourishing Condition of the Church, now more than ever; while the other Party, taking up the like Cry of the Danger of the Church, tell us, that now a real visible appearance of Danger to the Church is before us; and that not only to the Church of *England* as such, but even to the whole Interest, and Safety of the Protestant Religion in *Britain*; that this Danger is imminent, and unavoidable from the great Growth and Increase of *Popery*, and profest *Jacobitism* in the Nation. This indeed they give but too great Demonstrations of from the spreading of Popish Agents among us, whose profest Employment it is to Amuse, and Impose upon the poor Country People, as well in Matters of *Jacobitism*, as of Religion; and the great Success these Emissaries of Satan have obtain'd in several Parts of *Britain*; but especially in the North. Now tho' we cannot but acknowledge, but that much of this Alarm is justly Grounded, and that the Endeavours of *Popish* and *Jacobite* Agents, and Emissaries in diverse Parts of *Britain*, are too apparently Successful; yet as wise Men could never see into the reality of such Danger, as was by some People pretended to be Impending over the Church in the Time of the late Ministry; So neither can we allow that Popery is so Evidently at the Door at this Time, as that we should be Apprehensive of having the Church of *England* immediately Transvers'd, and the Protestant Religion in *Britain*: And one great Reason for this Opinion is, that Her Majesty, who is a Zealous Professor of the Protestant Religion, and has been Bred up in the Bosom of the Church of *England*, is so Rooted in Principle, and has Declared from Her very Infancy such Horror and Aversion to Popery, that it cannot Enter into any true Protestant Thoughts to apprehend any thing of that Kind, while Her Majesty lives. *BUT* Lord have Mercy upon us! *What if the Queen should die?*

From Religious Matters, come we next to consider Civil Interest, Liberties, Privileges, Properties; the Great Article that in the late Revolution, went always Coupled in the Nation's Negative, with that of Religion, as if they were woven together; and was always Cry'd upon by the Mob in one Breath, (*viz.*) No *Popery*, no *Slavery*. The first of these concerns our Civil Interest; such as the Publick Credit, by the Occasions of a long and Expensive War, and to prevent Levying severe Taxes for the Carrying on the War, such as would be Grievous to Trade, Oppressive to the Poor, and Difficult to be Paid. The Parliament for the Ease of the Subjects, thought fit, rather to lay Funds of Interest to raise Money upon, by way of Loan; Establishing those Interests, payable as Annuities, and Annual Payments for the Benefit of those who Advanc'd their Money for the publick Service. And to make these things Current, that the publick Credit might be Sacred, and the People be made free to Advance their Money, all possible Assurances of Parliament have been given, that the Payments of Interests and Annuities shall be kept punctually and Exactly according to the Acts of Parliament, that no Mis-applications of the Money shall be made, or Converting the Money received upon one, to make good the Deficiency of the other; and hitherto the Injunctions of that Kind have been exactly observ'd, and the Payments punctually made, which we call the Credit of the Nation. At the first of the late Change, when the New Ministry began to Act, the Fright the People were put in upon the Suggestion of some, that all the Parliamentary Funds should be wiped off with a Spunge, was very Considerable; and the Credit of those Funds sunk Exceedingly, with but the bare Apprehension of such a Blow; the Sums being Infinitely great, and the Number of Indigent Families being Incredibly many whose whole Substance lay in those Securities, and whose Bread depended upon those Interests being punctually Paid. But wiser Men saw quickly there was no Ground for those Fears; that the New Ministry stood upon a Foot that could no more be Supported without the publick Credit, than those that went before them; that Especially while they were under a Necessity of Borrowing further Sums, they behoved to Secure the punctual paying of the Old; and by making the People entirely Easie, not only take from them the Apprehensions they were under of Losing what they Lent already, but make them forward and willing to Advance more to this Purpose. They not only Endeavoured to give the People all possible Satisfaction that their Money was Safe, and that the Funds laid by the Parliament in the former Ministry, should be kept Sacred, and the Payments punctually made, but took care to obtain Parliamentary Securities, by real Funds to be Settled for the Payment of those Debts contracted by the former Ministry, and for which no Provision was made before. This was the Establishment of a Fund for Payment of the Interests of the *Navy* Debt, Ordnance, Victualling, Transport, &c. to the Value of Seven or Eight Millions; which is the Substance of what we now call the South-Sea Stock. By this means the publick Credit, which, it was Suggested, would receive such a Blow at the Change, as that it should never recover again; and that it would be Impossible for the New Ministry to Raise any needful Sums of Money for the Carrying on the War, or for the publick Occasions, recovered it self so as that the Government hath ever since found it Easie to Borrow what ever Sums they thought fit to Demand in the same manner as before. Now that these Loans are Safe, no Man that weighs the Circumstances of the Ministry and Government, and the Circumstances of the People, can Doubt; the first being in a constant Necessity of Supporting the publick Credit for the Carrying on publick Affairs, on any suddain Emergency that may happen; and being liable to the Resentment of Parliament, if any open Infraction should be made upon the Funds, which touches so nearly the Honour of the Parliaments, and the Interest of most of the best Families in the Nation. While this is the Case, we think it is not Rational to believe that any Ministry will venture to attack Parliamentary Credit, in such a manner; and this will Eminently be the Case as long as Her Majesty sits on the Throne. Nor can a thing so bare-fac'dly Tyrannical and Arbitrary, and above all Dishonourable and Unjust, be Suggested, as possible to be Attempted in the Reign of so Just and Consciencious a Prince; So that we may be very willing to allow that there is not the least Danger of the publick Faith being Broken, the publick Credit lost, the publick Funds stopt, or the Money being Mis-apply'd. No Cheat, no Spunge while Her Majesty. *BUT* Alas for us! *What if the Queen should die?*

From this piece of Civil Right, come we to those Things we call Liberties, and Privileges. These may indeed by joyned in some Respects; but as we are Engag'd in speaking particularly to such Points, wherein our present Dangers do, or do not appear, It is proper to mention them apart. *Privileges* may be distinguished here from Liberties, as they respect Affairs of Trade, Corporations, Parliaments, and Legislature, *&c. Liberty*, as they respect Laws, Establishments, declared Right, and such like. As to the first, from the Revolution to this Time they have not only been Confirm'd, which we had before; but many Privileges added to the People; Some of which are Essential to the well-being of the Kingdom. All the *Quo Warranto's* against Corporation Privileges, the High-Commission Court against the Church's Privileges extending Prerogative in Detriment of the Subjects natural Right; and many such things, which were Fatal to the Privileges of this Protestant Nation, were laid aside and received their just Condemnation in the Revolution; and not so only, but the Privileges obtain'd since the Revolution by Consent of Parliament, are very considerable; such as the Toleration to this part of *Britain*, and the Establishment of the Church of *Scotland* For the North part, in matters of Religion; such as the Triennial Election of Parliaments, In Civil Affairs, such as the several Corporations Granted upon really useful Foundations in Trade; as the *Bank Company*, &c. and such like. These and many more, which may be Named; and which these are Named only as Heads of late Secured to us by Law; and those Laws yet again made sure to us by the Honour and Veracity of Her Majesty, and as long as Her Majesty's Life is spared to these Nations, we have great Reason to believe we shall rather Encrease than Lose our Privileges. *BUT what if the Queen should die?*

Our *LIBERTIES*, which come next in Order, may be Summ'd up in what we call *Legal*, and *Natural* Right; or such as by the natural Consequence of a Free Nation and a just Government; or such as by mutual Assent and Consent of Soveraign and Subject, are become the Legal Right of the latter. These, needless to be Enumerated here, are Summ'd up into One; or are expresly Enacted by Statute Law, and thereby become Fundamental to the Constitution. These receive no Wound, but one of these two ways, either by open Infraction, and Contempt of Right, or by Dispensing Arbitrary Power; both of which by the many Assurances from the Throne, by the constant Jealousies of Parliaments, and the full Liberty they have more of late, than ever, taken to Examin into, and Censure Breaches of the Laws, We are very well assured shall not be Attempted in Her Majesty's time: Nay, on the contrary, the Superiority, and Influence of Parliaments over and upon the Management of publick Matters; Nay, even their Influences upon the Royal Majesty of the Soveraign, has been such, and has in such a manner Insensibly Increased of Late, that the like has never been known, or Practised in this Nation for some Ages before. We see Her Majesty declines Extending Her Perogative, either to the Detriment of Her Subjects, in Cases Civil, or Religious; and wherein it might be so Extended; nay, when even the Parliament have desir'd Her to Extend it: So that we have a great Satisfaction in the Safety of our Established Liberties, and that no Tyrannical Arbitrary Invasions of Right shall be made during Her Majesty's Reign. *BUT what if the Queen should die?*

In like manner for our Properties, our Estates, Inheritance, Lands, Goods, Lives, Liberties, &c. These are effectually Secured by Laws of the Land, and the Soveraign in this Country, having no Right, but by Law to any part of the Subjects Estate, Causes that Estate to be called *PROPERTY*. The Kings and Queens of *Britain* are Monarchs limited to Act by the Laws. When they Cease to Rule by Law, the Constitution is Broken, and they become Tyrants and Arbitrary, Despotick Invaders of Right. This is Declared by the Revolution, wherein the Right of the Subject are openly, not set down only, but Claim'd, Demanded as what Justice required should be Granted to them, and as what the Soveraign as aforesaid has no Right, no Pretence, no just Authority to take, or detain from him. This is the Great Capital and Fundamental Article of *Magna-Charta*, and the Foundation upon which all the Laws Subsequent, and Consequential to *Magna-Charta* have been made [𝔑𝔬 𝔉𝔯𝔢𝔢𝔪𝔞𝔫 𝔰𝔥𝔞𝔩𝔩 𝔟𝔢 𝔗𝔞𝔨𝔢𝔫 𝔬𝔯 𝔍𝔪𝔭𝔯𝔦𝔰𝔬𝔫𝔢𝔡, 𝔬𝔯 𝔟𝔢 𝔇𝔦𝔰𝔰𝔢𝔦𝔷𝔢𝔡 𝔬𝔣 𝔥𝔦𝔰 𝔉𝔯𝔢𝔢𝔥𝔬𝔩𝔡, 𝔬𝔯 𝔏𝔦𝔟𝔢𝔯𝔱𝔦𝔢𝔰, 𝔬𝔯 𝔉𝔯𝔢𝔢 𝔠𝔲𝔰𝔱𝔬𝔪𝔰, 𝔬𝔯 𝔟𝔢 𝔒𝔲𝔱-𝔩𝔞𝔴𝔢𝔡, 𝔬𝔯 𝔈𝔵𝔦𝔩𝔢𝔡, 𝔬𝔯 𝔬𝔱𝔥𝔢𝔯𝔴𝔦𝔰𝔢 𝔇𝔢𝔰𝔱𝔯𝔬𝔶𝔢𝔡; 𝔫𝔬𝔯 𝔴𝔢 𝔴𝔦𝔩𝔩 𝔫𝔬𝔱 𝔭𝔞𝔰𝔰 𝔲𝔭𝔬𝔫 𝔥𝔦𝔪, 𝔫𝔬𝔯 𝔠𝔬𝔫𝔡𝔢𝔪𝔫 𝔥𝔦𝔪, 𝔟𝔲𝔱 𝔟𝔶 𝔏𝔞𝔴𝔣𝔲𝔩 𝔍𝔲𝔡𝔤𝔢𝔪𝔢𝔫𝔱 𝔬𝔣 𝔥𝔦𝔰 𝔓𝔢𝔢𝔯𝔰, 𝔬𝔯 𝔟𝔶 𝔱𝔥𝔢 𝔏𝔞𝔴 𝔬𝔣 𝔱𝔥𝔢 𝔏𝔞𝔫𝔡. *Magna-Charta*, Cap. xxix.] The Words are Plain and Direct; and as to the Subject, we are now upon, they require no Comment, no Explication. Whatever they do, as to Pleading in Law. The Proof of the Subject's Rights to the free Possession of his own Property, is also the less needful to Enlarge upon here, because it is acknowledged in full and express Terms by the Soveraign, as well in Practise, as in Expression. Her Majesty adhering strictly to this, as a Rule, has from the beginning of Her Reign, made it Her *Golden Rule*, to Govern according to Law. Nor while the Establishment of the Crown it self is Built upon the Legal Constitution of this Nation, can it be otherwise here: That Prince that Governs here and not by Law, may be said, rather to Oppress, than to Govern, rather to Over-rule, than to Rule over his People. *NOW* it cannot without great and unjustifyable Violence to Her Majesty's just Government, be Suggested, that we are in any Danger of Oppression during the Righteous Administration of Her Majesty's Reign. The Queen Raises no Money without Act of Parliament, keeps up no Standing Army in time of *Peace*, Dis-seizes no Man of his Property, or Estate; but every Man Sits in Safety under his own Vine, and his Fig-tree; and we doubt not but we shall do as long as Her Majesty Lives. *BUT what if the Queen should die?*

Possibly Cavils may Rise in the Mouths of those whose Conduct this Nice Question may seem to Affect, that this is a Question unfit to be asked, and Questionless such People will have much to say upon that Subject; as that it is a Factious Question, a Question Needless to be Answered, and Impertinent therefore to be askt; that it is a Question which respects things remote, and serves only to fill the Heads of the People with Fears and Jealousies; that it is a Question, to which no direct Answer can be given, and which Suggests strange Surmises, and amuses People about they know not what, and is of no use, but to make People uneasie without Cause.

As there is no Objection, which is Material enough to make, but is Material enough to Answer; so this, altho' there is nothing of Substance in it, may Introduce something in its Answer of Substance enough to consider: It is therefore most necessary to Convince the considering Reader of the Usefulness and Necessity of putting this Question; and then likewise the Usefulness, and Necessity of putting this Question *NOW* at this time; and if it appear to be both a needful Question it self, and a seasonable Question as to time, the rest of the Cavils against it will deserve the less regard. That it is a needful Question, seems justified more abundantly from a very great Example, to wit, the Practise of the whole Nation, in Settling the Succession to the Crown. This I take to be nothing else, but this: The Queen having no Issue of Her Body, and the Pretender to the Crown being Expelled by Law, Included in his Father's Disastrous Flight, and Abdication; when the Parliament came to Consider of the State of the Nation, as to Government as it now stands; that King *William* being lately Dead, and Her Majesty with universal Joy of Her People, being reciev'd as Queen, the Safety, and the lasting Happiness of the Nation is so far Secur'd. *BUT what if the Queen should die?*

The Introduction to all the Acts of Parliaments for Settling the Crown, Implies thus much, and speaks directly this Language (*viz.*) to make the Nation Safe and Easie, in Case the Queen should die: Nor are any of those Acts of Parliament Impeach'd of Faction, or Impertinencies; much less of Needless blaming the People, and filling their Heads with Fears and Jealousies. If this Example of the Parliament is not enough, Justifying to this Enquiry the well known Truth, upon which that Example of Parliament is Grounded, is sufficient to justifie it, (*viz.*) That we all known the Queen *MUST die*. None say this with more Concern and Regret, than those who are forwardest to put this Question, as being of the Opinion abovesaid, that we are effectually Secured against the Pretender, and against all the terrifying Consequences of the *Frenchify'd* Govournours during Her Majesty's Life. But this is Evident, *the Queen is Mortal*, tho' crown'd with all that Flattering Courtiers can bring together, to make Her appear Great, Glorious, Famous, or what you please; yet the Queen, yea, the Queen Her self is *Mortal*, and *MUST die*. It is true, Kings and Queens are called Gods; but this respects their Sacred Power: nothing supposing an Immortality attending their Persons, for they all *Die* like other Men, and their Dust knows no Distinction in the Grave. Since then it is most certain that the Queen *MUST die*, and our Safety, and Happiness in this Nation depends so much upon the Stability of our Liberties, Religion, and aforesaid Dependencies after Her Majesty's Life shall End, it cannot be a Question Offensive to any who has any Concern in the Publick good, to enquire into what shall be the

State of our Condition, or the Posture of our Affairs, when the Queen shall die; *but this is not all neither.* As the Queen is Mortal, and we are assured she must die; so we are none of us certain, as to be able to know when, or how soon that Disaster may happen, at what time, or in what manner. This then, as it may be remote, and not a long time; *God of his Infinite Mercy grant it may be long first, and not before this difficult Question we are upon, be Effectually and Satisfactorily Answered to the Nation*: So on the other side, it may be *near*; None of us know how *near* the fatal Blow may befal us soon, and sooner far than we may be ready; for to day it may come, while the cavilling Reader is objecting against our putting this Question, and calling it Unreasonable and Needless; while thy Word is in the very Mouth, mayest thou hear the fatal Melancholly News, *the Queen's Dead.* News that must one time, or other be heard; the Word will certainly come some time, or other, to be spoken in the present Sense, and to be sure in the time they are spoken in. How can any one then say, that it is improper to ask what shall be our Case, what shall we do, or what shall be done with us *if the Queen should die?*

But we have an other Melancholy Incident, which attends the Queen's Mortality, and which makes this Question more than ordinarily season-able to be ask'd at this time; and that is, that not only the Queen is Mortal, and she *MUST die*, and the time uncertain; so that she *may die*, even to Day before to Morrow, or in a very little space of time: But Her Life is under God's Providence, at the Mercy of *Papists* and *Jacobites* People; who the one by their Principles, and the other by the Circumstances of their Party are more than ordinarily to be Apprehended for their bloody Designs against Her Majesty, and against the whole Nation. Nay, there seems more Reason to be Apprehensive of the dangerous Attempts of these desperate People, at this time, than ever, even from the very Reasons which are given all along in this Work, for our being Safe in our Privileges, our Religious and Civil Rights during Her Majesty's Life; it would be mispending your time to prove that the *Papists* and *Jacobite* Parties in this Nation, however they may, as we have said, be under Tyes and Obligations of Honour, Interest, and Gratitude, *&c.* not to make attempt upon us during the Queen's Life; yet that they are more Encouraged at this time than ever they were to hope and believe, that when the Queen shall die, their Turn stands next. This we say, we believe is lost Labour to speak of: The said People, the *Popish* and *Tory* Party will freely own and oppose it. They all take their Obligations to the Queen, to End with Her Majesty's Life. The *French King*, however in Honour, and Gratitude he may think himself bound to Encourage the *Pretender* to insult Her Majesty's Dominions, while the Queen with whom he Personally is Engaged by Treaty,[8] shall remain alive, will think himself fully at Liberty from those Obligations when the Queen shall die. If we are misinform'd of the *French* Affairs, and of the Notions they have in *France* of these things, they are generally no otherwise understood then that the King of *France* is Engag'd by the Peace now in View, not to disturb Her Majesty's Possession during Her Reign and Life; but that then the *Pretender's* Right is to be receiv'd every where. The *Pretender* himself, howsoever, as abovesaid, he may despair of his Success in Attempting to take Possession during the Queen's Life, will not fail to assume new Hopes at Her Majesty's Death: So much then of the hopes of *Popery* and *French* Power; so much of the Interest of the *Pretender* depending upon the single Thread of Life of a Mortal Person; and we being well assur'd that they look upon Her Majesty, only as the Incumbent in a Living, or Tenant for Life in an Estate, what is more Natural, than in this Case for us to apprehend Danger to the Life of the Queen; Especially to such People, who are known not to make much Consciencies of Murthering Princes, with whom the King killing Doctrine is so Universally receiv'd, and who were so often Detected of villanious Practices, and Plots against the Life of Queen *Elizabeth*, Her Majesty's famous Predecessor, and that upon the same Foundation, (*viz.*) The Queen of *Scots* being the *Popish Pretender* to the Crown; what can we expect from the same Party, and Men acting from the same Principles; but the same Practices. It is known that the Queen by Course of Nature may Live many Years, and these People have many Reasons to be Impatient of so much Delay. They know that many Accidents may Intervene to make the Circumstances of the Nation at the Time of the Queen's Death, less favourable to their Interests than they are now; they may have fewer Friends, as well in Power, as out of Power by length of time, and the like: These, and such as these Considerations may excite Vilanious and Murtherous Practices against the precious Life of our Soveraign (God Protect Her Majesty from them) but while all these Considerations so Naturally offer themselves to us, it seems most Rational, needful, seasonable and just, that we should be Asking and Answering this great Question, *What if the Queen should die?*

Thus far we have only asked the Question it self, and shewed our Reasons, or Endeavoured to Justifie the Reasonablness of the Enquiry. It follows that we make some brief Essay as an Answer to the Question. This may be done many ways; but the Design of this Tract is rather to put the Question into your Thought, than to put an Answer into your

Mouths. The several Answers which may be given to this Important Question may not be proper for a publick Print; and some may not be fit so much as to be spoken. The Question is not without its Uses, whether it be Answered or no, if the Nation be sufficiently Awaken'd; but to ask the Question among themselves, they will be brought by thinking of the thing to Answer it one to another in a short Space. The People of *Britain* want only to be shewed what imminent Danger they are in, in Case of the Queen's Decease: How much their Safety and Felicity depends upon the Life of Her Majesty, and what a State of Confusion, Distress, and all Sorts of dreadful Calamities they will fall into at Her Majesty's Death, if something be not done to Settle them before Her Death; and if they are not during Her Majesty's Life secured from the Power of *France* and the Danger of the *Pretender*.

From
Defoe's *Review*
(1705–10)

A REVIEW
OF THE AFFAIRS OF FRANCE:
WITH OBSERVATIONS ON
TRANSACTIONS AT HOME.

Thursday, September 6. 1705.

IN my last, I brought the Question of *Jure Divino* upon the Stage; I did not examine the thing it self, *for that I reserve to another place*; but I am debating what can be the Intent and Meaning of starting and asserting this Doctrine, among the Church of *England* Men, at this time of Day.

I think, I made it plain, that there can be no other Design in arguing the Inherent Right of Government, but to argue that the Queen has no Right at all.

I think, 'tis very rational to argue, That if they deny this, they must deny their Imaginary King, and fall with the Revolution into the *Violent Suspicions* of the Cheat[1] put upon the Nation in his Birth, which are mentioned in the P. of *O*'s Declaration. In short, they must either renounce the Claim of that pretended King, or protest against the Title of the Queen, or Damn their Doctrine of Divine Right, *and let them take which of the three they please.*

1. If the last, then to what purpose do they bring that upon the Stage, which they will be driven to the Necessity of renouncing again, and so talk something which signifies nothing, and argue on purpose to be laught at?

2. If they are for rejecting their pretended Birth, and blasting the young hopes of the Family as a Spurious Imposture; then what can they say for themselves, that they do not conform to the Present Government, and take the Oath to the Queen? Since, if that Prince, *as they call him*, be a Phantosm, a Meteor of Popish Exhalations, an *Ignis Fatuus*, a Light without Fire, a Birth of projected Treason to this Nation; then their

Divine Right must die under the Midwife's Hands; or it will immediately center in the Queen, and fly to her for Protection.

3. If they are for maintaining Divine Right, and the Prince of *Wales* [2] too; then let them tell us, if they can, what Title upon their foot, the Queen can have to the *English* Crown?

Her Majesty in the mean time, is exceedingly oblig'd to these Gentlemen; and above all, to the High Church of *England* Clergy, that joyn with them in these preposterous Projects, and the Mystery remains yet unriddl'd, how they will reconcile it to the rest of their pretensions – Indeed the High Church Men may see here, to what Necessities, Exigencies, and Scandalous Shifts the Party is driven; and had they any Eyes, they might see whose work they are doing.

Can it be possible, that they can be *Englishmen*, who, in so Scandalous a manner Mortgage their Integrity, their Loyalty and their Character as *Englishmen?* Pray, Gentlemen, let us ask, *who are you?* Let the World see you, let us furnish our selves with your Character from your own Mouths.

1. Are you Protestants? Can it be possible you should be so, and yet form such a Mine against your Religion? Can you, as Protestants, for the maintaining a giddy Notion of other Mens Brain, covet to come under the absolute Dominion of a Popish Prince? Can you do Justice to God, to yourselves, your Country, or your Posterity, in Sacrificing the Truth committed to your Charge, in behalf of all these, to a wild Modern Invention, a *Chimera* made up of False Principles, and worse Conclusions, which being in it self wholly immaginary, is set on foot by a Party, on purpose to render Ridiculous, to Banter, and Buffoon the Settlement, both Politick and Religious in these Nations?

Can it be possible that Englishmen and Protestants, can so betray their Principles, and Sacrifice Religion to their private Resentments? Is all our Claim to Liberty, and Property of Estates on one hand, and of Conscience on the other, come to this? What then shall we say to Religion, and how easily can Men form it by their Fancies and Interest? What have your Fathers Fought for, your Martyrs Dyed for, your Laws been made for? Can you so easily give up your Inheritance, and bring in that Popish Authority, which in the late Revolution, was Suppress'd with so much Zeal, and so Universal a Concurrence of the whole Nation?

I cannot forget what I happened to hear Delivered at the Bar of the House of Lords, in a Message from the Commons, in Convention just upon the Revolution –

Mr. *H—den* [3] carried up the Message, and the Words were as follows: 'My Lords, I am Commanded by the Commons of *England*, Assembled in Convention, to Acquaint your Lordships with a Resolution, pass'd *Nemine Contradicente* by them, and Order'd to be Deliver'd to your Lordships, *viz.*,

'*That it is Inconsistent with the Constitution of this* Protestant *Kingdom, to be Govern'd by a* Popish *Prince.*'

This is a Declaration which ought to be wrote in Letters of Gold; no *Protestant*, no *English* Man ought to be Ignorant either of the Substance, or the Circumstance of them; they ought to know not only that it is true in Fact, but that it has been Declar'd so by Parliament; they ought to know that the Constitution of the *English* Nation is so understood by all the True Defenders of its Liberty, and Exposers of its Laws.

Who are you then, Gentlemen of the High Church, that you should push at things inconsistent with the Constitution of *England*, and contrary to the Express Declaration of the Representative of the Nation, consent to have us under the Government of One, whose Right is absolutely Inconsistent with the Constitution – Will you be call'd Protestants who are willing to come under the Power of a Popish Prince? Is this consistent with the Safety and Good of the Protestant Religion, and with the Care every Christian ought to have of it?

If you are Protestants, you must at the same time be mad Men, worse than any in *Bedlam;* whose Understandings are uncapable of judging what is, or is not proper for the Preservation, or Destruction of the Religion and Liberty of your Native Country.

2. Are you *English* Men? It has been undoubtedly the justest Character of *English* Men, of any could ever be given them, that they are Tenacious of Liberty, and Positive in the Maintaining the Privileges granted by their Kings, obtain'd by their Sword, and Handed down to them from their Fathers.

The Doctrine of Divine Right does not only lead us by the Hand to a Popish Prince, but also to a Popish Tyrant; whoever he is, that shall Rule by absolute Authority, Indefeazible and Independent, must be a Tyrant; 'tis in his Nature, and this gives him a loose, all the Bonds and Obligations of Laws, Oaths, Compacts and Consequences are taken off; the Brute is let loose on the Man, and the Reins given to that lust of Rule, which, I believe, I do no wrong in saying, is mix'd in our very Natures, and runs thro' the whole Mass, as the Effects of that Pride and Ambition which fill'd our first Parents, and is convey'd to us their Posterity, by an uninterrupted Descent.

> *Nature has left this Tincture in the Blood,*
> *That all Men would be Tyrants if they cou'd,*

Not Kings alone, not Ecclesiastick Pride,
But Parliaments, and all Mankind beside:
If we forbear our Neighbours to Devour,
'Tis not for want of Will, but want of Power;
'Tis all a General Epidemick Taint,
Ambition's Natures Darling –[4]

Would any Men in their Senses then, having Bounds and Limits set by Legal Authority, and most just Prescription to this Unhappy Error in Nature, strive of their own accord, to trust Nature with more Power than she ought to be Trusted with; take off the just Weights of Law, and Constitution, which in all Ages have help'd to Crush and keep down this Swelling Vapour of Ambition – Sure they can never be *English* Men, that would prompt that Mischief among us? That would draw up the Sluces of the Laws, and turn the Stream of Pride and Intolerable Tyranny, upon the Liberties of this Nation?

To perswade Men that are in Power, that their Power is unrestrain'd, is to be sure to have it unrestrain'd; 'tis Effectually to prompt them to Exert it beyond all Restraint; to Contemn Law, Trample upon Liberty, and Destroy all the Branches of Constitution.

This is some part of the Picture of this Monster of *Jure Divino*, but this is not the main Reason why it is shown at this time of Day; Would you know the meaning why we are so fond of *Jure Divino*? Why we are running back to the foolish abdicated Spectre of Tyranny? The Reason is plain, because this once bewildring the Fancies of the People, will Effectually Overthrow the present Constitution, Dissolve the Succession, Annihilate all our Declarations of Right, and Limitations of the Crown.

In short, if *Jure Divino* comes upon the Stage, the Queen has no more Title to the Crown than my Lord Mayor's Horse; all the People are bound by the Laws of God to Depose her, as an Usurper, and Restore their Rightful and Lawful King *James* III. all the Risque of Liberty, *Protestant* Religion, Property, Wives and Children, or such like Trifles, *to the Contrary in any wise notwithstanding*.

And *now 'tis out*, here's the Riddle Expounded; here is the Comment upon this Worthy Text; this is the *Rehearsal*[5] Transposed; this is *Jacobitism* in Miniature; the true Effigy of a *Jure Divino Protestant*; let all the Men in *England*, put a fairer Construction upon it if they can; I am positive in this, and must be excused the Tautology of Repetition, *Jure Divino* can have no other End in it; its Professors can have no other End in starting it at this Time; they must Preach this Doctrine directly against the Queen's Title, or it will fall to the Ground, even in their own Management.

And now, Gentlemen of the High Church, *What must we say of you?* What sort of Monsters will ye make your selves? *Have you taken the Oaths to the Queen?* Have you taken the Abjuration? Have you Entred your selves into the Lists of the Revolution? You ought to Tremble at the Repetition of the Abjuration, while you pursue the Interest you have Abjur'd; while you profess your selves to believe Her Majesty an Usurper, at the same time that you Swear Allegiance to her? Were ever such things practis'd among the most Unpolish'd *Pagan* Nations of the World? The Perjury is horrid, the Hypocrisie of it without Precedent, and the Consequences must be most Pernicious.

Are you the Gentlemen that cry out of Hypocrisie in the Occasional Conformity of the *Dissenters*? Here is Occasional Conformity in its proper Dress, in its Original Colour; here is that Occasional Conformity, that cannot be practis'd without Hypocrisie, and that of the Worst and Blackest Sort, and most fatal to the Nation. [. . .]

Tuesday, September 11. 1705.

I Endeavour'd in some of the last Papers to Expose to View, the plain Design of a Party of Men, against the Title of Her Majesty to the Crown; I confess, I long waited and expected to see it come to this. I shall say no more to the Unaccountable *Brass* of the Projectors, for they seem hardned in Resolutions, to provoke, if possible, a Government resolv'd in Methods of Moderation, Candor and Forbearance, beyond all possible Bounds.

Nor shall I pretend to Charge our Governors with Unseasonable Lenity, in suffering the Title of the Prince to be Disputed every Day, and an Exotick Impostor Encroaching upon her, in the Triumphs of a Party.

But the End of all this is to open the Eyes, if possible, of the *English* Nation; who, Deluded with the Ænigma of the Churches Danger, are amused with the Fright, and Directed by a Party, to look to the wrong Point of the Compass for the Stone.

He shall never be judge of the Weather, that looks out of a Leward Window; the way to see when a Cloud is coming, is to look to Windward; Storms ride upon the Wings of the Wind; there can come no Showers of Fire and Brimstone upon this Church and Nation, but what come with a *French* Gale; Does the Wind blow a *Jure Divino* Gale? Look for Tempests upon the Crown, Gusts of Party Wind will Attack the Queens

Title; *stand fast Church of* England, for if the Crown be blown off, you sink in the Fall; if that Totters, your Foundations Tremble, and an Earthquake will not sooner thro' down the Monument, than you will certainly fall in the Destruction of the Revolution Establishment.

And pray Gentlemen consider, how can it be otherwise? What was it the Church of *England* call'd over the Prince of *Orange* for? Was she in Danger, or in no Danger? The most surfeited High Churchmen ever I met with, will allow there was Danger then, when *Magdalen* College was fallen,[6] and a High Commission threatn'd all the rest; if there was no Danger, why did you call him over? If there was, why would you go back again? Upon the Foot of the Revolution, stands all the Safety of the Church, from those very Dangers which the Prince of *Orange*, our late Glorious King *William*, was call'd over to prevent; and restoring his Line, back'd with *French* Power, *French* Popery, and *French* Maxims in Government, can never foretel any more Security. – Are you of the Opinion the Church is in Danger? And would you flye from a Protestant to a Popish Prince to secure it? I cannot but think a little Help would clear up the Eye-Sight of this deluded Nation in this ridiculous Case.

But who meddles with the Title of the Queen, *says the Gentlemen of the High Party*? We are content she should be Queen, but we would have her be our Queen; we would have her be a Church of *England* Queen; and we would have her pull down all the Enemies of the Church of *England*; not set up Presbyterian Tyranny at her own Door, and leave the Church to the Mercy of Occasional Conformity at home.

Well Gentlemen, let us joyn Issue a little upon these Heads too; you say you are content she should be Queen, and you do not meddle with her Title to the Crown; you have no Design to Depose or Disturb her. To convince the World of this, it is absolutely necessary, that you declare your Abhorrence of that antiquated, newly revived, imaginary Doctrine of Divine Right; since (*as I think*) 'tis plainly proved, it can have no other Retrospect than the Title of the Queen. It is utterly impossible it should have any other Meaning than to prove, that her Majesty has no Title to the Crown; that the true Divine Right of the Crown, is in the Person of King *James* III. as they count him.

If ye will come off of this, and declare your selves to believe, that Parliamentary Authority has a Superiour Right to that of Primogeniture or Inheritance, and can, and may Lawfully limit Succession; that the Revolution was a Legal Re-assumption of an abused Authority, and removing it, because of Male Administration, to the Hand of another. If you will come over to this, something may be, there may be Hopes of you.

But while you pretend to preach the Doctrine of Divine Right, a Teeming Monster in the Womb, of which are all the Legions of Tyranny, absolute Power, Non-resisting Submission, and the like, never talk of being willing the Queen should Reign. The present Government is as inconsistent with absolute Dominion, as it is with Jacobitism; and I pretend to be able to prove, That entire positive Subjection, Non-resistance, and Submission, as natural a Consequence of a *Jure Divino* Title, as the Light is the Consequence of the Sun.

He that Claims a Right from God himself, Superiour to all Humane Authority, must of Necessity Claim the Entire Absolute Subjection of all Humane Power to his Command; he Rules under God, only is Subjected to his Laws, no *Postulata* of Government binds him; 'Tis Treason to Debate the Right of his Commands, as it is to Debate his Right of Commanding: The Question with him is not, Whether what he Commands be Reasonable and Just, but whether he had a Title to Command, or no? And this Title being Divine in its Original, must be Uncontroulable in its Execution; this Prince holding Immediately from God, is Unaccountable, Absolute, and Arbitrary, AND THAT'S A TYRANT.

I am told, a certain Author, who now Vigorously Contends in Print for this Divine Right of Kings, so far agrees in this being the Consequence, that he Denies it to be a Crime for Kings to Tyrannize; and Declar'd, That if he was a King, and his Subjects should Disobey or Dispute any of his Commands, he would make no Difficulty of Destroying such People, Men, Women, and Children, to any Number, and on any such Occasions; and I think this Gentleman much in the right of it, for a Power by Divine Right, and such sort of Justice is certainly all of a piece.

Thus *Moses* Govern'd the Children of *Israel*, by Immediate Divine Authority, and when he found them fallen into Idolatry, he falls upon them with the Arbitrary Sword of Power, and kill'd 30000 of them for the Fault; and so may any Prince do with the same Justice, who receives the Sword from the same Hand, in the same Immediate manner; to Disobey such a Prince, is Disobeying God Almighty in his Immediate Commands. Thus when *Samuel* told God Almighty of the Slight they put upon his Rule, the Answer he receives, is a plain owning of the Immediate Authority of God in that Government: *They have not rejected thee,*[7] *but they have rejected me,* says God.

He now that would bring up the Government of the Prince, to the same Dignity of a Government immediately deputed, and the Methods dictated by God himself, must of Necessity lead us to as absolute a Subjection to that Prince, as if the Pillar of Smoke by Day, and the Pillar of Fire by Night, were upon the Doors of his Pallace.

Divine Right of Government, must imply the Divine Debt of Entire Submission, and a *Jure Divino* King, and a Passively Obedient People are Synonimous in Nature, tend to the same thing, and are constant Attendants one on the other.

From hence I draw this Conclusion, and I think 'tis very just – That to start the Doctrine of Divine Right in *England*, is a Design, if possible, to restore Tyranny to this Nation, and to distil such Notions into the Heads of the People, as may suppress the Desire and Love of Liberty, and make absolute arbitrary Government Familiar, and Eligible to them: This I think so Natural, that I cannot see what Objection can lie against it.

To obey God, is Natural Religion; No Reserve, no Condition, no Reluctance, or Hesitation, can be allow'd in our Obedience to our Maker; his Right to Govern us, is fixt in his Power of forming us; and as he is our Creator, he has an absolute indefeasible Disposing Right over us; to disobey, merits immediate Death here, and for ever; he is Lord over us by all Sorts of Right, Creating, supporting, defending, preserving, and providing, and no Man so brutish as will not own

> *First Cause he is, and that First Being gave,*
> *And it is highly due,*
> *That he who gave us Breath, we should*
> *At our Last End pursue.*[8]

Who ever then can claim a Right of Government, immediately from Heaven, without any Interposition of Human Concert, Assistance, Compact, or Consent of Parties, has an absolute Inherent Right over the People he Governs; may Destroy or Preserve them at Pleasure, and the Subjects ought not only not to resist, but not so much as complain.

This is the Result of Inherent Right, or *Jure Divino*; and this is certainly the End and Design of preaching up this Doctrine at this Time of Day; for the Consequence of Divine Right, being Divine Tyranny, it more particularly suits these People, who in all their Proceedings have run on to Extremes every way, tending to that Manner of Government.

Absolute Rule must be Tyrannical, and I hope to prove it beyond all Objection; and they that preach this Doctrine to *England*, must expect to have it accepted, just as the People have in all Ages receiv'd Tyrants themselves, that is, without Contempt: Never let such People expect but

Nature will always *rebel against Principle*, when once it comes to be prest; and why, Gentlemen, will ye strive to *rouse Nature*, when you know from your own Memorial,[9] *page* 12. that she cannot bear it?

They that preach Divine Right in these Nations, against Parliament Limitation, would do well to consider, whether they can ever bring this Nation to bear it or no; they may perhaps be wheedled in to listen to the Doctrine, but they will never practise the Obedience – They may bear the thing, but they will never bear the Men; they have sometimes gone a great way in the Pretence in *England*, but Nature always rise against Principle, when they came to the Practice; it is in vain to talk of Speculative Government, when they are reduc'd to Practice. No Nation under Heaven, that had two Grains of Reason in its Exercise, could ever bear a Tyrant, much more this enlightned People of *England;* the Name of Tyrant is rooted so deep, the Aversion to it so strong, and the Reasons against it so great, that they might justly, any one, Despair in the Attempt.

Let Government be never so Sacred, and the Line of Governours *Jure Divino*, Tyrants are no Messengers from Heaven but when sent in Judgment to a Nation; there's no Divine Right can legitimate a Tyrant; he ceases to have a Right upon his perverting the End, for which the Government he was born to, was Ordain'd and Appointed.

But I diligently avoid descending to Argument, if I should grant Governours as Sacred as Government, and the Inherent Right in all its Extent as it is proposed, the Matter would not differ here; the Question before me is, Why this Matter is now debated? And how it can suit with any Man's Duty to the Queen, whom we all acknowledge to Reign by the Sacred Authority of Parliamentary Limitation, which Parliamentary Limitation is the Supreme Authority of this Nation; all Power that pretends to supersede it, is Tyranical; and the Doctrine of Divine Right, tending in its own Nature, to Tyranny and absolute Dominion? The starting that Doctrine at this time of Day, can have no other Design, but the introducing Tyrannick Power into *England.*

Thus the Project of Divine Right, stands fairly charg'd with these Designs, as the natural Consequences of the Proposal.

1. Denying and Invalidating the Title of the Queen.
2. Superseding Parliamentary Authority.
3. Introducing Arbitrary Tyrannick Power, in its full Exercise.

So that Revolution, Liberty, Settlement, Protestant Succession, Queen, House of *Hannover*, and all the Priveledges and Birthrights of this Nation, have their Fate laid out in this Exotick Scheme; and these are your Men that take Care of the Church of *England*, that cry Out of her Danger!

and would bring in Tyranny to support her; as if Arbitrary Power was a safer Kind of Government, and more for the Good of the Church of *England*, than a Limited, Legal Monarchy, which if it be true, is the severest Satyr upon the Church that can be made, and must be very little for her Reputation.

Saturday, July 13. 1706.

ONE Word to railing Accusations, and then, *Satan*, I have done with thee – The Man of Noise, and the Cause, that it upheld by Bullying and Sophistry, are equally contemptible to me; and I do not think it worth my Readers while to disturb them with the Absurdities of the *Rehearsal*; Railing is his Talent, and he is in the right of it, for his Party are no otherwise to be upheld.

But having debated at large his *Jure Divino* Principles, in the Book bearing that Title and now finish'd; and if I mistake not, shown some of its inconsistent Nonsense in its true Colours, I cannot help speaking a Word to the Subject here.

The Gentleman,[10] I speak of, asks me; if the QUEEN has any Divine Right, and if the Duke of *Marlborough* is not fighting for that Right? and wherefore the QUEEN is call'd Sacred, and then what the Duke of *Marlborough* is fighting for, and the like; and among the rest, puts an unscholar-like Proposal to me, *viz.* to prove a Negative – *Viz.* When there was a Time, that People were without any Government, which *first*, is a Contradiction, and *secondly*, is a thing I never alledg'd, nor is it at all material here –

Now not to answer some People, *as Solomon says*, in their Folly, and make them wise in their own Conceit; I shall lay my Disputant by, and only state the Matter plain, let them come off from the Difficulty, if they can.

To prove, when the People were without Government, tho' it be nothing to the purpose, yet the Scripture is plain in it. When there was no King in *Israel*,[11] but every Man did what was right in his own Eyes?

This also may be prov'd, and is more to the purpose; that there was a Time when Nations had no other Government, but what was of their own erecting; and I would be glad the *Antagonists* would tell me, who was King when the Tower of *Babel* was built – And when God scatter'd the People, who were the Kings of every separate Band – and what

Government they were under, when *journying thro' the Plain, they said one to another, go to, let us make Brick,* &c. Gen. 11. 2. 3.

And after all, if there ever were any such Kings, as these Dreamers of Dreams allow, appointed immediately by God Almighty, Where is the Race? What King in the World is now of the Line? Who can challenge the Inheritance? I undertake to prove, that none of the Line reigns in *Europe* – And tho' it be a Negative, I think, 'tis effectually done by proving the Intersections of Blood, Bastardy, or Usurpation upon every one of the Royal Lines now reigning in *Europe*.

The malicious Wretch now turns the Argument to the Royal Line of *England*, either designing to draw me into a Snare, or presuming, I shall shun the Debate, for fear of using too much Freedom.

Alas! how mistaken are these People? Her Majesty is a Fountain of Royal Wisdom and Justice, and no Man need fear speaking the Truth; the *English* Crown stands upon the Basis of Legal Constitution, and triumphs over the ruins of Tyranny. Here is no need of Pretences of a Divinity that is not to be found; and Her Majesty laying no Claim to this sham mock Title, no Man need be shye of the thing.

I am therefore free to lay down the following Propositions, which I offer to prove.

1. No King or Queen in the World has a Divine Right to the Government of any Nation or People, personal and inherent in Him or Her, by Succession, Inheritance, Line or Devolution.

2. To say, the Kings or Queens of *England* have an inherent Divinity of Title in their Persons by Lineal Succession, is a horrid Plot upon Her Majesty's Person and Government, and a plain Suggestion, that the QUEEN has no Title to the Crown of *England*.

3. The Doctrine of Divine Right of Princes to govern, implies such Obligations to unlimited Obedience, as lays the Foundation of a Necessity upon Subjects, to submit to all Manner of Tyranny.

4. The Commands of a Prince, who reigns *Jure divino* Inherent and Personal, may not be disobey'd or disputed, howsoever contradictory to Reason or Nature; because that would be to rebel against God – But the Commands of a King or Queen of *England*, if contradictory to Reason or Nature, may be disputed or disobey'd – *Ergo*, The Kings or Queens of *England* do not reign by Inherent, Personal, Divine Right.

And yet after all, the QUEEN of *England* has a Divine Right, and is a Sacred Princess. Government is Divine, and Her Majesty's Title to execute it, is Divine; Government is without doubt of Divine Original, as Reason is the Daughter of Nature, Nature the first-born Daughter of

Heaven – Government is founded in Reason, Reason is the immediate Creature of the most High; God Almighty begat Nature by the Breath of his Mouth, fix'd its Eternal Law in his unalterable Decree; Nature begat Reason, Reason begat Government

God gave Man the Earth for his Possession; in that Possession he included the Government, for to have given a Body of Men the Possession of a Country, but give the Dominion of it away from them, had been not to give it them all; in this Possession, is their original Power seated. Lords of the Soil are always Lords of themselves; if it be otherwise, 'tis by Usurpation and Invasion; and that is a Force upon Reason, and thwarts the Order of Nature.

Hence the Free-holders are the Foundation-Branch of Constitution; and here all the Governments in the World began; the Right of Possession always had the Right of Government, which is the Band and Guard of that Possession – Reason thus finding it self possess'd of Property, dictated Government for its Regulation and Security, and this is a Right, whose Divinity cannot be disputed.

Even God himself holds by this Tenure; his Right to rule over us, is founded upon his Property in us – *The Earth is the Lords*, says the Text – *Who shall say unto him, what doest thou?* he governs the World, because the World is his own.[12] The Divine Right of his Authority is fix'd in the Article of Creation; *He made us, and not we our selves*, Psalm 100. What follows therefore, *we are his People, and the Sheep of his Pasture*.

In this Right of Property, the *English* Government is establish'd and its Original is certainly divine – And therefore it is, that the Title of Sacred is not put upon the QUEEN till her Coronation; which Coronation is the publick Consent and Homage of her Subjects; and the *French* Word for Coronation, is SACRE – Or consecrating the King; which explains it very well, and is nothing, *the Formalities of the Priests excepted*, but proclaiming the King, and asking the People; if they are willing, he *should reign over them*? I appeal to Coronation-Forms for the Truth of this.

This is her Majesty's Divine Right, *Viz*. The Establishment of the Crown by the legal constituent Parts of Government – This is a fair and just Supersedeas[13] to all Claim of Blood, Line, Descent, or pretended Divine Right whatsoever. This Divine Right, the QUEEN has, and whoever says, this is not sufficient, or that the Parliament of *England* has not a legal Power to limit the Succession, that is to displace, dis-inherit, put by, state, and re-instate, as they see fit, is an Enemy of *England*, and a Traytor to its Constitution.

This is Her Majesty's Right, *'tis truly Divine*, Her Majesty needs no other; Her Majesty can have no other; the Duke of *Marlborough* fights to maintain the Sufficiency of this Title; and concurring Heaven gives a loud Testimony to the Justice of the Claim by Miracles of Victories, and by striking the Enemies of this Possession with Terror and Amazement.

Will any Man then ask what Right the QUEEN has, and what the Duke of *Marlborough* fights for – This is the Divine Right, and Descent of Blood, Line, inherent Regality and the like; all truckle to the supream Authority of Constitution-Power built upon Law, and that upon Property, directed so by Reason; the Exemplification of Nature, and that of *GOD*.

Let any Prince in the World show such a Divine Right as this! all that pretend to rule by any other Claim, are Usurpers; and the Consequence of their Pretence is always Tyranny; 'tis in the Nature of the thing, and we have had too much Evidence, that it has always been in their Design.

This is an Abridgment of my Notion of Divine Right; I have been larger upon the Subject elsewhere; and shall therefore make no more Returns to the Cavills of the Opposer, who in this, is a true Pun upon his Title, a meer *Rehearser* of himself – But to this Hour, dares not make any Return to three modest Questions; one of which I repeat, and which till he replies to, I shall say no more to him.

If the Kings of *England* have an Inherent *Divine Right* of Succession to the Government – What Title has her Majesty to the Crown? And for what reason, but to invalidate that Title, is the Doctrine of Divine Right now Started? [. . .]

Thursday, August 15. 1706.

I Have often resolv'd to meddle no more with the dull Repetitions of the Champions for the Doctrine of *Jure Divino*; I think it is sufficiently exposed, and I see nothing to add to the matter; it deserves Ridicule rather than Argument.

But I am push'd upon more speaking, by one that thinks he has started something unanswerable; and that in his Objection against the Right of Freehold, having the Right of Government annexed; and to shake this, he asks an old controverted Question, and a thing many times answer'd, *Viz.* Which was prior, Dominion or Property? To which I readily answer, Property was first in Man, and yet I allow, that

Government was instituted by God Almighty too; nay, I'll call *Adam* a King, or anything he pleases; but I must tell him, God gave *Adam* Livery and Seisin,[14] a free Possession, before he deputed Government to him – And the giving him the Government, was a meer Consequence of the Property; he was a rightful Freeholder, and by Vertue of his Freehold, rightful Lord – And when his Posterity were planted in the several Parts of the World, their Possession was their Freehold; and as they had one, they had a Right to settle the other.

I do therefore no where say, Government was instituted by God; for it is founded in Nature and Reason, Principles in Man immediately infused by his Maker with his Life – But the Form of Government was certainly his own – And there was a Time, when Form of Government was not, *viz.* before Government was in its Exercise – If thus *Adam* was a King, or what ever Sort of Governour you please to call him, there was a Time when he was not so.

Speaking of this, which I take to be a just Distinction, 'tis plain, Property was before Dominion; for God gave *Adam* the Possession of the World, and his Dominion was the Consequence of that Possession.

Thus the wondrous Difficulty is clear; the first Possession of the several Lands, which the Posterity of *Adam* took by Direction of their Maker, or otherwise at their Travail from *Babel*, was doubtless a Freehold, and few better Tenures can now be shewn; with this Possession went the Government, or God had given them nothing – Their Dictates to the Government of themselves were as natural as their Apetites to eat and drink; The Form, Manner, and Circumstances, *such as the Person or Persons governing, &c.* was wholly their own, and fairly left to them by their Maker, in that he no where prescrib'd it.

I can see no Contradiction in this, and the eternal Cavils of the Objector can never shake this Foundation; upon it all the Forms of Government in the World stand, and the *English* Constitution is the exactest Exemplification of it imaginable. [. . .]

Tuesday, November 11. 1707.

Miscellanea.

I Have a Debate before me for this Part of the Paper, which the Author of the *Rehearsal* has open'd the Door for in the World, and which I have undertaken to answer him upon, if he please to go on.

Viz. Whether there cannot be a happy Union among us in *Britain*, without a Union of Principles?

But I must adjourn the Debate a little, to speak to a new Question which he has advanc'd in the World,

Whether the *Jure Divino* of Monarchy is not proved from the Antiquity of it; and that because Monarchy was in the World before Common-Wealths, therefore they are only of Divine Original.

But I think, with Submission to Mr. *Rehearsal,* that this is not the Main of the Question, and therefore I would humbly propose to him to state this Question another Way, and if he pleases to take it thus – In the Answer to which will manifestly appear the Design of the Doctrine.

Whether suppose, Monarchy was the first Government in the World, therefore Kings are absolute, and may tyrannize over their People?

Whether suppose, Monarchy was the first Government in the World, therefore the People must not be allow'd to repell Violence with Force?

When he has taken up the Point thus fairly, I shall undertake to prove, that a People oppress'd and abus'd by the Lust, Tyranny and arbitrary Will of even a Legal Prince, may take up Arms in Defence of their Liberty, may dethrone, depose, or dispose of that Tyrant, and establish their own Liberty, by setting up another Prince in their Room, or erecting any other reasonable Government, in the Stead of it – And I'll undertake to prove,

1. That the Nature of Government implies it.
2. That all Nations have practis'd it.
3. That GOD Himself has approv'd of it.
4. And that if it be not so, then there is not one Lawful Monarch now Reigning in the World, nor has there been One since the Line of King *David.*

After this, I shall state another Method for Mr. *Rehearsal* to go upon, if he will please to stand by his argument, and bring it to a Head.

That supposing for Argument Sake only, that all he tells us of the Original of Monarchy were true; That it was in its Original Sacred, and in its Exercise Absolute; that an undisputed Obedience was required, and that to resist, were to resist the Ordinance of GOD.

This cannot affect us in these Ages of the World, unless he can prove, for any Prince now reigning, an un-interrupted Succession of Blood, from some Monarch who had such a Divinely Instituted Original; and that therefore to push his Argument now, is but to proclaim War against all the Kings of the Earth, as Usurpers over Men, and Traytors to GOD; reigning in Prejudice of some or other Person, who has an inherent Right of Blood immediately deriv'd from GOD's Institution, Indefeizible in its Nature, and Sacred in its Original.

And tho' this Heir of Eternal Right has his Title, neither discover'd to the World, nor to himself, and may be in Quality a Chimney-sweeper, in Nature a Scoundrel, and abject to the meanest concievable Degree, yet he has the Sacred in his Blood, his Claim is inherent, and all the World must lie in Confusion, till they find him.

This, and infinite Absurdities will follow such a Scheme, and therefore I think, Mr. *Rehearsal* may employ his Talent to much better Purpose, than to start such ridiculous Stuff as this in the World.

As to his Argument about the *Jus Divinum* of *Episcopacy*,[15] being also built upon the same Hypothesis, I leave it to the Decision of those Gentlemen, whose Business it more particularly is, tho' I think, it is effectually answer'd in several late Tracts, which Mr. *Rehearsal* cannot be ignorant of, and which if he could be ignorant of, I could recover his Memory about.

Tuesday, November 25. 1707.

I Had not meddled with this Subject now but that it appears levell'd, *first* at the Revolution, and *secondly* at her Majesty's Government; since if this old abdicated Doctrine be granted, they would soon boast over both as Usurpation.

I stated the Case in a late *Miscellanea*[16] on that Subject, to which I referr, and leave this Question to be answer'd at their Leisure, for I suppose they won't make abundance of Haste in it; Whether supposing Monarchy to be the original Government, whether therefore Tyrant Monarchs must not be resisted?

I have advanc'd in former Papers also, that it has been the common Method of Divine Justice in the World to pull down Tyrants, by the Hands of those very People that have been oppress'd by them, and to retaliate the Murthers and Violences they have committed in the same Manner, they have committed them.

Adonibezec, who had cut off the Fingers and Toes of threescore and ten Kings, by the meer Barbarity of his Nature, and unbounded Insults of his Pride, had the same Punishment appointed him by Heaven's Justice in the very Circumstance of it, *Judges* 1. 7. And no Regard was had to his Royal Dignity and Crown.

Ahab, who spilt the innocent Blood of his Subject *Naboth*, meerly to satisfie the Lust of a Tyrant, in coveting his Inheritance, and cast his murther'd Body out into the Streets to the Dogs, had the Dogs licking his Blood, *perhaps the same Dogs too*, in the very same Place, when Vengeance following his Tyranny, he fled wounded, and dying out of the Battle of *Ramoth Gilead*, 1 *Kings*, 22. 38. And *Jehu* was rewarded for the Destruction of that Tyrant and his Houses.

Haman,[17] a Prince, tho' not a King, and an Instrument as well as an Exciter of the Murther of the Captive *Jews*, we find hang'd and all his Sons, on the same Gallows he had prepar'd for the Destruction of innocent *Mordecai*.

This would make a good Application to his most Christian Majesty,[18] and I wish he would permit himself to read that Scripture in the 31*st* of *Isaiah, v.* i. *Woe unto thee that spoilest, and thou wast not spoiled, and dealest treacherously, and they dealt not treacherously with thee; when thou shalt cease to spoil, thou shalt be spoiled, and when thou shalt make an End to deal treacherously, they shall deal treacherously with thee.*

Shall I descend to prophane History, and show the Nation's deposing Tyranny; not a Nation in the World but gives us faithful Instances of the Hand of Divine Justice following Tyrants, even by a visible Stroke of Justice, and pursuing them to their Destruction, by the very People they have oppress'd; nay, this very King of *France* himself enjoys the Crown of that Kingdom, by the Power and Valour of that very People, who pulled down the House of *Valois*[19] for their Cruelty and Persecution? Shall we search the Judgments of GOD on that bloody House, how their Monster of Persecution and Hypocrisie, *Charles* IX. dy'd mad; how *Henry* II. was kill'd by a Wound in the Eye, having promised to glut his Eyes with the Blood of his Subjects; how *Henry* III. who basely murther'd the Duke of *Guise*, by causing him to be assassinated as he went into the Council-Chamber, was afterwards basely murther'd, being stabb'd in his

Tent by a *Jacobite* Fryar,[20] after having been declared a Tyrant, and formally deposed by his People?

Should we search the *Persian*, *Græcian* and *Roman* Empires, from *Sardanapalus* down to *Tarquin Julius Cæsar*, and afterwards down to *Adolph of Nassau*? How are the Histories of all those Times full of Instances of the miserable Ends of Tyrants, and Invaders of the Nations Properties?

From the Beginning of History it is remarkable, that Nations have all along thought it just as well as proper to pull down Oppression; and therefore if it be objected, that this is to put the Sword into the Hand of Subjects to insult Government, and raise that worst of Crimes, Rebellion – Let me mingle the sad Story with a little Mirth, as well as History; some of the Lines I suppose, the Author may have seen before.

> When Kings against the *King of Kings* rebel,
> And the *Crown'd Christian* turns an Infidel;
> When *Mortal Man* his Maker once defies,
> We may *the Man*, tho' not *the King*, despise;
> The just Distinction's here exactly shown,
> Between the *Man* that wears it, and *the Crown*.
> For if to Blood and Rapine *they descend*,
> And by their *Right Divine* the Crown defend,
> Trample on Justice, and suppress the Law,
> And think the Crown *must injur'd Subjects awe*;
> Nature directs the Nations *what to do*,
> And Nations Nature's Dictates always *will pursue*:
> The Sanction of the Crown's at once transferr'd,
> *Blood calls for Blood*, and Nature will be heard;
> The Crown no more can such a Wretch defend,
> He's damn'd *by Natures Law*, his Reign must end:
> What tho' by Strength of Hand *he keeps* the Crown,
> He's no more King, *tho' he possess* the Throne;
> *Tyrant* and *King* are vastly different things,
> We're robb'd *by Tyrants*, but we are rul'd *by Kings*;
> *These* may uphold, but those o're-turn a State,
> *That* is the Man, and *This* the Magistrate;
> Our Safety must *on this* Distinction rest,
> For *this* we must obey, and *that* we should resist.
> *If it be ask't*, how the Distinction's known,
> Oppression marks him out, *the Nations* groan;
> The Laws *dispens'd*, the *Injuries*, the *Blood*,
> Are Languages *by all Men* understood:
> The *Voice of Bondage* and *Destruction's* known,
> And summons all Men to defend their own;
> Freedom's *the common Right* of all Mankind,

And *they that slight it*, leave their Sence behind;
No Laws of GOD our Properties expose,
Kings *are our Guards*, those Freedoms *to enclose*;
And they who *what they should defend*, invade,
Forfeit their Office, have their Trust betray'd
To him, *that first employ'd them*, shall account,
As Soveraign Power does Human Power surmount.
  Nor that alone; but *they* that are opprest,
Shall take that Power *away*, which he possest;
So far shall punish Mischiefs done before,
As to prevent the willing Wretch from more;
Shall take the Soveraign Glory from his Head,
And *set up Right* to govern in his Stead.
  The Laws of Nature dictate to the Sence,
That all Men claim the Right of *Self-Defence*;
Even *they that swear* a larger Debt to pay,
Insult their Maker, if they thus obey;
Subjection's *always* to be understood,
Saving the Laws of Nature and of GOD.
Immortal Power has the superiour Sway,
This *People* must observe, and *Kings* obey;
If *the Crown'd Wretch* rebells and fights with Heaven,
The Voice of Nature speaks, *the Signal's given.*
People *must never* with th' Invader joyn,   ⎫
His *Crown falls off* of Course, his Scepter's vain, ⎬
By *whatsoever Right* he came to reign.   ⎭
  From this just Cause *it always* comes to pass,
Let *the Fool Man* be ne're so much *an Ass*;
The Laws of Nature *ne're so much* opprest,
The Passive Wretch be *ne're so much* a Jest;
The just Dominion of Eternal Right
Dissolves the Mist *at last*, and clears his Sight.
  The Passive Contradictions *are so plain*,
Such vile direct Absurdities maintain;
They bring *the wheedl'd Wretch* to such a Case,
He may be damn'd *in spight of Soveraign Grace*:
  Suppose *a Tyrant* dooms a Man to die,
And *bids him hang himself*; if he'll obey,
Let Mankind answer for his Future State,
'Tis my Opinion, all Men know his Fate;
Those Men will *damn him too*, if he refuse,
Th' unhappy Wretch is left *no Room to chuse*;
Fate has hedg'd up his undirected Way,
He dies, if he'll refuse; *he's damn'd*, if he'll obey.[21]

If this does not clear up the Title, that Tyrants may be deposed, and Subjects may by Force resist Violence, and take up Arms to recover their Liberties, both Civil and Religious, tho' 'twere against their own Lawful Soveraign, I may give you some more Fragments hereafter.

Tuesday, December 13. 1709.

Because this Paper is seen in some Parts of the World, where such a Man as Dr. *S—l* [22] has not been heard of – and where the Sound of his late Harangue is not found, it seems necessary to tell, what to us here in *London* will be no News – *Viz.* That on the *Fifth* of *November*, being the Anniversary for Gun-powder Treason, one Dr. *S—l* preach'd at St. *Paul*'s Cathedral, from those Words in 2 *Cor.* xi. 26. *In Perils among false Brethren*; wherein having plentifully rail'd at and anathematiz'd the *Dissenters*, and left them in Custody without Bail or Mainprize, with the Devil and his Angels – He particularly asserts two Things.

1. The Doctrine of Passive-Obedience – which he most remarkably justifies from the late Revolution.
2. The Hereditary Right of her present Majesty to the Crown.

In my last I have most humbly petition'd him to do two other Things at his Leisure, for the publick Satisfaction.

1. To reconcile the Battle at the *Boyn* to the Doctrine of Non Resistance, and to assoil the Parliament of *England*, and the Church of *England*, from the Breach made in that Principle in the War in *Ireland*.
2. To tell us – by what Part of Hereditary Right her present Majesty possesses the Crown of *Great Britain* and *Ireland*.

Now I must in Reason give the Doctor some Time to reply, and therefore I shall respite the Discourse – And as what may not be improper to the Purpose – for the farther Information of the People – I shall play the Expositor a little – and show you from Scripture, that even in the first Ages of Monarchy in the World – the Superiority of Laws to the Sovereign was not only claim'd by the People as their Right, but was acknowledg'd by the Monarch as the Peoples Due, and as a Debt they could not with-hold – And this is the famous Story of *Darius* [23] casting the Prophet *Daniel* into the Den of Lions.

It is evident, That *Sardanapalus*, the great *Assyrian* Monarch proving an effeminate luxurious Tyrant, was resisted by the Great *Arbaces* the

Median – and was depos'd, burning himself afterwards in his great Golden Palace; *of which hereafter.* Hereupon the *Median* Empire was erected, which afterward was joyn'd with the *Persian*, and *Darius* was their King in the Time of the Captivity, and *Daniel* the Prophet was a Favourite in his Court – I have indeed made this publick[24] once before, but few having seen it, and the Occasion being thus renew'd, I perswade my self, it will not be unacceptable to repeat it.

The Limitation of Power and Superiority of Laws in Matters of Government have an Original in the very early Ages of the World; and the Holy Text give such an Instance of the limitted Power of Kings, and their Subjection to the Laws of their own making, that I know no Instances in the World can come up to it.

The Princes and Rulers, under *Darius* the *Median* King, having resolv'd the Destruction of the Prophet *Daniel, laid their Contrivance thus*, to get a Law made, that no man should pray to *any God*, or make any Request to *any Man*, but to the King, for such a Time, *Dan.* 6. *v.* 7. Now knowing that *Darius* was so fond of *Daniel*, that he would not be directly prevail'd upon to hurt him, they form this Project, and tender it to the King in their Council, or Assembly, or Parliament, call it which you please; and they bring in an *Bill of Occasional Conformity*, and desire the King to *pass it*, not discovering their Persecution-Design against *the Innocent*, who they certainly knew would not omit his Duty, and consequently would fall into the Snare.

That this was a National Law, *or Act of Parliament*, the Text is happily particular in, *Verse* 7. *All the Presidents of the Kingdoms, Governors, Princes;* there's the House of Lords; *Counsellors and Captains;* there's their House of Commons, *consulted together to establish a Royal Statute.* Where I observe,

First, To make a Statute, requir'd the Assembling and Consulting of the Princes, Counsellors, Great Men, *&c.* as well as the King, so that Legislation was thus early vested in the Persons to be govern'd.

Secondly, The King had nothing to do, but to approve and sign the Decree, the making it and consulting about it, requir'd the Assembling the Heads of the People.

Thirdly, When the Parliament, or Assembly of Princes and Counsellors, had made a Law, and the King had sign'd it, *even the King himself* could not alter it, so that the making of Laws was in the People, and when made, they will be superior even to the King himself.

Fourthly, Nay, the King himself had not Power, *after a Law was made*, so much as to suspend its Execution on the Criminal; all which are deducible directly from the Example in the Text.

Nor is the King's signing this Decree or Statute left here to his Arbitrary Choice; *but the Text is plain.*

The Princes, Counsellors, *&c. assemble together to the King, v.* 6. That is, in our Parliament-Terms, *both Houses joyn'd in an Address to his Majesty;* for the Reason of his passing this Law, they tell him, *They have all consulted together,* or because they have all consulted . . . . as appears by the very next Words.

Verse 8. *Now, O King, establish the decree, and sign the writing;* or in our Phrase, since both Houses have unanimously pass'd this Act, we hope, your Majesty will not refuse your Royal Assent, *for we have all consulted together about it.*

And to confirm this, and prove that it is no forc'd Construction, See the next Words, *v.* 9 *WHEREFORE King Darius sign'd the writing and the decree,* even for that Reason.

Now observe the Treatment these People gave their King: Upon the ripening of the Plot, they find *Daniel* praying, as they knew before they should, at the Window of his Chamber, looking towards *Jerusalem*, as was the Custom of their Country, from the Words of *Solomon* in the Dedication of the Temple, *Hearken thou to the supplication of thy people Israel, when they shall pray towards this place,* 1 *Kings* 8. 30. Away they go to the King, and first demand a Recognition of the Law from him, *v.* 12. *Then they came near, and spake before the King concerning the King's Decree, Hast thou not sign'd a Decree, that every Man that shall ask a Petition of any God or Man within thirty days, save of thee, O King, shall be cast into the Den of Lions?*

Well says the King, I have, and you know when it is done, I cannot undo it; for *according to the Laws of the* Medes *and* Persians *it altereth not;* then they tell him the Story of *Daniel*, how he had not regarded the Law, nor the King's signing it, *v.* 13.

Now observe the King's Conduct, *v.* 15. *Then the King, when he heard these things, was sore displeas'd with himself,* i. e. for passing such a Law unadvisedly, without making some Proviso or Exception for his beloved *Daniel; and he set his Heart on Daniel to deliver him, and he labour'd to the going down of the Sun to deliver him.* This Passage is a most significant Expression of the Extremity of the King's Affairs, and how he labour'd between the Affection he had for the Prophet, and his Respect for the Law.

He labour'd till Sun-set, where we may suppose, *I believe without any Arrogance,* that he labour'd by perswading the Great Men to spare him; it is plain, he did not labour with himself to be willing and easie to deliver him up, but the Words are express, *he labour'd to deliver him.*

Note here, the King had no Dispensing Power; the Criminal, the Law condemns, must be executed, even the King himself could not reprieve him.

And tho' the King suspended the Execution but one Day, see the Unweariness and Clamour is rais'd THEN, that is, at the going down of the Sun, *these Men assembled unto the King.* Now mark the Emphasis; they do not come with another humble Address to his Majesty, that the Laws might be put in Execution, but they come with a Claim of Right, *KNOW O KING, that the Laws of the* Medes *and* Persians *is, that no Decree or Statute, which the King establishes, may be changed;* as if they had said, Sir, we come to demand our Rights and Liberties according to the known Laws of this Land; and to tell you, Sir, that to dispense with the Laws of the Land is illegal, and is not in their Power. The King took their Meaning presently, and knowing he could not contend with them, or in meer Veneration to the most sacred Authority of the Law, gives them no Answer, but delivers up *Daniel* to their Mercy.

His Concern for him, when he was in his Enemies Hands, appears, *v.* 18. *Then the King went to his Palace, and passed the Night fasting, neither were the Instruments of Musick brought before him, and his Sleep went from him.* Here's his Concern for him illustrated farther; by his running to the Den of Lions in the Morning, to know how it far'd with him, his Joy at his Knowledge of his Deliverance, and his severe Revenge upon his Accusers, as may be seen at large, *v.* 19, 20, 21, 22, 23, 24.

Here's an original Monarch, whose sacred absolute Power and Dominion could not save a Favourite from the Force of the Law, tho' falsly accus'd. Here's the due Sovereignty of the Law so acknowledg'd, and recogniz'd, as no Prince in *Europe* could stoop to.

Not King *Charles* I. parted with his beloved *Strafford,* and Star-Chamber; not King *Charles* II. granted the *Habeas Corpus* Act; not King *James* parted with his Crown, or King WILLIAM with his Blue Guards,[25] with a fortieth Part of the Reluctance, but the Law was pass'd, and the King had no Power to alter or suspend it.

Thus the Superiority of the Law to Kingly Power was acknowledg'd in the *Medes* and *Persians* Monarchy; and King *Darius,* tho' as Potent a Prince as most that ever reign'd, vail'd his Crown to the Regency of Law, and acknowledg'd himself unable to alter it, or suspend its Execution.

Thursday, August 31. 1710.

I Was designing, as may appear in my last, to have Examin'd farther the Address of the *London* Clergy, and the particular manner, in which, *at least to me*, they seem to Recognize the great Doctrine of Resistance, and promise to practise it.

But if by Examining the General System, these Things may be brought to a right Understanding, I think it is the more peaceable Way; and therefore having a great desire to make this Paper a Reconciler of Differences, I shall now, tho' it take me up more time than usual, enter into a full Enquiry after, and search to the Bottom, the present Debates, which so much Agitate our Minds, about *Hereditary-Right* and *Non-Resistance.*

I know I am going about a very difficult Work, yet the difficulty lies not so much in the Argument, as in the Temper of the People I am arguing with, to whom it is neither grateful, nor as they think, for their Convenience, to be undeluded.

However, I shall set about the Work, and with this Assurance, that if it miscarry, it shall not be for want of Demonstration – And if you will not receive it, the Negative shall not be for want of Obstinate Blindness.

I know I am to struggle with, 1. *Your Pride*, from whence flow strong streams of Opinion-Wisdom, 2. *Your Politicks*, from whence proceeds the Maxim, that 'tis your Interest to disagree; and 3. *Your Inclination*, visibly pleas'd with Strife, and fond of Contention –

As my difficulties from hence will be the greater, it behoves me to lay down every Thing so plain, that if possible, it may leave no room for those to take hold, who are fondest of Contradiction.

If my Stile therefore, appears a little more Laconick; if my Periods are shorter than usual, and I seem to affect being Sententious; you will bear with my being less Polite, for the sake of my being less Impertinent.

Our present Disputes, *alas how trifling!* are resolv'd into two Generals – Which if they are Overthrown, 'tis humbly conceiv'd, the Particulars drawn from them, will fall of themselves.

1. Whether her present Majesty's Title to the Crown is Hereditary, or subject to Parliamentary Limitation?
2. Whether Resistance in any Case whatsoever be Lawful in the Subject against the Prince?

If in my Examination of these Things, I shall make it clear to you, that *Hereditary Right* and *Parliamentary Limitation*, are the same thing, That *Resistance*, and *Non-Resistance*, have no specifick difference in them – And that a right understanding of this, would reconcile us all; it will be a very keen Satyr upon our Folly, and shew that this whole Nation has *made a great Noise about nothing*.

This is the Labour I am going to undertake, I see no difficulty in the Thing itself, the Demonstration is easie – The Argument plain, and the Contraries have in themselves, a propensity to Unite.

But how to open the Eyes of a People, who in both these Points are born Blind; *Hic Labor hoc Opus*.[26]

London, like *Niniveh*, has so many Thousand Souls that know not their Right-Hand from their Left, in this Matter, that it were pity not to inform them; but it has also *so much Cattle, Jonah, 4. 12. i.e.* So many Brutes that will not be inform'd, that 'tis enough to make a Man of more Resolution than I, despair.

An Ass is so much an Ass, that if you turn him seven Years to Grass, you will never take him up a Horse – And *Solomon's* Fool[27] tho' bray'd in a Mortar, wou'd in spite of the Mollifying Operation, come out a Fool, just as he went in.

Sed nil desperandum,[28] it must have some good Effect, to set Things in a clear View, must first, or last, be a benefit to some Body; If a Hand be set up at a Cross-Way, pointing out the right Road; tho' 'tis of no use to him, that makes no use of it, yet 'twill for ever remain of use to him, that is not willing to go out of the Way.

At the worst, it shall divest the hardned Age of all excuses for their Errors, and Posterity shall never say, in defence of their Fathers, that they were not told it, or that they knew no better.

One Thing more before I begin, and I'll have done with Preambles.

I must pay Homage here, to the two greatest helps I have receiv'd in this great Work; and therefore in Justice to the *London* Clergy, and to the Itinerate Dr, I must acknowledge, that their great Labours, the one in their late wonderful Address, and the other, in his great want of ADDRESS, endeavouring to lay open the difference of these Things, have very much Contributed to confirm me in this Great Truth, That there is no difference in them at all – And so I come to my Point.

And First of Hereditary Right.

And here to avoid shifters, and shifting too, I lay down, That by Hereditary-Right, I mean without Circumlocution, the Hereditary-Right of the present Queen, to the Crown of *England* – The Hereditary Right of all those her Majesty's Predecessors, Kings or Queens of this Kingdom, who have gone before her, or Successors that shall come after her.

Mr. *Asgill*[29] will Pardon me I hope, for pursuing his most Excellent Method, in which he has so unanswerably prov'd, the Divine Hereditary Right of the Elector of *Hannover;* and if I borrow any thing from him, I shall do Justice to the Lender, and always pull off my Cap, and make my Leg[30] for his License, in applying it to the uses and purposes he has fitted it for.

That Ingenious Author, has, in searching the Original of the Title of the Kings of *Israel,* and the Right they had to their Regal Authority, happily found out the Entail, in these Prophetick Expression of the Old Patriarch *Jacob,* when he took leave of his Sons – And the World, both together.

> *The Scepter shall not depart from Judah, or a Law-giver from between his Feet, until Shiloh come.*[31]

> *Here I crave leave for a Digression, tho' perfectly remote to my Case, being a Duty in Solemn Recognition of the Glorious fulfilling this promise of the MESSIAH, in the coming of* our Lord Jesus Christ *into the World – And which, if any of the Jews would please to consider – It would either convince them, that the promised MESSIAH is already come, or put them to some difficulty, to make out what they say they believe,* viz. *That the Prophecies of the Old Testament are Divine; and they may as well give over expecting him, as not believe he is come.*

> *They all grant that in this Text, by SHILOH, is meant the MESSIAH who shall come, and that the Scepter shall not depart, till the MESSIAH shall come.*

> *They must also allow, that the Scepter is departed from Judah, they have neither King, nor Law-giver among them, neither ever have had since the Destruction of their City and Temple by the Romans.*

> *Wherefore the MESSIAH must be already come, or that Prophecy was false,* and *so not,* nor *can ever be* fulfill'd[c] – But this by the Way.

> I now return to the Case in Hand.

If I make a just Abridgment of Mr. *Asgill's* Argument, it is – That this being a Settlement of the Inheritance upon the Tribe, what ever Branch of the Tribe at any time posses'd it, whether in a Right, or Collateral Line, his

Title was Hereditary, and that it was not necessary that the immediate Heir, *that is the Eldest Branch*, should be the Heir *in Tail*, since the first Settlement was an Entail upon, *and special to* the Tribe, yet not limitting it to the Eldest Branch of that Tribe – And his Instances are apposite to the Point, *viz.* 1. That God passed by the Eldest Branch of the Royal House, *viz. Shelah*, (who was *Judah's* Eldest Son – *Er* and *Onan* dying without Issue) and took *Pharez* who was the Younger, and by a second Wife, of whose Race *Jesse* the Father of *David* proceeded, in a Direct Line. And 2. That in pitching upon this Younger Branch, the Entail was not fix'd upon the Eldest Branch, even of *Jesse*, but upon *David* the Youngest, his seven Elder Brothers being all brought and presented before him – And thus Again in many succeeding Princes of *Judah*, as of *Solomon* in particular – And yet the Entail being settled upon the Tribe, not on any particular Branch – The Possession of any Branch of that Tribe, was truly Hereditary.

Thus far Mr. Asgill

I shall run the Parallel to its full extent, in the Succession of our Kings and Queens, to the Crown of *England*; and tho' perhaps I may not find so excellent a Period, from whence to begin the Entail of the Crown of *England* (now *Britain*) as that Prophetick Inspir'd Declaration of the Patriarch *Jacob*, in behalf of the Tribe of *Judah*;

Yet if I produce an Indisputable Title, Recogniz'd by all the World, and continued by that Prescription, which in all other Cases is allow'd sufficient, to the Possession or Inheritance of any Estate in these Nations, I shall have as clear a Foundation, as any Title in the World can make out.

I might content my self with saying, that the Title of our Sovereigns is sufficiently confirm'd, in that it is not disputed either within the Realm, or without, by any Pretender, by any dormant Claim, or by any suppos'd Injury whatsoever – I mean now, not the Descent of this or that particular Branch of the Family, but the Right of the Royal Family itself.

The Royal Family of *England* being, after the *Saxon* Invasion, rejoyn'd with the *British*, after the *Danish* Invasion rejoin'd with the *Saxon*, and after the *Norman* Conquest again rejoyn'd with the *English*; seems to me, to continue in the same Race or Tribe where it was found, wherever History can trace the least appearance of a Royal Power.

Not that this at all proves the Divine Original of the Race, or of their Title to the Crown, unless it could appear, that the first Entail was a Settlement from Heaven, like that of *Judah* among the Tribes.

Saturday, September 2. 1710.

AND now, Gentlemen, having told you, that I am come in to Acknowledge the Doctrine of Hereditary Right – Before you boast of me too much, as a Convert, give me to leave to explain my self.

I gave you in my last, an Abridgment of Mr. *Asgill*'s Scheme, of the *Hereditary Right* of the Kings of *Israel*, who tho' they frequently succeeded over the Heads of the Eldest Branch, were nevertheless Hereditary by vertue of the great Entail of the Crown, upon the Tribe of *Judah*; by which, *not this* or *that* Branch, had the Entail fix'd upon special to them, but the whole Tribe, exclusive of all the rest of the Tribes; so that every Member of that Tribe, had a Capacity of Inheriting, as well as the Elder Branch, and God reserv'd the Nomination in himself, as in the Case of the House of *Jesse*, who was of the Younger Branch of the House of *Judah*, of *David*, who was the Youngest Son of Eight, in the House of *Jesse*, and of *Solomon*, who was a Younger Son of the House of *David*, and the like.

And why should we differ any longer about Words, and Quarrel about Circumstances, let us see, not how far asunder we can go, but how near together we can come – It is easie enough to find our what we differ in; but where's the Man that tries how far we can agree? This would be the Way to heal us – While the other Temper makes us all but *State-Tinkers*, who pretending to mend one Breach, make two.

Our Brethren the *Hereditary-Right Men*, own the *Legal Provision*, made by Parliament; they own, or else *Væ! vobis Hypocritæ*,[32] the Parliamentary Limitation of the Crown, to the House of *Hannover*, tho' it cuts off the Elder Branches, of the Houses of *Savoy*, *Orleans*, &c. Let the Addressors speak, whether they do, or not: On the other hand, we own the Hereditary Claim of the Queen, within the said Parliamentary Limitations; What is it then that we differ about? I profess solemnly I see nothing between us, but that we all mean the same thing, only cannot be so Complaisant to our own ease, as to express our selves the same Way.

Let us see then, if we can bring these differing Systems to speak the same Language, that our Lectures of Politicks, being not read in an unknown Tongue, they *that occupy the Place of the unlearned*,[33] may know when to say *Amen* to them – And that Trumpet of the State, giving a more certain Sound, all Men may know when to prepare themselves for Peace or War.

I shall go back in my next, to search into the great Charter of the *English* Crown – Perhaps it may not be found so very Authentick, as to be declar'd from Heaven, equal to that of *Israel*, by the Voice of *Jacob*, and by the immediate Direction of God himself, to the Prophets *Samuel* and *Nathan* – But the undisputed Inheritance of the Royal Family of *England*, from *Edgar* the first *British* Monarch, having a prescription of above 1300 Years, this *Vox Populi*, will be allow'd to pass for *Vox Dei*;[34] nor will there be any need to Debate it, or search farther for its divine Original, a difficulty I leave to those that pretend to it: I choose another Foundation, equally subservient to the Ends of Government, and equally entitling the Possessor of the Crown to our Allegiance; and this I call the Laws of the Land –   *I State it thus.*

The ROYAL FAMILY of *Britain*, having the Crown entail'd by the Laws, the Inheritance is to them, and to every of them; and they have an undoubted Right to the Possession, (upon such Terms, and Subjected to such a Tenure only, as is contain'd in the said Entail.) By this Entail the Crown is setled upon the Family indeed, but is not thereby Limitted to this or that Branch of the Royal Line, but every individual Person of the Blood Royal, has a Capacity of Inheriting, and the Right of Nominating to that Inheritance, is reserv'd in the Parliament – The Crown is nevertheless an Inheritance; the Parliament of *Britain* having a reserv'd Right of Limiting the Descendants to the Possession – and this is what I mean by *Parliamentary Hereditary Right.*

Now I defie all the Clan of *Jure-Divino* Biggots, to offer me an exception to this, *as to Fact*; or to prove that this is not the only Hereditary Right, our Crown can claim, *and this indeed is enough*; this is what we call *Constitution* – And this is what our Addressors mean, *if they mean any thing*, When at one end they talk of the Queen's Sacred-*Hereditary* Title to the Crown, and at the other end talk of Adhering to the Protestant Succession – Which is indeed reconcileable to this System; and I am persuaded, I may say without Arrogance, can be reconciled no other Way.

As for those, who would fain understand *Hereditary Right* to signifie Descent by a *Right Line*, a Phrase much in use in the time of the Famous *Bill of Exclusion*,[35] and found very useless soon after – Her Majesty will be less Angry with me, for saying she makes no such Claim, than with them, for saying no other Claim can be Legally made.

It is evident, the Queen was actually Queen, in her Capacity of Succeeding, while her Father was alive, and had the Crown fallen by the Demise of King *William, King James being yet alive,* Her Majesty had been our Lawful Rightful Sovereign, by the same *Hereditary Title,* that she is now; *the Reason is plain*, for that the Parliament, in whom the Right of Limiting the Inheritance is plac'd, had Nominated her Majesty to Inherit, with a *non-obstante* to her Father, or any other of his Children, whether Males or Females being then alive.

This is farther evident, by the Deed of Settlement, made by the Nation at the Revolution; wherein there is no new Entail of the Crown – (Whether there was a Right in the Convention to have made a new Entail, or not, is not the present Question) But the Old Entail is follow'd, and the Right of the Royal Family to the Crown, being own'd as the Foundation, the Remainders of the Inheritance are declar'd by the Parliament, (in whom the Right of Declaring those Remainders, is allowed to be) to such and such Branches, as by their Act of Limitation does appear – And these Branches thus Inherit, and if you will have the Word (Hereditary) you shall, they become *Hereditary Descendants* to the Crown, by *Authority of Parliament* – And what is this but PARLIAMENTARY HEREDITARY RIGHT, as I call'd it before?

And now, pray Gentlemen, What are we falling out about? How are we making Men Offenders for Words? How are we *Darkning Counsel by Words without Knowledge*?[36] 'Tis all the same thing, mean't by either Side, but dully and darkly express'd to *Dum-found* one another, and puzzle a Cause, which in itself, is the plainest in the World – If therefore you have a Mind to differ for Trifles, you must; but *who is for Peace, let him come in hither* – Here is a Method of Reconciliation, both Sides come over to both Sides; the Negatives and Affirmatives meet, the Extreams Kiss, the Opposites shake Hands, and we are all one again, if you please: If you will not unite now, *Mark them that sow Divisions.*[37]

You *Tories* say, the Queen has an Hereditary Right to the Crown – Well, we *Whigs* say, the Queen has a *Parliamentary Hereditary Right* to the Crown – *Vice Versa*.

We Whigs say, the Parliament has a Right of Limiting the Succession of the Crown, and therefore we own the Settlement on the House of *Hannover*: *You Tories say*, you acknowledge and adhere to the Succession of the House of *Hannover*, and therefore you own the Right of Parliament to limit the Succession.

And where is our Difference now? That we should fall out at this Mad rate? – What are we Scolding for, and Brangling about? – We have a fine House, and we all agree such a one is, and shall live in it, Proprietor, but the Familly cannot agree, whether he shall go in at the Fore-Door, or at the Back-Door; and so while all are willing he should go in, and Dwell in it – Yet the peaceable Possession is interrupted for that Trifling Debate.

If any Man will differ with me after this, about *Parliamentary Right* and *Hereditary;* I shall only desire him to tell me first, Which is farthest, from the *Exchange* to *Whitehall,* or from *Whitehall* to the *Exchange?* – A difficulty that can't be express'd, is no difficulty – My Answer is short; *Parliamentary Right* is *Hereditary,* and *Hereditary Right* is *Parliamentary,* and her Majesty is our Rightful Queen by both – He that expresly denies her either of these, is Guilty of Treason by the Act of Parliament, Entitled an Act for the better securing her Majesty's Person and Government, and ought to be Hang'd for a Traytor – And I say, *Currat Lex.*[38]

Thus Foolish have we been, and as Beasts in this Case; Bullying our Sovereign with what *is,* or *is not* her Majesty's Title, till we have made our selves a Sport, and a Laughing-Stock to them, who says *she has no Title at all* – Nor can this Dispute be a Service to any Body else, for nothing can tend more to make the Pretender's Claim clear, than to make the Queen's obscure; nothing can tend more to make *Jacobitism* easie, than to make the Queen's Right difficult to explain.

The System I have laid down, brings the Thing to a Point; there's now but one Debate left, and that we are all willing to have left; and there we must all be on one Side against the *Jacobites, viz.* Whether the *Parliament* has a Right to Limit the Descendants to the Inheritance, or whether the Crown must, *Jure Divino,* Descend in a Right Line, in spight of unquallifying Circumstances.

This is the true Debate, between *Jacobitism* and *Revolution* – 'Tis hard we should have any other Debate; the Parliament has set Queen *Ann* on the Throne, in Contravention of this Opinion of Descent *by Right Line,* and I doubt not the whole Power of *Britain* will Maintain her there – Her Right is made Hereditary by Authority of Parliament, the Entail remains special to the Family still, and is so far Hereditary – 'Tis only limited in the Person of the Queen by Parliamentary Authority – Thus upon the Demise of the Queen, and on default of Issue by her Majesty, the Remainder is Limited and Declar'd to Descend to the House of *Hannover* – And after it is Limited in the Line of *Hannover,* to such only as shall be Protestants; and in Default of such, the Inheritance may again be declar'd by the same Authority, in Bar of any Right of Line, and with a *non-obstante*[39] to any Claim of the immediate Heir – To such, or such, as that Parliament shall Determine, only keeping to the General Entail on the Blood Royal – And still this Descent is an Inheritance, and the Descent of the Estate may be call'd Hereditary – And so we will, by my Consent, differ no more about Words – But her Majesty is own'd by us all, to have a Parliamentary Hereditary Right to the Crown.

I had purpos'd here, to have run through our *English* History, to have shewn you how many Intersections of the immediate Line of Descent have been made, by Parliamentary Authority in this Kingdom; And how far Parliamentary Authority has always Interpos'd, between the Right Line, and the other Branches of the Blood Royal, in the Inheritance of the Crown – All which have been adjudg'd Legal by Parliament; and the Title of the Princes so Reigning, might still in this Sense be call'd *Hereditary* – All which serve only to tell us, that Parliamentary Limitation, does not destroy *Hereditary Right*, or *Hereditary Right* destroy *Parliamentary Limitation*, but both together make the firmest Title in the World, under this new United Name of a *Crown Parliamentarily Hereditary*.

Tuesday, September 5. 1710.

I Promised in my last, to Examin the great Charter of the Royal Family of *Britain*, by Virtue of which, the general Entail of the Crown, appears to be settled, as I have already observ'd – And by Virtue of which Entail, the subsequent Re-settlements have still, notwithstanding the Inter-sections made in the *Right-Line*, been always reserv'd to some or other Branch of the Blood Royal, tho' frequently without any Regard to the Doctrine of Primo-geniture – I shall make some entrance now into this Work – Because I have a great Mind, if I can, to explain this mighty Mystery, of the Right of our Sovereigns, and put an end to the Differences that are risen among us, about the Affair of Parliamentary-Right, and Hereditary-Right; of which I have Advanc'd for Truth, and will Maintain it, that they are the very same Thing, understood alike by the whole Nation; and that our Differences about them are a meer Strife of Words, with no manner of substantial Signification.

It is evident in History, that the *Saxons* having by Conquest, how Treacherously and Unjustly I will not Examin here, possess'd this Nation, and driven the Ancient *Britains* to the Refuge of the Mountains, and inaccessible Retreats of *Wales, Cornwall, Cumberland*, &c. The *Saxons*, I say, Divided this Kingdom, or part of *Britain*, from them call'd *England*, into a Heptarchy of Kingdoms, over which they Establish'd, by the Ancient *Gothick* Principles of Government, their Respective Kings.

What I call the *Gothick* Principles of Government, needs very little Explication, and may, as it serves to my present purpose, be Abridg'd thus; That the Nobility and Commons in these Ancient Governments, always, either Collectively or Representatively, had certain reserv'd Rights which the Kings were Sworn to Maintain, as the *Postulata* of Government, and on the Foundation of which, Royalty on one Hand, and Obedience on the other, were Reciprocally Founded – The Disputes that may arise about the Original Title, are needless to be Examin'd here; nor is the Divine Right of the first Kings of the *Saxons, Hengist* and *Horsa*, or their Successors, capable of any Demonstration, and therefore the Dispute here is perfectly needless.

That they were Captains and Leaders of Armies, who as Mercenaries, hir'd themselves out to fight for Pay, is no question – That when by their Power they reduc'd these Kingdoms, they became Kings, is Matter of Fact – And when we need make no Objection against the Foundation, since we make none against the Superstructure; no doubt the Kings Succeeding have as much a Right to Reign over this Kingdom, as we the People have to possess the Land; and that is a Title, we may very well be quiet with.

The Divided State of these *Saxon* Kings began to wear out, when *Egbert* King of the *West Saxons*, having subdu'd five of the seven Kingdoms, caus'd the whole to be call'd by a new Name, *Englelond, i. e.* the Land of the Angles, from whence Mr. *Camden*[40] tells us, came the Latin Word *Anglia* – This it seems was about the Year 800 – And 150 Year after this, King *Edgar* having Subdu'd all the rest, became Monarch of *Great Britain*, receiv'd Hommage of all the Petty Princes remaining in that famous Story, of his being Row'd in his Barge or Pinnace upon the River *Dee*, by a Boat's Crew of Kings, himself holding the Helm.

And here is the *English* Title to the Crown in the *Saxon* Line begun; in his Time, we read of several Parliaments or Wites-motes[41] held, being the Assemblies of the Wise Men of the Nation, by whom his Authority was Recogniz'd; and from him to *Edward* the Confessor, you have a Line of Kings of the *Saxon* Royal Family, tho' with various Intersections of the direct Line, as in *Edmund Ironside, Edgar Atheling*, and King *Harold*; then by the *Norman* Conquest, and even in that Conquest King *Rufus* and *Henry* I. Reign'd, their Elder Brother *Robert* being then alive – After this Usurpation by Conquest the *Saxon* Line was restor'd again in *Henry* II. – This *Henry* was made King, his Mother *Maud* the Empress being then living – And Mr. *Tyrell*[42] observes, the Consent of the Nobles, *i. e.* the Parliament, prevail'd against the Claim by Blood: *Edward* III. was made King, his Depos'd Father *Edward* II. being alive; *Henry* IV. then Duke of *Lancaster*, in the same manner upon the Deposing or

Abdication of *Richard* II. comes to the Crown, *Richard* II. being still alive; King *John* then Reign'd, and is recogniz'd by Parliament; the Right of the immediate Line, being in Prince *Arthur* his Eldest Brother's Son, and his Daughter *Eleanor*, who was living all his Reign; *Henry* III. Succeeded his Father in this pretended Ursurpation, the Lady *Eleanor* being still alive, in whom the immediate Descent was by Nature a Title, if that had been regarded – From the Reign of *Henry* VI. to *Henry* VII. the Crown was toss'd in a Blanket, as we may say, or Shuttle-cock'd about from Side to Side, between the Houses of *Lancaster* and *York*, till they were both United in the Old *British* Race of *Owen Tudor*, Marryed in the Person of *Henry* Duke of *Richmond*, of the House of *Lancaster*, to *Elizabeth* Daughter of *Edward* IV. of the House of *York*.

Here the Lines being United, the *British* Race of Kings are restor'd, in the Sirname of *Tudor*, they are joyn'd with the *Saxon*, and again Recogniz'd by Parliament in the Preamble to the Act 1 *Hen*. VII. cap. 1. and 1 *Hen*. VII. cap. 6. and from this Prince, the Inheritance of the Crown of *England* Descended to the Family of *Stuart*, the Royal Blood of the Kings of *Scotland*: The *English* Line failing in Queen *Elizabeth*, the Reminder of the Entail was only found in *Margaret*, Daughter of *Hen*. VII. and her Heirs, who being Marry'd to *James* IV. King of *Scotland*, left one Son who was afterwards *James* V. Father of Queen *Mary*; also she left one other son by the Duke of *Lenox*, whose Son, *Henry* Lord *Darnly*, Marry'd the said Queen *Mary*, and by her, had *James* V. whose Descent was particular in this, that his great Grandmother both by Fatherside and Motherside, was the same Person, *viz.* the Lady *Margaret* Daughter of *Henry* VII.; yet this King *James* was allow'd King, while his Mother was yet alive, and continued so many Years.

All these Things make it evident, that the Crown of these Kingdoms can be no otherwise Hereditary, than by the Inheritance being Entail'd on the Royal Family, and special to the Family, is not prescrib'd to this or that particular Branch, but being reserv'd to the Blood Royal, the declaring the Inheritance rests in the Parliament: And thus I make out my *Parliamentary Hereditary Right*, let him that Disputes it, Contradict me if he can.

EXPLANATORY NOTES

Some Reflections On A Pamphlet Lately Publish'd (1697)

Advertised for 'yesterday', in the *Foreign Post* for 29 November–3 December 1697. The first of Defoe's three contributions to the Standing Army debate. See Introduction pp. 17–20.

page

37   1   *Hard Words . . . Ears:* Samuel Butler, *Hudibras*, Part 1 (1663), Canto 1, lines 9–10.

39   2   *Mr. ABCDEFG*: The Dedication to Trenchard and Moyle's *An Argument Shewing*, etc. is signed 'ABCDEFG'.

     3   *Common Wealths Man*: a republican.

     4   *like Jehu*: see 2 Kings 10:16.

41   5   *Mr. Stephen's unmannerly Books*: The Rev. William Stephens (1647?–1718), Rector of Sutton, was a violently Whiggish author and preacher. His *Letter to the Author of the Memorial of the State of England* (1705) was later answered by Defoe in *Remarks on the Letter to the Author of the State-Memorial* (1706), which cast doubt on the genuineness of his Whiggism.

     6   *A Ferg—, a Man—*: 'Ferg' is perhaps meant to suggest Robert Ferguson, an independent clergyman and political intriguer, much concerned in the Popish Plot and Monmouth's rebellion. Macaulay writes of him as 'a bitter malcontent'.

43   7   *è contra*: conversely.

     8   *Charibdis*: The legendary whirlpool which, with the sea monster Scylla on the opposite shore, threatened mariners in the Straits of Messina.

44   9   *No Legislators*, etc: see Trenchard and Moyle, pp. 6–7.

45   10   *in totidem verbis*: in so many words.

46   11   *Oportet Mendacem esse Memorem*: a liar needs to have a good memory.

     12   *Pretorian Soldiers*: the Praetorian Guard, household guards of the Roman emperors.

     13   *Selimus Depos'd and Murther'd his Father*: Defoe may be thinking of the Sultan Murad (Amurath) who, on succeeding his father Selim II in 1574, had his brothers (not his father) killed.

47   14   *Ship Money*: Ship money was an old-established levy on maritime towns and counties to strengthen the navy in time of need. The action of

page   Charles I, in 1635, in extending it to inland areas was one of the grievances which led to the Civil Wars.

47   15   *course Allay*: coarse alloy.

48   16   *Sally*: Sallee, a Moroccan seaport at that time infested by pirates.

    17   *Epethite*: epithet.

50   18   *Enfans perdue*: (more properly perdus) 'lost children'.

    19   *Iniskilling and London Derry*: Eniskillen and Londonderry were, from
late 1688, the two great centres of Protestant resistance to the royalist
armies in Ireland. The 105-day siege of Londonderry, begun when
Protestant apprentice boys seized the keys of the city and shut the
Ferry Gate against the forces of the Earl of Antrim, is famous.

51   20   *Treaties of Westphalia and Nimeguen*: Respectively, the treaty which
in 1648 brought an end to the Thirty Years' War and the treaty
which in 1678 ended a six-year war between France and the United
Provinces.

    21   *Mr. Johnsons false Heraldry*: The Rev. Samuel ('Julian') Johnson, pillo-
ried for his opposition to popery during the reign of James II, wrote
in his attack on Bishop Burnet's *Pastoral Letter* of 1689, entitled *Notes
upon the Phoenix Edition of the Pastoral Letter* (1694), p. 4: 'I would fain
know whether the word Popish added to tyranny makes it better or
worse? . . . To put a bad Name upon Tyranny is false Heraldry.' (Defoe's
meaning is, evidently, that armed force is armed force, whether one
calls it an army or a fleet.)

52   22   *Pointy*: Jean-Bernard-Louis Desjean, Baron de Pointis (1645–1707),
naval commander. He seized Nueva-Cartagena from the Spanish in
1697.

54   23   *Charenton*: In 1567, during the French civil wars, the Huguenots under
the Prince de Condé took possession of Charenton, a suburb of Paris
through which most of its grain supply flowed.

55   24   *Ferdinand II*: Ferdinand of Styria (1578–1637), who became Holy
Roman Emperor as Ferdinand II in 1619.

    25   *Gustavus Adolphus*: Gustavus Adolphus II (1594–1632) king of Sweden.
In 1630, during the Thirty Years' War, he intervened as the champion of Protestantism against the Catholic League in Germany,
winning spectacular triumphs before his death on the battlefield at
Lutzen in 1632.

    26   *Carolus Gustavus*: In 1655 Charles X of Sweden attacked John Casimir
of Poland, who had refused to recognise his accession to the Swedish
throne.

    27   *Barnavelt's Principles . . . De Witts*: Upon the death of the Dutch stad-
holder William II in 1650 the grand pensionary Jan de Witt (1625–72),
a republican in the tradition of an earlier grand pensionary Jan van
Olden Barneveldt, opposed the dynastic pretensions of the House of
Orange, as represented in the infant Prince William (later King of
England).

56   28   *Duke of Monmouth*: In 1685 the followers of the Duke of Monmouth,
in his rising against James II, were defeated by James's army at
Sedgemoor in Somerset.

57   29   *Deceptio visus*: optical illusion.

    30   *Quatenus*: 'as' or '*qua*'.

page

57   31   *Popish Successor*: the Old Pretender, James Francis Edward Stuart (1688–1766), the (possibly supposititious) son of James II. He was called James III by the Jacobites after his father's death in 1701.

59   32   *his Royal Declaration*: William of Orange's Declaration, drawn up in Holland with the aid of Bishop Burnet, reached England at the end of October 1688.

An Argument Shewing, That A Standing Army (1698)

Advertised as 'this day' in the *Flying-Post* for 1–4 January 1698. The second of Defoe's contributions to the Standing Army debate.

page

64   1   *knows not Joseph*: see Exodus 1:8.

        2   *Discourse of Militia's*: i.e. Andrew Fletcher's *A Discourse Concerning Militias and Standing Armies* (1697).

        3   *A Second part of the Argument*: a continuation of Trenchard and Moyle's *An Arguement Shewing, etc.* published in December 1697.

65   4   *Medium*: compromise.

66   5   *Prince of Parma's Army*: The military organisation of the Spanish Armada in 1588 was in the hands of Phillip II's minister Alexander Farnese, Prince of Parma.

        6   *Guard du Corps*: life guards.

        7   *Guards du Terres*: (Defoe's inaccurate French) yeomanry.

        8   *King of Bohemia*: In August 1619 James I's son-in-law Frederick of the Palatinate accepted the crown of Bohemia. A year later, however, after his defeat at the battle of the White Mountain, a Spanish army invaded the Palatinate.

        9   *Relief of Rochel*: In 1627 Charles I despatched a fleet to relieve the Huguenots, besieged in La Rochelle. When, however, the expedition arrived at the Isle de Ré, just off La Rochelle, the Rochellese proved unwilling to throw in their lot with their would-be deliverers.

      10   *One neighbour*: i.e. France.

67   11   *Peace of Nimeguen*: see note 20 to *Some Reflections*, p.266.

      12   *1672*: France and England declared war on the Dutch in 1672, and the French army quickly overran the Netherlands.

      13   *they would be good for nothing*: As early as his first poem, *A New Discovery of an Old Intreague* (1691), Defoe was highly satirical about the militia.

      14   *Principiis Obsta*: stop things in their beginning.

68   15   *Count Colocedo ... Count Mansfield*: Count Don Carlos Coloma was Spanish ambassador to England during the reign of James I. Count Ernst von Mansfield was a German soldier of fortune who served as a general under James I's son-in-law Frederick; see note 8 above. In 1624 he was brought to England to command the army then being prepared for intervention in Europe, an appointment which enraged the professional soldiers.

      16   *Tho' his government ... Horses*: from the poem 'A Dialogue between the Two Horses', frequently attributed to Marvell.

page

68   17   *the Peace*: A peace between England, France, Spain and the United
Provinces was signed at Ryswick in October 1697.

69   18   *Pacta Conventa*: agreements between William and the Convention
Parliament, the body which offered him the crown.

      19   *in hac verba*: (properly *haec*), 'in these very words'.

70   20   *the Year 1680*: At the motion of the moderate Tory leader Robert
Harley, the Commons voted in December 1697 to disband all troops
raised since September 1680.

      21   *Purbeck fancied Invasion*: The *Second Part of an Argument* (p. 21) refers
to 'the Purbeck invasion, which was so private that it was seen only
by an old man and a boy: and yet though the country thought the
Government against them, we had above forty thousand volunteers in
arms in two or three days time'.

      22   *Battle of Newport*: Maurice of Nassau defeated the Austrians at
Nieuwpoort on 2 July 1600.

72   23   *the Power of the Sword … him if need be:* In the passages in italics,
Defoe seems to be giving a close paraphrase of Andrew Fletcher's *A
Discourse Concerning Militias and Standing Armies* (1697), p. 6.

73   24   *the Barons growing poor … the like*: a close paraphrase of Fletcher's
Discourse, p. 10.

75   25   *no Weapon … cou'd ever Prosper*: see Isaiah 54:17.

76   26   *the 10th Penny*: The tyrannical Duke of Alva attempted to impose a
10 per cent sales tax on the Netherlanders, but without success.

77   27   *Coat and Conduct money*: a tax levied on the counties by Charles I to
pay the cost of clothing troops and their travelling expenses.

      28   *Quo Warrantoes*: A *quo warranto* ('by what warrant?') was a writ against
a defendant, whether an individual or a corporation, calling on him
or it to show by what right he or it laid claim to something. In October
1683, by a *quo warranto* judgement, Charles II deprived the City of
its liberties and the Livery Companies of their charters.

      29   *In the year … Privileges of the City*: At the swearing-in of the new City
sheriffs on 28 September, the royalist lord mayor had trained bands
stationed near the hustings, and their colonel pulled a Whig councillor
down off the hustings and threw another, Henry Cornish, out of the
hall. A number of suits were brought against him for this behaviour.
There is a good account of the affray in M. E. Campbell, *Defoe's First
Poem* (Bloomington, Indiana, 1938), p. 155.

A Brief Reply to the History of Standing Armies (1698)

Probably published in early December 1698. The third of Defoe's contributions
to the Standing Army debate.

page

83   1   *And should … Murmur too*: This line, adapted in Defoe's *The True-
Born Englishman* (1701), Part 2 (line 672), first appeared in his *A New
Discovery of an Old Intreague* (1691), p. 12.

page

83   2   *Lord Strafford*: Sir Thomas Wentworth, first Earl of Strafford (1593–1641), began his political career as a strong critic of Charles I's ministers, but in 1629 he went over to the King's party.

       3   *Noy*: William Noy (or Noye) (1577–1634). Originally a defender of the subject's liberties, on becoming Attorney-General to Charles I in 1631 he became an active supporter of absolutism.

84   4   *For Parliament*-Men . . . *for't*: from the poem 'A Dialogue between the two Horses', frequently attributed to Marvell.

       5   *Lords S— D—, Mr H—, Mr H—*: it is not clear exactly whom Defoe has in mind.

       6   *whole Club of Mistaken Politicians*: Defoe is more explicit in *The Two Great Questions Further Considered* (1700) that Trenchard and John Toland ran a republican and Socinian 'club'.

85   7   *Strada and Bentivoglio*: Famianus Strada, author of *De Bello Belgico* (1632–47). Guido Bentivoglio, author of *The Complete History of the Wars of Flanders* (1554; London 1654).

       8   *Duke D'Alva*: Fernando, Duke of Alva (1508–83), tyrannical Governor of the Netherlands under Philip II of Spain.

       9   *D'Egmont presented the Petition*: The Count of Egmont was sent on a special mission to Madrid in 1665 to open the eyes of Phillip II to the hatred aroused in the Netherlands by the attempt to make them into a Spanish dependency and introduce the Inquisition.

86   10   *Loss of Dunkirk*: Dunkirk, won from the Spanish by Cromwell, was in 1662 sold to France by Charles II.

87   11   *one Reply*: Defoe is probably referring to his own *An Argument Shewing* of 1698.

88   12   *the Peace purchased now*: The Peace of Ryswick (1697), which brought to an end the War of the League of Augsburg.

90   13   *Dundalk*: King William's general the Duke of Schomberg made a landing in Ulster in August 1689 but halted his advance at Dundalk. Over the ensuing winter his troops suffered many casualties from disease.

92   14   *Iniskilling Men* After the landing of William of Orange in England in 1688 King James's troops were moved towards Ulster to prevent an uprising, but the Protestants succeeded in their desperate struggle to hold Eniskillen.

     15   *P. of O.*: Prince of Orange's.

     16   *A Book was printed*: Defoe probably means Andrew Fletcher's *A Discourse Concerning Militia's and Standing Armies* (1698).

93   17   *For Disputants . . . rail*: from the Epilogue to Dryden's *All for Love*.

     18   *To tell us . . . fram'd*: see Trenchard and Moyle, pp. 20–1.

     19   *Duke Schomberge*: Frederick Herman, Duke of Schomberg (1615–90) was a German soldier of fortune who became King William's most trusted commander.

95   20   *The Gentlemen who argue . . . Final*: this corresponds loosely to pp. 44–5 of Trenchard's *Short History*. 'Final' is Final Ligure.

98   21   *two Socinian Books*: One of the two books would have been *Christianity Not Mysterious* (1696) by John Toland, who was also involved in the publication of Algernon Sidney's *Discourses Concerning Government* in 1698.

page
98   22   *Ludlow's Memoires*: Edmund Ludlow's *Memoirs* were published posthumously in three volumes in 1698-9.

23   *O. C.*: Oliver Cromwell.

24   *Book for the Liberty of the Press*: perhaps Matthew Tindal's anonymous *A Letter to a Member of Parliament: Shewing that a Restraint of the Press is inconsistent with the Protestant Religion* (1698).

25   *Opening of the Parliament*: Parliament convened on 6 December 1698.

The Original Power of the Collective Body of the People of England (1702)

Advertised as 'this day' in the *Post-Man* for 25-7 December 1701. For a commentary on this pamphlet, see Introduction, pp. 21-3.

page
102   1   *Contemptible Imposter*: i.e. the Old Pretender. See note 31 to *Some Reflections*, pp. 266-7.

103   2   *Cess*: cessation (?).

104   3   *great Collective Body*: Defoe presumably means the 'Convention Parliament' (not strictly a Parliament) which offered the throne to William III.

4   *President*: precedent.

106   5   *Original Right*: It will be noticed that the title is here reworded.

6   *Jure Populi Anglicani*: or rather *Jura Populi Anglicani: or the Subject's Right to Petition set forth, occasioned by the Case of the Kentish Petitioners* (1701), thought to be by Lord Somers.

7   *A Vindication of the Rights of the Commons of England*: the title of a tract by the high Tory Sir Humphrey Mackworth (1701).

8   *Vindication of the Rights of the Lords*: i.e. *A Vindication of the Rights and Prerogatives of the Right Honourable the House of Lords* (1701), sometimes attributed to Lord Somers.

107   9   *Salus Populi suprema Lex*: The welfare of the people (is) the supreme law.

10   *And Power . . . Original*: from Defoe's *The True-Born Englishman*, line 819.

108   11   *that foolish Maxim*: Mackworth writes in his *Vindication*, p. 5, that 'the several and respective powers vested in the King, Lords and Commons, are mutual checks and mutual boundaries to one another, but are not to be limited by any authority besides their own'.

12   *by Petition*: e.g. in the case of the Kentish Petition. See Introduction p. 20.

109   13   *Banter'd*: mocked.

110   14   *Legion Libels*: a reference to *Legion's Memorial* (1701), reprinted in *Political and Economic Writings*, vol. 2.

15   *That Kings . . . Subject free*: from Defoe's *The True-Born Englishman*, lines 804-5.

111   16   *the Complaint which a late Author brings*: Mackworth writes (p. 40) that if a subject, in a petition to the Lord Chancellor, should presume 'to desire the Lord Chancellor to turn his plausible speeches into just and righteous decrees, I presume his Lordship might legally commit him to the Fleet [prison] for such an indignity to the court'.

page

111 17 *the Fleet*: the Fleet prison and its liberties, off Farringdon Street. It was by this time mainly a debtor's prison. Defoe himself spent several brief spells in it.

18 *must concern that part of the Country*: Mackworth writes (p. 38): 'It can never ... be admitted as legal, or so much as consistent with the interest and safety of England, for the Freeholders of any particular place or country, to direct the proceedings of Parliament'.

113 19 *Determination*: termination.

114 20 *Humanum est Errare*: It is human to err.

117 21 *the late Parliament*: the Parliament which sat from December 1698 to December 1700 and which made trouble for King William over the Standing Army question.

22 *a certain Treatise*: i.e. Mackworth's *Vindication*.

119 23 *These things ye ought to have done*: see Matthew 23:23.

24 *Lords denying ... the House*: In 1701 Lord Haversham offended the House of Lords by his vehement defence of Somers and Halifax against impeachment.

25 *Forty Years hence ... at Truro*: Mackworth says (p. 20) that the Lords might be tempted to frustrate a general impeachment by timetabling it for an absurdly near or an absurdly distant date, and that, though this is a very remote possibility, a wise constitution should guard against it.

120 26 *The Governments ... Original*: Defoe's *The True-Born Englishman*, lines 806–19.

27 *de Novo*: all over again.

122 28 *Soccage*: a form of tenure without knight-service.

123 29 *permissu Superiorum*: by permission of his superiors.

124 30 *Annihilated ... the Peers as a House*: In 1649, immediately after the execution of Charles I, the Rump Parliament abolished the House of Lords.

31 *a late Author*: i.e. Mackworth

125 32 *By their Works ye shall know them*: see Matthew 7:20, 'by their fruits ye shall know them'.

33 *Treaty of Partition*: the secret treaty signed by William III and Louis XIV in 1698, making a prospective division of the Spanish dominions in the event of the King of Spain's death.

126 34 *Dissolution of the last Parliament*: King William dissolved Parliament on 11 November 1701.

35 *Indignity ... French King*: The recognition by Louis XIV of the Old Pretender as King of England.

127 36 *Kentish Gentlemen*: see Introduction, p. 20.

Some Remarks on the First Chapter in Dr Davenant's Essays (1704)

Advertised as 'now published' in the *Daily Courant*, 6 December 1703. A rejoinder to Davenant's *Essays upon Peace at Home, and War Abroad* (1703), the first chapter of which was visibly directed against Defoe's *The Original Power of the Collective Body of the People of England* (1702) (see above, pp. 101–28).

Charles Davenant (1656?–1714), a self-styled Doctor of Law, was an MP and an authority on public finance. He was recruited by Harley round about 1700 as a Tory propagandist and made a considerable impression with his *The True Picture of a Modern Whig* (1701), but in 1701 he came under suspicion of being in French pay.

page

132   1   *Peace and Union*: The Queen in her speech to Parliament on 9 November 1703 enjoined 'Perfect peace and union'.

       2   *Sir Humphrey Mackworth*: Tory politician and projector (1657–1727). Defoe is referring to Mackworth's *Peace at Home; or a Vindication of the Proceedings of the House of Commons on the Bill for preventing Danger from Occasional Conformity* (1703). He in fact replied to this pamphlet of Mackworth's in *Peace without Union* (1703).

134   3   *a Scheme*: Mackworth's *A Vindication of the Rights of the Commons of England* (1701).

       4   *a subsequent Author*: Defoe perhaps means Lord Somers and his tract *Jura Populi Anglicani* (1701).

       5   *this Author*: Mackworth.

136   6   *a certain H—se*: see note 34 to *The Original Power*, p. 271.

138   7   *For tho' we value ... with you*: Adapted from the ballad, probably by Defoe, known as *A New Satyr on the Parliament*, the first line of which is 'Ye True-Born Englishmen proceed'. The ballad, a satire on King William's recalcitrant House of Commons, was published in May or June 1701.

139   8   *Declaration and Proscription*: In 1581 Philip II of Spain denounced William of Orange as a traitor and enemy of the human race and offered a large reward to anyone who would rid the world of such a pest.

       9   *Fam. Strada*: the *De Bello Belgico* (1632–47) by Famianus Strada.

140   10   *Balthazar Garrad*: William was shot dead on 29 June/9 July 1584 by Balthazar Gerard, a Burgundian.

       11   *Catholick League*: The Catholic League, under Henri le Balafre, Duc de Guise, and his two brothers, Charles, Duc de Mayenne, and Louis, archbishop of Rheims, was formed in 1576 to destroy Calvinism in France.

141   12   *Answer to Sr. H—M's. Vindication*: Defoe's *The Original Power of the Collective Body of the People of England* (1702), which defends the right of the People to have the last word, was a retort to Mackworth's *Vindication of the Rights of the Commons of England*. The paragraphs in quotation marks on pp. 141-2 and 145–7 are from *The Original Power*.

142   13   *Bodon Down*: Macaulay, in his *History of England*, vol. 1, chapter 9, relates how, on 16 November 1688, Lord Delamere took arms in Cheshire, convoking his tenants to stand by him, and 'his force had trebled before he reached Boaden Downs'.

       14   *the Gentlemen at Nottingham*: On 22 November 1688 announcements from the nobility, gentry and commonalty of Nottingham and York were published, declaring adherence to the Prince of Orange.

143   15   *January, 1688*: i.e. 1689, according to modern reckoning, which regards the year as beginning on 1 January.

147   16   *I make no question ... Foundation of Power*: This quotation, with the exception of the paragraph beginning 'But he that possessed the least

Freehold', corresponds to Defoe's *The Original Power of the Collective Body of the People of England.*

148   17   *King William in his Declaration*: on 30 September 1688 the Prince of Orange issued a declaration, explaining his reasons for his proposed invasion of England.

18   *Declaration of the French King*: Early in November 1700 Louis XIV issued a Declaration, letting it be known that he accepted the King of Spain's will, on behalf of his grandson.

19   *Duke of Austria*: The Emperor Leopold finally proclaimed the right of his younger son, the Archduke Charles, to the Spanish throne in 1703.

From Memorandum to Robert Harley (1704)

Internal evidence suggests that this belongs to July or August 1704. See Introduction, p. 36, for a discussion.

153   1   *supreme ministry*: i.e. Prime Minister.

2   *refined*: subtle.

3   *Richlieus*: Cardinal Richelieu (1585–1642) was chief minister during the reign of Louis XIII of France and a leading architect of absolute monarchy in that country. Defoe was reading a biography of Richelieu at this time and repeatedly refers to it in the *Review.*

4   *Mazarines*: Cardinal Jules Mazarin (1602–61), a protégé of Richelieu, was chief minister during the minority of Louis XIV.

5   *Colberts*: Jean-Baptiste Colbert (1619–83), controller-general of finance, was one of Louis XIV's greatest ministers. He helped found the Académie des Inscriptions et Belles-Lettres and the Académie des Sciences and did much to build up the French navy.

6   *Spencers . . . Gavestones*: Hugh Despenser, Earl of Winchester, and Piers Gaveston, Earl of Cornwall, were favourites of Edward II.

7   *Leicester*: Robert Dudley, Earl of Leicester, was a favourite of Queen Elizabeth.

8   *Somerset*: The Duke of Somerset became Protector after the death of Henry VIII.

9   *Buckingham*: The Duke of Buckingham was a favourite of James I.

10   *Lord Cromwell*: Thomas Cromwell, Earl of Essex, held many high offices under Henry VIII.

154   11   *Sir Francis Walsingham*: Secretary of State under Queen Elizabeth.

12   *of course*: in the natural course of things.

13   *Overkirk*: Hendrik van Nassau, Heer van Ouwerkerk, one of King William's inner circle, eventually becoming a field-marshal.

14   *The King of Sweden*: Gustavus Adolphus II (1594–1632), King of Sweden: champion of Protestantism during the Thirty Years War.

15   *new post*: Harley became Secretary of State on 18 May 1704.

155   16   *Gehezai*: the untrustworthy servant of Elisha, see 2 Kings 5:20–7.

17   *old Prince of Orange's*: Maurice, Prince of Orange (d. 1625), Stadholder of the Dutch Republic.

page
156 18 *Momorency*: Henry II, Duke of Montmorency (1595–1632), revolted against Richelieu but was defeated and executed.

158 19 *Milton*: The poet Milton acted as Latin Secretary to Cromwell's Council of State and was continued in the post after the Restoration.

20 *insurrection in Hungary*: Hungarian rebels were ravaging the territory of England's ally Austria.

21 *war in Poland*: Sweden had invaded the Polish territories of Augustus II, King of Poland and Saxony, thus incapacitating him from helping in the conflict with France.

159 22 *misunderstandings between the two kingdoms*: The Scottish Act of Security, passed in 1703, reserved Scotland's right, should Anne die without a surviving heir, to choose a different monarch from England. The resulting tension nearly led to war and was a decisive factor in bringing about the Union of 1707.

23 *Letters Writ by a Turkish Spy*: famous fictitious and satirical memoirs of a Turkish spy in Paris, published in seven volumes from 1687 onwards and attributed to the Genoese Giovanni Paolo Marana. A *Continuation* of these letters published in 1718, is probably by Defoe himself.

24 *Lord N—m's*: Daniel Finch, second Earl of Nottingham (1647–1730), who was Secretary of State 1702–4. Defoe visited his office in 1703, when under interrogation over *The Shortest Way with the Dissenters*.

25 *Sir George Rook*: Admiral of the Fleet Sir George Rooke (1650–1709).

160 26 *first Occasional Bill*: A Bill against Occasional Conformity (the first of several) was introduced in Parliament in November 1702 but defeated in the Lords.

161 27 *Scylla . . . Charybdis*: see note 8 to *Some Reflections*, p. 265.

Reasons against the Succession of the House of Hanover (1713)

Advertised as, 'this day' in the *Evening Post* for 17–19 February 1793. This is the first of three provocative pseudo-Jacobite or anti-Jacobite tracts which Defoe published between February and April 1713 and which led to his prosecution. (See Introduction, pp. 30–32.)

page
165 1 *Si Populus . . . Decipiatur*: If the People wants to be deceived, let it be deceived.

169 2 *Monmouth's Men in the West*: the followers of the Duke of Monmouth in his rising in the West country in June 1685.

3 *Example of the King of Poland*: In 1704, under the influence of Charles XII of Sweden, the Saxon king of Poland Augustus II (1697–1734) was deposed, his throne being given in the following year to Charles's protégé Stanislaus Leszczinski.

170 4 *the Lady Jane*: In June 1553, a few weeks before his death, the devoutly Protestant Edward VI was persuaded by the Duke of Northumberland to settle the succession on the latter's daughter-in-law Lady Jane Grey, daughter of the Duke of Suffolk and a convinced Protestant. Her nine-

page

day reign ended when, on 3 August, the Catholic Mary Tudor entered London in triumph and the country declared for her in virtue of her strong hereditary claim to the throne, as elder daughter of Henry VIII.

172   5   *the Suffolk Men*: i.e. the supporters of Lady Jane and her father.

       6   *Britain*: i.e. Briton.

175   7   *Gallies*: i.e. galleys.

       8   *Digesture*: digestion.

176   9   *Menage*: management.

178   10   *Abjuration Oath*: The Abjuration Oath, imposed by Act of Parliament in 1702, required all office holders and clergy to renounce allegiance to the Pretender; but it also demanded assent to the Act of Settlement of 1701, according to which any successor to the Crown of England had to 'joyn in Communion with the Church of England as by Law established'. Despite objections by the Commission of Assembly, the Abjuration Oath continued to be imposed under the Act of Union of 1707, and, as Defoe frequently insisted to Harley (see for instance his letter of 1 January 1707), it caused great resentment on the part of the Scottish Presbyterian clergy.

179   11   *Famous E. of Sunderland*: Robert Spencer, second Earl of Sunderland (1640–1702).

181   12   *amuse*: deceive.

182   13   *P. of O*: Prince of Orange.

184   14   *History of the Kings of England, Vol. Fol. 287*: i.e. *A Complete History of England, with the Lives of all the Kings and Queens thereof*, etc., by Oldmixon, White Kennett, *et al.* (3 vols, 1706), vol. 1, p. 287.

186   15   *1688*: according to the modern style of dating, 1689.

And What if the Pretender should come? (1713)

Advertised as, 'this day' in the *Evening Post* for 21–4 March 1713. The second of the three pseudo-Jacobite or anti-Jacobite tracts which Defoe published between February and April 1713 and which led to his prosecution. (See Introduction, p. 30–2.)

page

190   1   *openly grants his Legitimacy*: Defoe had written in the *Review* for 16 September 1712: 'I have nothing to say here to his [the Pretender's] Legitimacy of Birth, I always thought that to be a Dispute we have no manner of Concern in, I take it to be no Damage to our Establishment, that he be taken for the true Son of King *James*, nor did I ever lay any stress upon the Thing call'd his Legitimacy'.

192   2   *Scanderberg*: George Casteriotis, known as Scander Beg, leader of an Albanian rising against the Ottoman Turks in 1443.

       3   *New Treaties of Barrier and Guarantee*: In January 1713 Britain signed a new barrier-treaty with the Dutch.

199   4   *taking the Abjuration*: see note 10 to *Reasons Against the Succession*, above.

       5   *House of P—s*: i.e. House of Peers (or Lords).

page

199   6   *robb'd of their Birthright*: Under the terms of the Treaty of Union Scottish peers were not entitled to sit in the House of Lords simply by virtue of their titles but were to elect sixteen of their number to represent them.

201   7   *Comme une Coup de Grace . . . Une coup d'Eclat*: (properly *un coup*) as a final blow . . . a spectacular blow.

       8   *most Part of the Money*: i.e. most of the money invested in government stocks.

       9   *the Payment on both Sides*: i.e. payment of interest, and levying of taxes.

203   10   *Carlisle*: See the *Review* for 20 May 1710: 'When the Inhabitants of Carlisle in their famous Address, Ann. 1686 . . . gave the late King James Thanks in *Totidem Verbis*, for his Standing Army'.

204   11   *Nose them*: impudently confront them.

205   12   *talk of Security*: Defoe, in the *Review* for 19 February 1713, writes that it is in the interest of the Jacobites to argue that the Pretender, if allowed to rule, would have the utmost care of the Funds and public credit. '*These are good Words*; but as personal Security is not generally thought a good Establishment for a Joynture or an Annuity; far less can it be for a Nation, and I do not see what Security the Jacobites can offer us for the Performance.'

206   13   *Quam si Non . . . Ansis*: 'Which, if he does not obtain, he at least has had many opportunities to'. (Source untraced.)

An Answer to a Question that No Body thinks of (1713)

Advertised as, 'this day' in the *Evening Post* for 2–4 April 1713. The third of the three anti-Jacobite tracts which Defoe published between February and April 1713 and which led to his prosecution.

page

209   1   *Roper and Ridpath*: Abel Roper, the editor of the Tory *Post-Boy*, which ran from 1695 till 1714; and George Ridpath, editor of the *Flying-Post*, which he ran from 1695 till 1713.

       2   *Tom T—men*: Tom Turdmen, or nightsoil collectors.

213   3   *the Ninth Electorate*: The House of Brunswick-Luneburg, otherwise known as Hanover, was made an Electorate (the ninth) in 1692.

215   4   *that Text*: Ephesians 2:20.

216   5   *Act of Settlement*: the Act of 1701 (12 & 13 Will. III c.2) settling the succession to the crown of England upon the Electress Sophia of Hanover and her heirs, on condition that they be Protestants.

218   6   *little Encroachments*: In March 1712 Parliament passed an Act of Toleration for Scottish Episcopalians. Those benefiting under it were required to take an oath of abjuration of the Pretender, but the Tories secured the inserting of a clause imposing the same condition on ministers of the established (Presbyterian) church. This act was followed in May 1712 with one restoring lay patronage in Scotland. These measures were greatly resented by the Kirk.

       7   *Memorial of the Church of England*: The virulently high-church *Memorial of the Church of England* (believed to be by James Drake) was published

page
in 1705, causing a hue-and-cry after its author and being condemned by the grand jury in London to be burnt as a 'false, scandalous and trayterous libel'.

226 8 *Personally is Engaged by Treaty*: Under the Treaty of Utrecht, Louis XIV recognised the Protestant succession in Britain and agreed that the Pretender should never re-enter France.

From the **Review (1705–10)**

6 September 1705

page
231 1 *the Cheat*: i.e. the fraudulent pretence that James II's queen was the true mother of the child baptised as James Frances Edward Stuart.

232 2 *the Prince of Wales*: the Old Pretender was often referred to as the Prince of Wales even after his father's death.

3 *Mr. H—den*: Richard Hampden, son of the famous John Hampden of 'ship money' fame.

234 4 *Nature has left this Tincture . . . Darling*: a variant of the opening lines of Defoe's *Jure Divino* (1706). (A further variant is to be found in Defoe's *The History of the Kentish Petition* (1701), in *Political and Economic Writings*, vol. 2.)

5 *the Rehearsal*: a reference to the journal, at first known as *The Rehearsal of Observator*, conducted by Charles Leslie from 1704 till 1709. (See Introduction, pp. 27–9). But Defoe is playing on the title of Andrew Marvell's *The Rehearsal Transpros'd* (1672).

11 September 1705

236 6 *when Magdalen College was fallen*: When the president of Magdalen College in Oxford died in 1687, James II forced the fellows to elect the Bishop of Oxford, a Catholic convert, to succeed him, and twenty-five fellows were expelled for resisting this.

237 7 *They have not rejected thee*: see 1 Samuel 8:7.

238 8 *First Cause he is . . . pursue*: a slightly adapted quotation from one of Defoe's own manuscript verse 'Meditations'.

239 9 *your own Memorial*: the anonymous High-Church *Memorial of the Church of England* (1705) by James Drake, on p. 12 of which one reads: 'The Principles of the Ch—ch of E— will dispose Men to bear a great deal; but he's a Madman that tries how much. For when Men are very much provok'd, Nature is very apt to Rebel against Principle, and then the Odds are vast on Nature's side'.

13 July 1706

240 10 *the Gentlemen*: i.e. Charles Leslie, in the *Rehearsal* for 3 July 1706.

11 *no King in Israel*: see Judges 17:6.

242 12 *the Earth . . . thou?* : a general reference to the Book of Job.

13 *Supersedeas*: the technical term for a stay of legal proceedings. Here, a supersession.

page

15 August 1706

244 14 *Livery and Seisin*: Livery is the act of giving seisin or possession.

11 November 1707

246 15 *Jus Divinum of Episcopacy*: divine right of episcopacy.

25 November 1707

16 *late Miscellanea*: the passage so headed in the *Review* for 11 November.

247 17 *Haman*: see Esther 7.

18 *his most Christian Majesty*: i.e. the king of France.

19 *pulled down the House of Valois*: The accession of the Bourbon king Henri IV in 1589 brought to an end the rule of the House of Valois in France.

248 20 *Jacobite Fryar*: Henri III of France was assassinated by a young Dominican friar, Jacques Clement, on 1 August 1589.

249 21 *When Kings ... he'll obey*: In these lines Defoe has stitched together passages from Book IV and Book VI of his *Jure Divino*, rewriting them freely.

13 December 1709

250 22 *Dr. S—l*: Dr. Sacheverell. Henry Sacheverell (1674–1724), a virulently High-Church Oxford cleric and enemy of the Dissenters, was one of those lampooned in Defoe's *The Shortest Way*, and his impeachment and trial in 1710 was one of the great events of Queen Anne's reign.

23 *Story of Darius*: See Daniel 6.

251 24 *I have indeed made this publick*: Defoe is reproducing the lengthy footnote on Daniel and Darius in his *Jure Divino* (1706), Book VIII, pp. 8–10.

253 25 *Blue Guards*: In February 1699, under the terms of the disbanding Bill, King William was compelled to send home the famous Dutch Blue Guards, who had fought under him in every major battle of his career.

31 August 1710

255 26 *Hic Labor hoc Opus*: more correctly *hoc opus, hic labor est* (this is the task, this is the undertaking); Virgil, *Aeneid*, 6.129.

27 *Solomon's Fool*: see Proverbs 27:22.

28 *Sed nil desperandum*: but let us not despair.

29 *Mr. Asgill*: John Asgill (1659–1738). In 1710 he published *De Jure Divino*, claiming right for the Hanoverian succession.

256 30 *make my leg*: make obeisance.

31 *The Scepter ... come*: see Genesis 39:10.

2 September 1710

258 32 *Vae! vobis Hypocrite*: woe to you, hypocrites!

33 *occupy the Place of the unlearned*: see 1 Corinthians 14:16.

259 34 *Vox Populi ... Vox Dei*: Voice of the People ... voice of God.

35 *Bill of Exclusion*: In May 1679, at the time of the Popish Plot, a bill excluding the future James II from the succession to the throne passed its second reading, whereupon Charles II prorogued Parliament. In

November a more stringent bill was passed by the Commons but rejected by the Lords.

260   36   *Darkening Counsel . . . Knowledge*: Job 38:2.

     37   *Mark them . . . Divisions*: Rom 16:17.

261   38   *Currat Lex*: let the law take its course.

     39   *non Obstante*: notwithstanding.

5 September 1710

263   40   *Mr Camden*: The antiquary William Camden writes in his *Britannia* (ed. and trans. Edmund Gibson, 2 vols, 1722, vol. 1, col. clxviii) that Egbert, King of the West Saxons, issued an edict about the year 800 that the Heptarchy should be called 'Englelond, i.e. *the land of the Angles*. From hence came the Latin name Anglia . . .'

     41   *Wites-motes*: The witenagemot, or Anglo-Saxon assembly of the higher clerics and laymen, elected the king.

     42   *Mr. Tyrell*: James Tyrell (1642–1718), author of *The General History of England, both Ecclesiastical and Civil* (3 vols, 1697–1704).

TEXTUAL NOTES

The textual policy for *Political and Economic Writings of Daniel Defoe* is described in the General Editors' Preface printed above, pp. 3–4. Bibliographical details of each work will be found in P. N. Furbank and W. R. Owens, *A Critical Bibliography of Daniel Defoe* (London: Pickering & Chatto, 1998), referred to as 'F&O' in the notes that follow. The numbers in the left-hand column refer to the Pickering & Chatto page numbers.

Some Reflections on a Pamphlet Lately Publish'd (1697)

The copy-text is the first edition of 1697 (F&O 7), identified here as 1697a. This has been collated with the second edition, which was probably published in the same year and is identified in the following list as 1697b.

40a F.] 1697b; T. 1697a

An Argument Shewing, that a Standing Army (1698)

The copy-text is the first edition of 1698 (F&O 8). This has been collated with the text included in *A True Collection of the Writings of the Author of the True-Born Englishman*, 1703, and with the text included in the second edition of *A True Collection*, 1705.

61a 2 Chron ... Jerusalem] 1698; *omitted* 1703, 1705
63a *wrest*] 1703, 1705; *write* 1698
64a it seems] 1703, 1705; in the Case it seems 1698
66a and at ... place,] 1703, 1705; and in another 1698
67a *footnote*] *added* 1705
68a all from the] 1703, 1705; all the 1698
69a Argument] 1703, 1705; thing 1698
70a Prince generously] 1703, 1705; Prince 1698
71a the] 1703, 1705; an 1698
74a Prince] 1703, 1705; P. 1698
77a *footnote*] *added* 1705
77b *footnote*] *added* 1705

A Brief Reply to the History of Standing Armies (1698)

The copy-text is the first edition of 1698 (F&O 12(P)), identified here as 1698a. This has been collated with the 'second edition', also of 1698, identified in the following list as 1698b.

95a begins, unless . . . us] 1698b; begins 1698a
98a World. And . . . to him.] 1698b; World. 1698a
98b People. And . . . Speaker.] 1698b; People. 1698a

The Original Power of the Collective Body of the People of England (1702)

The copy-text is the first edition of 1702 (F&O 31). This has been collated with the text included in *A True Collection of the Writings of the Author of the True-Born Englishman*, 1703, and with the text included in the second edition of *A True Collection*, 1705.

103 Cess, if] 1703, 1705; Cest of 1702
105a Language] 1703, 1705; Errors of Language 1702
107a *And . . . Original.*] 1703, 1705; 'And . . . Original. *True Englishman*, p. 28. 1702
108a That] 1703, 1705; And that 1702
110a That . . . free.] 1703, 1705; "That . . . free. *True Born Englishman*, P. 1702
114a *what if I should say*] 1703, 1705; *some have thought* 1702
119a *footnote*] *added* 1705
119b Original.] 1703, 1705; Original. *True Englishman*, p. 47. 1702
120a *footnote*] *added* 1705
121a Because] 1703, 1705; For as much as 1702
121b Note, I] 1703, 1705; I 1702
122a But . . . Parliament.] *added* 1703
124a Revolution, in which . . . employed.] 1703, 1705; Revolution; That the Ministery of the late Reign, *for whose Misbehaviour we thought we had a just Right to call in Foreign Aid, and to suppress whose exorbitant Power we took up Arms against our Prince*, should not only not be punish'd as they deserv'd, but be still capable of acting in the Ministery again, and of representing in Parliament that very People they had Betray'd. 1702.
127a *footnote*] *added* 1705
127b *footnote*] *added* 1705
128a Posterity.] 1703, 1705; Posterity. *D.F.* 1702

Some Remarks on the First Chapter in Dr Davenant's Essays (1704)

The copy-text is the first edition of 1704 (F&O 48(P)). No substantive emendations have been made to the text.

From **Memorandum To Robert Harley [1704]**

The manuscript is in the British Library: Lansdowne MSS. 98, ff. 23–45, unsigned but in the handwriting of Defoe (F&O 272).

   This document was first printed by G. F. Warner in the *English Historical Review*, Vol. 22 (1907), and is reproduced in *The Letters of Daniel Defoe*, ed. George Harris Healey (Oxford, 1955), pp. 29–50. Only the first three sections have been included, since the remaining two ('Some Considerations with Relation to the Affaires of Hungaria and Poland' and 'As to Poland') deal, not with constitutional matters but foreign affairs. It has been thought best to modernise the text rather than attempt, as Healey did, to reproduce the idiosyncracies of Defoe's manuscript. Some missing words have been supplied in square brackets.

Reasons against the Succession of the House of Hanover (1713)

The copy-text is the first edition of 1713 (F&O 146).
173a no] all

From the **Review**

The copy-text is the first edition (F&O 250) as reproduced in *Defoe's Review*, facsimile ed. Arthur W. Secord, 22 vols (New York, 1938). No substantive emendations have been made to the text.